What People Are Saying About

Chicken Soup for the Soul:
The Golf Book

"An assortment of eloquently written and heartwarming short stories for which the experienced player, novice, or even non-golfer can relate with a sense of déjà vu and awe."
~Michael Marion,
PGA Master Professional

"I found that I wanted more of them to read. The stories being brief (but amazingly, entirely complete!) made it all the more fun."
~Leigh Bader,
PGA of America National Merchandiser of the Year

"A refreshing inside the ropes look at the game we love by folks who love the game."

Founder/CEC ...ion

D1114014

"Se...
Chicken Soup and golf is good for anybody's soul."
~Gary McCord,
CBS Commentator & Author

Chicken Soup for the Soul

for the Soul.

The Golf Book

Chicken Soup for the Soul: The Golf Book
101 Great Stories from the Course and the Clubhouse
by Jack Canfield, Mark Victor Hansen, Max Adler

Published by Chicken Soup for the Soul Publishing, LLC www.chickensoup.com

The publisher gratefully acknowledges the many publishers and individuals who granted Chicken Soup for the Soul permission to reprint the cited material.

Front and back cover photos courtesy of Jupiter Images. Interior photo courtesy of PunchStock.

Cover and Interior Design & Layout by Brian Taylor, Pneuma Books, LLC
For more info on Pneuma Books, visit www.pneumabooks.com

Distributed to the booktrade by Simon & Schuster. SAN: 200-2442

Publisher's Cataloging-in-Publication Data
(Prepared by The Donohue Group)

Chicken soup for the soul : the golf book : 101 great stories from the course
 and the clubhouse / [compiled by] Jack Canfield, Mark Victor Hansen [and] Max
Adler.
   p. ; cm.

 ISBN-13: 978-1-935096-33-7
 ISBN-10: 1-935096-33-8

1. Golfers--Literary collections. 2. Golfers--Anecdotes. 3. Golf--Literary collections.
4. Golf--Anecdotes. I. Canfield, Jack, 1944- II. Hansen, Mark Victor. III. Adler, Max,
1981- IV. Title: Golf book
PN6071.G62 C54 2009

810.8/02/0352   2009922157

PRINTED IN THE UNITED STATES OF AMERICA
on acid∞free paper
17 16 15 14 13 12 10 09   01 02 03 04 05 06 07 08

Chicken Soup for the Soul® and Golf Digest® present

The Golf Book

101 Great Stories from the Course and the Clubhouse

Jack Canfield
Mark Victor Hansen
Max Adler

CSS

Chicken Soup for the Soul Publishing, LLC
Cos Cob, CT

Chicken Soup

www.chickensoup.com

for the Soul

Contents

Foreword *by Dr. Bob Rotella* xiii

❶
~Subtle Breaks~

1. Coming Back, *Philip Beard* 1
2. Bwa, *Jaime Diaz* 5
3. "Why Is Golf Mean to Me?" *Nick Henry* 10
4. The Third Side of Lee Trevino, *Guy Yocom* 14
5. Driving David Sutherland, *Brett Avery* 19
6. Oliver Twist Hits the Links, *Bruce McCall* 23
7. A Ray of Hope, *John Buccigross* 27
8. Inside the U.S. Open Contest, *John Atkinson* 31
9. Perpetual Promise, *John Strege* 34
10. Tour Pros Worry About the Chunk Too, *Mark Long* 36

❷
~Apexes~

11. My Guilty Ace, *Peter Richmond* 45
12. You're Away, *Ron Fitzsimmons* 48
13. You Can't Bring a Baseball Swing to the Golf Course,
    Jared Slater 51
14. Anything Can Happen, *Kenny G* 56
15. An Iowa Steamer, *Dr. Sam Christensen* 59
16. Shopping to Buy Woods on a Snowy Evening,
    Harris Green 61
17. Ernie's Last Game, *Kay Connor Pliszka* 62
18. Playing Augusta National, *Tom Cunneff* 64

19. Hot Dogs and Sansabelts, *Brian Amos Fox* 67
20. Low and Left, *Robert Bruce* 69
21. America's Course, *David Shedloski* 72

❸

~Working the Ball~

22. Never Ever Say Never, *Fred Funk* 79
23. Chalas's Chance Encounter, *Jim McCabe* 82
24. A Rough Start in the Business, *Craig McLean* 86
25. Being Put in One's Place, *Ronald Read* 92
26. The Compliment, *Tim Murphy* 95
27. Just About Perfect, *Tom Borda* 99
28. Bearer's Eye View, *Kaameran Stenberg* 105
29. No Complaints, *Ed Sherman* 109
30. The 16th Tee, *Max Adler* 112

❹

~Gamesmanship~

31. Girls Will Be Girls, *Ashley Mayo* 121
32. The Golf War, *Eric Stark* 125
33. Getting Sacked by #56, *Dwight Freeney* 128
34. Living With the Yips, *Vicki Griffin* 131
35. No Chance at the Course Record, *Nelson Bayne* 135
36. Golf Widow, *Trish Bonsall* 136
37. 11/22/33, *Matt Ginella* 138
38. Never Let a Big Gun Bring You Down, *Mark Soltau* 145

❺

~Fathers~

39. Appreciating Bad Golf, *Steve Rushin* 151
40. My Gift to My Son, *Mark Spangler* 155
41. Dreamer, *Whit Sheppard* 158

42. Pings Left in a Will, *Jason Kileen* 162

43. Two Feet Short, *Gregg Mills* 165

44. The Twenty-Seven Year Challenge, *George McDonald* 168

45. Generations Linked, *Harry L. Dauberger* 172

46. Hallowed Ground, *Mark H. Massé* 173

47. Emergency Nine, *Lyn Larsen* 176

48. In Michigan, *Thomas Munson* 178

49. We Played Golf Today, *E. Michael Johnson* 181

50. The Mediator, *Jackie Fleming* 185

51. My Little Girl Golfer, *Steve Eubanks* 187

❻

~Recovery Shots~

52. Quitting, *John Hawkins* 195

53. Get Legs, *John Tidyman* 198

54. A Walk in the Woods, *Neil Rosen* 200

55. Arnold Palmer's Greatest Rescue, *Caroline Stetler* 204

56. The Six Stages of Golf Grief, *Reid Champagne* 207

57. No Carts, *James Swigert* 210

58. Coming to Grips, *Robert Scott Nussbaum* 212

59. A Widow by Choice, *Terri Tiffany* 214

60. The Strongest Memory, *Timothy J. Larkin* 216

❼

~Swing Thoughts~

61. Trusting Instincts, *Gary Player* 221

62. The Charms and Challenges of Links Golf,
    Tom Watson as told to Nick Seitz 223

63. The Space in Front, *Tom Chiarella* 226

64. Golf and Music, *Josh Kelley* 231

65. Confessions of a Snap Hooker, *Mark Fowlkes* 233

66. Me and My No Problem Putter, *Don Patton* 236

67. If It Weren't for Golf, *John Gaski* 239

68. Golf in Duluth, *Bob Landfield*..242
69. Foreplay, *Paul Ehmann*..244
70. What It's All About, *Steven Floyd*................................247
71. Saturday Singles, *Ted Johnson*................................249
72. The Genealogically Isolated Golfer, *David Gould*..............252

❽
~The Lifelong Game~

73. Remembering Mr. Meticulous, *Nick Seitz*..........................259
74. Just Call Me Jack, *Bob Baker* 262
75. The First Lesson, *Al Barkow*................................266
76. Nine Holes in Eighteen Years, *Todd Kersting*..................270
77. Everybody Should Play, *Peggy Kirk Bell* 273
78. Shrivel Disobedience, *Jeff Patterson*..........................275
79. Band of Golfers, *Lieutenant Ross Troike*......................278
80. A Miracle, *Bob Carney*................................281
81. Mea Culpa, Riviera, *Tony Mohr* 284
82. Round of My Life, *Mark Rylak* 286
83. On Moe Norman, *Craig Shankland*................................288

❾
~Grinders~

84. Large Bucket, *Mike Stachura* 293
85. Strangers on the Range, *Neil Haldeman*..........................296
86. It Was Colder Than I Thought, *Y. John Lee*......................299
87. Chip and Putt, *Kevin Butler and Tamara Bowers*................301
88. Why Do We Dream? *Cliff Schrock* 303
89. A Costly Free Lesson, *Thomas Ashcraft*..........................307
90. Walking On, *Richard Weber* 309
91. Embracing Mediocrity, *Chris Hagen* 313

⑩

~Raconteurs~

92. Tomcat the Caddy, *Arnold Palmer* 321
93. Best Show in Sports, *Dave Anderson*................................. 323
94. Kilspindie, *Brian Clark*... 326
95. The Guy Who'd Play With Anyone, *George Palmer*............ 331
96. Golf and Love, *Emily H. Allyn*....................................... 333
97. The 670-Yard Ace, *Jay Rylant*... 336
98. What's at Stake in a Casual Encounter, *Leigh B. MacKay*.....339
99. The Stolen Driver, *Robert A. Hedesh* 343
100. The Mix-up at Dunbar, *Neil Falco* 345
101. Pace of Play, *Chris Hodenfield* 348

Meet Our Contributors.. 355
Meet Our Authors 372
Acknowledgments... 375
About Chicken Soup for the Soul 376
Share with Us... 377

Chicken Soup for the Soul

Foreword

S o much of golf writing focuses on the elite game. Daily news-papers, weekly and monthly magazines, websites updated by the minute—they all devote so much of their energy to following the world's best players around the globe, seeking context, uncovering meaning, reporting for us fans back home more than just what scores were shot and how much money was made.

And while this is a noble pursuit, the highest competitive levels always warrant the attention of that sport's history (comparisons of Tiger Woods and Ben Hogan must be drawn), it can become possible to forget that the true lifeblood of our beloved game is everyday play. The fact that most golfers play for their entire lives is what distin-guishes it from other sports. Sure, a man or a woman can inevitably find a recreational league for almost anything they once played in high school, but the scope of this type of activity pales in comparison to golf. One only needs to show up at a public course on a beautiful Saturday morning without a tee-time to find this out the hard way.

And what if every name on that starter's Saturday tee sheet had one great golf story? Essentially, this is the question the editors asked when setting out to create this book.

While it's thrilling to find within these pages prose from legends like Arnold Palmer, Gary Player, Tom Watson, and Fred Funk, as well as present pro-am anecdotes from celebrities like Kenny G, Dwight Freeney, and Josh Kelley, I think you will also encounter powerful truth and kinship in the stories told here by everyday golfers. A father of five biological sons ultimately finds a golfing partner as enthusias-tic as he in his adopted Chinese daughter. A woman conspires with members of her late husband's regular foursome to fulfill a final ash-scattering wish. A case of mistaken identity leads an American man on vacation in Scotland to find a very disappointed gallery awaiting him on the first tee. A son-in-law, after years of awkwardness and emotional distance, experiences a rare on-course moment that connects him forever with his father-in-law. Because reporters are so busy covering the pro game, sometimes they miss the most dramatic, poignant, ironic, and miraculous moments in golf. They come from people like you.

Let's begin our journey through 101 stories by first turning our attention on the next pages to Philip Beard, an award-winning novelist who recounts helping his convalescing father rediscover that most magical feeling in the world, a purely struck golf shot, in "Coming Back."

~Dr. Bob Rotella

The Golf Book

Chapter 1

Subtle Breaks

Golf is life. If you can't take golf, you can't take life.

~Author Unknown

Coming Back

Success seems to be largely a matter of hanging on after others have let go.
~William Feather

My father stares down at his hands.

Slowly, as if solving a Rubik's Cube, they find the overlapping grip he has been using for fifty years. He waggles the club hesitantly. When he swings, his upper body appears cemented on its axis and his hands don't get much above waist-high. The descending blow is more of a stab than a swing, and the ball ticks harmlessly off the toe of his club and dribbles directly right, crossing in front of the only other player who is on the practice tee this late on a September evening. Our fellow member is polite enough not to look back over his shoulder at us.

"See?" my father says. "They're all like that."

And then, as if to demonstrate, he slowly rakes another ball into his stance, stares down at his grip and does the same thing again. This time, as the ball rolls away, my father lets the club head fall with a heavy thud against the unmarred turf in front of him. This is his version of a temper tantrum.

A *lacunar infarction* is what the doctor called the mild stroke my father suffered four months earlier, so named for the crescent-shaped void of synapses deep in the brain that appears like a scar on the CAT scan. There were several of them on my father's scan, evidence that his increasing forgetfulness in recent years hadn't been the result of the natural aging process, but was instead caused by a series of tiny strokes that eventually led to the more significant one on Mother's Day. That morning, his face fell of its own weight, his tongue became a useless, oversized piece of chewing gum in his mouth, and his eyes showed something I had never seen in the forty years I had spent with him to that point: fear.

"Is your back okay?" I ask him now. My father has had a creaky back since I was a kid, the muscles at the base of his spine periodically clenching in a spasm so severe that my mother had to dress him for work. Staying home in bed was the recommended treatment, but self-made men all share a common aversion to sick days. "I just need to get up and move around," my father would say, hunched like a question mark and shuffling toward the front door in a three-piece suit.

"My back's fine," he answers. "Why?"

"You're not turning," I tell him.

"Hmm?"

"You're not making a turn. You're just sort of lifting your hands and swatting at the ball. Turn your shoulders."

I step behind him, mirroring his posture, and help him to rotate.

"Oh," he says. "Okay."

He takes a couple of practice swings that begin to look familiar to me.

"And transfer your weight, remember?"

"What?"

"Get your weight moving toward your right foot on the way back, then to your left foot on the way through."

"Oh, yes," he says as he continues to swing, starting to find a rhythm.

All of his motor functions were fine, we were told, and his therapy had been directed solely at his speech. The words were still there, but they needed help finding an unimpeded way back out. His sense of humor, which had never left him even in the most difficult of times, was in hiding as well. Conversations moved too quickly for him. Even if his wit was still intact, he knew enough to understand that the punch lines were coming too late and therefore were better left unsaid. During those first months, he preferred spending time by himself, which was what led my mother to suggest that he go try to hit some golf balls. "Don't be such a lump," she told him. "Go do something."

His first attempt, without me, apparently had been exasperating. "I'm spastic," he told my mother. "I can't even hit the ball."

"Take Philip with you next time," she suggested. "Spend some time with your son."

So that's why I'm here, watching. My father taught me to play not long after he learned the game himself, taking me with him any time I asked until, like all kids, I preferred playing with my friends. Years later, he taught me how to practice law. Not how to argue or evade or obfuscate issues, but how to get things done for people. And because of him, I was pretty good at it, and I'm sure he thought we would practice together until he retired or died at his desk. The day I told him I was leaving the firm to write novels, he put his hand out to me. "Good luck, Philip," he said, holding on a fraction of a second longer than our usual greeting or departure. "There will always be a place for you here if you ever decide you want to come back."

"It's coming back, Dad." I tell him now. "I can see it. Last thing, and then I'll shut up. Belt buckle to the target. You're turning back fine, but now you have to turn through."

"Okay."

He incorporates this final piece of advice easily into his last few practice swings. I can see his body remembering, and I find myself swallowing hard at the simple beauty of it. Then he taps a ball toward him from the pile.

His stance suddenly looks comfortable, athletic even, for a man in his seventies, and when he takes the club back he turns it to almost parallel, pauses, unwinds and pinches the ball perfectly off the soft turf that is just now starting to dew.

"There, Dad," I say amidst the rush of pride. "Feel the difference?"

In the months that follow, my father will gradually re-inhabit his body. He will rejoin the conversation during family dinners, and he'll go back to the office. The same year my first novel is released, my father and his partner will celebrate forty-five years of practice together at a dinner party for a hundred people, and he will give a speech that makes everyone laugh. I can't take credit for any of that. His doctors, modern medicine and my mother's dogged patience are what brought him back to us. But this is my contribution, this one moment when his eyes open a little wider than they have in some time, watching the ball rise high, backlit and shrinking quickly against the fading blue sky.

"Yes," he says. "That one felt good."

~Philip Beard

Bwa

Admit it; you've tried to nail that little truck that picks up the balls at the driving range. No one ever thinks they are going to hit the thing, until they do. Only then does anyone think about the guy inside. For some of the best years of my golf life, I was that guy.

This was the late 60s. I was a teenager in Concord, then a mostly blue-collar suburb east of San Francisco, and my after-school hours and entire summer days were mostly spent at Concord Municipal GC (renamed Diablo Creek in later years), a non-descript track known for its wind and hardpan. As a fourteen-year-old during the Summer of Love, I wore my hair in a frizzy mop that made my bell-bottomed pipe stems seem even skinnier. But any Mod pretentions were offset by golf shirts with Penguin logos and my black-and-white winged-tipped spikes.

Picking up the range was my second job. I'd been fired from the first, as a dishwasher at the golf course's restaurant, for being too slow. Almost immediately, the world of commerce had positively confirmed that my nature was by turns procrastinating and methodical, a combination that would drive every boss in my future a little crazy. The traits also made me a poor range guy — and latrine cleaner, pro shop vacuumer, and golf cart re-charger. But I didn't get fired. Sometimes you just get lucky.

My salary was the then minimum wage of $1.65, but it was all about the perks: unlimited practice balls and free greens fees.

Retrieving the range balls from the remote areas of the range also did my game a lot of good. There was endless rapid fire chipping from every conceivable lie. Sometimes I would wield the club with only my weaker left arm, something I'd heard local hero Johnny Miller did. I also hit a lot of extreme cut shots over the high protective fence between the range and the 9th hole. Years later, when the Mickelson flop was astounding others, I remained haughtily unimpressed.

I probably spent the most time on the practice green competing with another adolescent golf bum or three. The standard putting bet was "quarter-dime"—25 cents to the winner of a nine-hole match, with 10 cents for every sink. To this day, a long session of "quarter-dime" is my best medicine for poor putting. We also played the chipping and pitching variation of H-O-R-S-E, with the player whose shot finished farthest away from the hole earning a letter.

Out on the actual course, I was an undersized short-hitter who would try to gain distance by slinging hooks designed to land in the hardpan "rough" and bounce a few times before angling back into the fairway. Our rounds were full of tour fixture mimicry—exaggerated Gary Player style forward presses, Doug Sanders backswings, Arnold Palmer whirly bird follow-throughs. A well-hit drive was often called a "TW Rip" after the then young and strapping Tom Weiskopf (though the term seamlessly transferred to the Age of Tiger). The silence of awkward moments—a drive OB or a skulled sand shot or a missed two-footer—were often relieved by someone affecting a high pitched Texas accent and uttering only one word—"Chris"—our impression of analyst Byron Nelson's way of engaging Chris Schenkel during ABC golf telecasts. Timed just right, it was hilarious.

Concord Municipal GC was rich in downtime atmospherics. There was the musty "back room," a junkyard of old clubs that smelled of shoe polish and wax and varnish, where we shined shoes, cleaned clubs and wondered out loud about life. The pro shop was like a bazaar, full of chatter from all sorts of regulars and oddballs, many spouting what they considered wisdom. I noticed that the good players practiced more than talked. One, Ben Smith, then a pin-machine repairman at the local bowling alley, used to hit balls for hours. He never seemed to have much success in local amateur tournaments, but in the mid 80s he would become a stalwart on the Senior Tour, finishing second twice.

The assistant pros, men sentenced to long hours behind the counter at low pay, became my guides into the game. There was Bill Krause, a former tour player who had the thick build and forearms of Jimmy Demaret. A Texan, Bill had a lot of Ben Hogan stories, and used him as his swing model. Whenever Bill had time to practice, I liked to sit behind him and take in what seemed at the time like unworldly power and control. After ending one session with three flushed 2-irons that shot out low before rising and gently falling to the left, Bill asked me, "You know what was wrong with those shots, don't you?" Stumped, I was silent. "That's right," he smiled. "Nothing."

Bill was succeeded by Jess Crawford, the most gifted player I was ever around in my youth, who was legendary in Northern California for the distance he could hit the ball. A sweet guy off the course, he was plagued by a Vesuvian temper. Once, after his shot on the short 8th missed the green, he reared back and hammer-threw his wedge all the way to the green. Carl Phippen, a fast-talking low handicapper who was one of the few not cowed into silence when Jess erupted, piped up, "Sorry Jess, no mulligans."

The most interesting assistant, and the one who most influenced me, was Paul Kujawa. He was an ex-decathlete and psychology grad from Cal Berkeley who had come to golf in his early twenties. He never became a good player, but he was an astute and dedicated teacher. He was a product of the rebellious times — liberal, progressive, endlessly questioning of the Establishment. Highly educated and a bit of an urban hipster, it was clear he felt trapped in Concord, and to some extent, in the conventional culture of golf.

While Paul's flavor didn't go down so easily with the older regulars, the younger crowd would gather round to listen to him hold court. One of his favorite screeds was on the shallow "bourgeois" values of middle class suburbia that he found so pervasive at the golf course. After we had run to the dictionary to look up the term, he changed it into a kind of code slang, the theatrically elongated "boo-wa." This was gradually compressed into "bwa." It became an all purpose word, used to express everything from disdain to approval to amazement. When Paul announced, "On the tee, Newsome two-some and Dingle single," he would add "Bwa" as a sort of bookmark. We all adopted the word, even at home. When told by my parents to clean my room, I might respond with an exasperated "bwa." Learning that his pet word had made its way into our daily jargon gave Paul the golf subversive immense satisfaction.

In line with stirring up the status quo, Paul enjoyed tweaking our hormonal hell. When I would linger in the pro shop by incessantly waggling the new clubs I coveted, he would chide me for "shaft shaking." Upon seeing me in the morning, he would often ask, with eyebrow raised, "Have you been a solitary Don Juan?" Without waiting for the answer, he would then go into his impression of a senile Irish priest agitated by what he had just heard in the confessional—"Oh Son! OH NO, SON!"

But it was Paul's interest in serious ideas that most rubbed off on me. He encouraged me to read about the game, which set me on a path that would eventually lead me to golf writing. In particular, the discussions we had about "Golf in the Kingdom," which he introduced me to, permanently shaped my sensibility about the game and its possibilities.

I didn't take as easily to my duties on the range. After getting the loose balls into rough piles, I'd go round and round in a rusted three-wheel truck dubbed the Orange Crate. The rolling ball picker it pulled was worn and unreliable, typically requiring several passes over the same area. To break up the monotony, I'd sometimes sing at the top of my lungs, knowing I'd be drowned out by the loud engine. I remember Leon Russell's "Roll Away The Stone" with its opening line, "Well, it's such a strange world that I've been living in" seeming particularly apt.

The Orange Crate didn't have a protective cage (it earned its nickname from how it handled) though I never got hit with more than a few hot grounders that hopped off my shins. The real problems associated with the job were a series of muddy drainage ditches bordered by wet slopes. One evening I fishtailed the Orange Crate into a ditch and couldn't get out. I went into the pro shop to get help. There I found only the head pro, Gordon Farris, and his friend Bud the Milkman, in the midst of finishing off a bottle of Jim Beam.

Gordon was a big man with a Gleason-esque air. He was a sharp dresser, favoring tropical pastels. I recall that day he wore maize paints and a lime green shirt of mesh material. Bud per usual had on his all-white milkman suit, nicely matching his white crew cut.

I was apologetic but Gordon was amiable, as he tended to be when lubricated. "C'mon, Bud," he said, "we can use the exercise."

Gordon and Bud tiptoed through the muddy ditch, placed their hands on the rear bumper of the Orange Crate and lowered themselves into the pushing position. "OK," Gordon instructed, "Give it some gas, and when I say 'Go' pop the clutch."

I did as directed, but after about five seconds the cart still hadn't moved. That's when I became aware of a lot of yelling and cussing.

I got out. Both men looked as if they had been dipped in a vat of dark ooze, only the whites of their eyes breaking up the monochromatic theme. I felt frozen as Gordon inspected himself in a slow burn that was pure Ralph Kramden. He said nothing, then stomped away. Bud, unwittingly but perfectly playing Norton, sheepishly followed.

I waited a few minutes and trudged to the pro shop like a condemned man. Paul was behind the counter. He didn't laugh. He didn't commiserate. He simply said all there was to say: "Bwa."

Still, I didn't get fired. Like I said, I was lucky.

~Jaime Diaz

"Why Is Golf Mean to Me?"

W hen asked "What does golf mean to me?" my knee-jerk Socratic response is "Why is golf mean to me?" Like many amateurs and pros alike, my on-course failures come in every shape and color; snaphooked tee shots, chunked approaches, skulled chips, unfortunate wardrobe choices, to name only a few. Fortunately, most of my humiliations have been witnessed by only my regular playing companions, who are equally, if not more, terrible. One exception however comes to mind.

My youngest brother has always been a great athlete. While I can still hold my own against him in other sports, it was clear from early on that he would be giving me four shots a side for a long time to come. Several years ago, we were lucky enough to have our educational paths cross when he was a freshman and I a third-year law student at the same university. He made the golf team and since I was losing my interest in legal studies, we saw a good deal of each other at the course.

It started out like any other Friday. I dragged myself out of bed at the crack of 11:00 for my 11:30 tee time, drove the two miles to the course, and met three other law school friends who had also made the wise decision to abstain from classes. The first seventeen holes progressed normally. A few pars, a few bogeys, a couple of "others." We had cheeseburgers at the turn (the best in town), several tasteless jokes—all in all, a typical round. Then we arrived to the par-5 18th. After the downhill tee shot you can either lay up or try to carry a large pond and hill that guard a multi-tiered green that's adjacent to the 10th tee and the clubhouse. I never viewed six as a bad score and was always ecstatic to end my round with a five. After my friend Toby sliced his into the cow pasture and exclaimed his customary profanity, I teed my ball. The result was one of my best—290 down the middle (okay, it's a severely downhill tee shot) and in great shape to have a go at it in two. Engulfed in the moment, I did not hesitate as I pulled 3-wood for my second shot. Imagine my surprise as the ball flew off the clubface on a direct line at the pin. Posing, eyes locked on the trajectory, I watched the ball land softly on the middle shelf and trickle up to the top shelf, stopping three feet from the flagstick.

As I strode triumphantly toward the green, I counted on one finger the number of eagles I had made in my life. Sure, there had been chances, but never anything inside of twenty feet. Like an adoring gallery, my friends slapped my back and offered the obligatory congratulations, even Toby who muttered, "Nice shot, loser." Reveling in what was sure to be a dramatic eagle, I was about 50 yards from the green when I noticed two foursomes of swaggering youngsters milling about on the 10th tee. The identical blue and white golf bags gave away their identity as the university golf team, my brother among them. I quickened my pace to call attention to my position which surely even they would admire and hopefully envy. "Hey Bro, check it out. Lying two!" I yelled perhaps a bit too loudly for this sleepy semi-private club. His face beamed his ever-present smile as he yelled back, "Knock it in, dude!"

My friends finished off their sixes and sevens so as to clear the stage for my crowning moment. I felt the eight sets of eyes from the 10th tee on me as I steadied myself over the putt. I took a deep breath and swung the putter back and through.

It missed badly to the right. Never had a chance, never even caught a piece of the cup. The energy of life drained from my limbs as I was dealt this most public of golf failures. My reaction was similar to Curtis Strange's at the 1995 Ryder Cup (walking off the green blank-faced with shock and shame) although inside I felt more like the Reverend in *Caddyshack* who raises his arms and putter towards the heavens in angry defiance of all the forces that have conspired against him. The golf team collectively just shook their heads and turned away, going back to their mindless undergraduate chatter. My little brother, smile now gone, looked at me and simply offered, "You'll make it next time." A small consolation for the choke of my life.

The day went on and the afternoon beers eased some of the pain. I also started to think about what my brother said. A perfunctory comment, but somehow it made the lesson clear. Just as in the rest of life, there is always hope in golf and it keeps us playing even when we are tempted to deposit our clubs into the nearest water hazard. I will play golf again. I will probably hit some good shots. I may even hit one as good as that 3-wood. And if I do, I'm gonna knock that putt in the dead center of the hole.

~Nick Henry

"I found the ball but I lost my clubs."

The Third Side of Lee Trevino

Thoughtfulness is a habit—
a way of life well worth cultivation and practicing.
~Brough Botalico

"Where you been?" boomed Lee Trevino as I rounded the corner of the clubhouse. "You're five minutes late. I could DQ you right now!"

Lee cackled and sat upright in his golf cart. He put down his *USA Today*, removed his reading glasses and reached for his bottled water. "You get lost?" he asked.

"Bad traffic and then a wrong turn," I said. "You give lousy directions."

"That means nobody else can find me, either," Lee laughed. He slid behind the steering wheel of the cart and motioned for me to sit next to him. "Come on. I'll take us down to my favorite spot where nobody can bother us. We'll talk some golf."

Lee was doing me a favor this warm July morning in 1999. He had agreed to do a story for *Golf Digest* with me as the writer, and he was coming through on short notice. A month earlier, my four-year-old daughter had been diagnosed with medulloblastoma, a malignant brain tumor as cruel as it is rare. Surgery was performed within twelve hours and the results were ghastly. In order to get all of the tumor, the neurosurgeon was forced to sever cranial nerves. The left side of my baby girl's face was now paralyzed, and so were her left arm and leg. The prognosis was difficult, and the worst was still to come: thirty-one radiation treatments on her brain and spine, followed by a year of chemotherapy. After that, I was told, you cross your fingers and pray, because a recurrence of medulloblastoma means the end.

I was calling on Lee because I didn't want to get on an airplane, not with my daughter being in tough shape and my wife as shattered emotionally as I was. Lee and his family spent a lot of time at his mother-in-law's house in the middle of Wethersfield Country Club, a convenient thirty-minute drive from my house in Connecticut. I'd worked with Lee on articles many times before, and after I explained the situation to Chuck Rubin, Lee's agent, Chuck arranged for me to see Lee within a week.

To this point I'd seen two sides of Lee Trevino. The first was the public side we've all seen, the wisecracking, witty, high-strung harlequin who entertained galleries like no one before him. But he also had a darker side that would manifest when people wrongly assumed that his everyman persona was an invitation to treat him like a first cousin. Lee could be snappish to people who pulled at him the wrong way at the wrong time. If someone shoved a program in his face and demanded he sign it, or cut him off when he was walking to a range or clubhouse, or asked him a silly question at the wrong time, he would verbally cut them off at the knees.

There were hints that Lee had a third side that not many people had seen. When his longtime caddy, Herman Mitchell, developed heart problems and was no longer able to work, it was rumored that Lee had paid for his care and recuperation, and had even given him a place to live. When confronted, Lee would give an update on Herman, but brushed his benevolence aside. He just wouldn't talk about it, even when reports of him helping others in the same way came to light.

Lee wouldn't let many people inside. The first few times I met with Lee at Wethersfield to do instruction pieces for *Golf Digest*, he was all business. He was cordial enough, but when we finished up and I dropped him off at his mother-in-law's house, that was it. There was no more small talk and no offering us something cold to drink.

But one day, after we'd wrapped up a story on driving—and I'll add here that no player I've ever seen hit the ball better than Lee Trevino—Lee invited me inside. He gave me a tour of his basement workshop, showed me how he'd tinkered with the many sets of irons and scores of rare and valuable Wilson 8802 putters that were in a barrel down there. He made us sandwiches. On the way out, he shoved several dozen balls and a handful of gloves at me. A few months later, when I saw Lee in Florida, he invited me out to his car. "I want to show you something," he said, and when we got there he popped open the trunk and handed me a Wilson 8802.

"I've watched you putt, and you need a good putter like this," he said. I'd earned his trust and friendship at last.

As Lee drove the cart down the hill from the clubhouse that day at Wethersfield, he gave no inkling he knew anything about the circumstances surrounding my daughter. He didn't say much as he parked the cart under a large oak tree on a remote part of the course. "Now, what's this story we're doing about?" he said.

"The idea is for you to identify the best players you've ever seen in every department of the game," I said. "Best driver, best iron player, best sand player, best putter and so on. Let's start with the best driver. You once told me Greg Norman is the best ever. You still believe that?" I turned on my tape recorder, the signal for Lee to start talking.

But Lee didn't say anything. After a moment I looked up at him expectantly, but he just stared at me. Then he reached down and turned off the tape recorder.

"I hear your kid is sick," he said.

"Well... yeah," I said awkwardly. "How did you..."

"Cancer, right? Brain tumor?" he said, his eyes narrowing.

"Yes."

"Maybe you should send her down to St. Jude's in Memphis. Has she been treated yet?"

I explained the surgery, and that her first of the thirty-one radiation treatments had taken place only a few days earlier.

"Listen," Lee said. "St. Jude's is the best. Everything they need to treat these sick kids is right on site—surgery, radiation, chemotherapy, physical therapy, everything. The families actually move down there while this goes on. And it's free. St. Jude's is the best, but they have one rule: They want the kid from the minute they're diagnosed. If you're in the middle of treatment somewhere else they won't take you, because they want to treat them their own way and track them from day one. They never violate that rule."

"Well, I guess we won't be going to St. Jude's," I said.

Lee put his arm around me. "I want you to know something. My whole career, I've had only one charity, and it's St. Jude's. I won the St. Jude's tournament three times, and I've done a lot for them down there. I don't talk about it, but let's just say I've done a lot for my favorite charity over the years."

Now Lee's eyes started to well up. He hugged me tighter. "I don't know if you're happy with the care you're getting up here or whether you have good insurance. Treating cancer isn't cheap. But listen: If you want to take your kid down to St. Jude's, I'll make a phone call. I'll ask them to help us. They have that rule, but if they don't break that rule for me after all I've done for them, well then, they've lost Lee Trevino."

I broke down over that. All of the fear and tension I'd concealed over the last month in order be strong came pouring out of me. In that time of crisis, many people had rallied with support. But having Lee Trevino on my kid's side was something else again. For him to stick his neck out like that, and immerse himself in something so unpleasant for someone he saw twice a year, was profound.

At that moment, under the shade of that big oak tree, Lee was like a spiritual being. All the energy, determination and force of will that had lifted him from abject poverty to one of the great athletes of all time, was now focused on my sick child. He exuded power, understanding, kindness and anger at the injustice of it all. I'd known about the two sides of Lee Trevino and now that wondrous third side was coming to the fore. Lee was transformed into a warrior angel eager to lift a terrible swift sword against something evil, with all his might and no reservations.

"We'll get her better," Lee murmured, patting my shoulder. "We'll get her better. There now, partner, it'll be all right. We'll get her better."

It wasn't necessary for me to call Lee, and who knows if St. Jude's could have accommodated such an awesome request, even from him. My daughter survived and despite some scares and setbacks, is with us still. Today, with sufficient time having passed that I can look back on those first dark days without my stomach churning all over again, I realize it wasn't just luck and the skill of many doctors that helped my child and our family survive. Prayers helped, too, and I've always felt that the magical third side of Lee Trevino was the greatest prayer of all.

~Guy Yocom

5

Driving David Sutherland

Golf is a game of days. And I can beat anyone on my day.
~Fuzzy Zoeller

One of the best days in David Sutherland's golf career happened in August 1989, in a series of events that still seems too dizzying to succeed. That day he hit zero warm-up balls, spent no time at the practice green and his heart was racing at the first tee. Yet he produced a level of play few competitors could duplicate in any circumstances.

If the Sutherland name seems familiar, it's because David's the younger brother of Kevin Sutherland, who in a dozen-plus PGA Tour seasons earned $10 million as well as the 2002 World Golf Championships-Accenture Match Play Championship. They were stellar players at Christian Brothers High School in their hometown of Sacramento, California, and became all-America selections at Fresno State. David followed his brother onto the tour, too, but a series of injuries curtailed his competitive career and led him to become the men's golf coach at Sacramento State.

Though for everything that older brother Kevin has done, nothing equals what David went through in 1989 on the final day of the 87th Western Amateur. Of all the amateur tournaments crammed into the summer, the Western is the only one that approaches the U.S. Amateur in prestige. Its list of past champions includes Charles

(Chick) Evans Jr., Marvin (Bud) Ward, Frank Stranahan, Jack Nicklaus, Lanny Wadkins, Ben Crenshaw, Curtis Strange, Hal Sutton, Scott Verplank, Phil Mickelson, Justin Leonard and Tiger Woods.

You don't make it onto that list by simply falling out of bed. Years of preparation go into surviving the Western's format: 36 holes of stroke play Wednesday and Thursday before a cut to the low 50 players, 36 holes Friday before a second cut to the low 16, then four rounds of 18-hole matches across Saturday and Sunday. Not a week for the timid.

David shot 70-78 the first two days at Point O'Woods G&CC in Benton Harbor, Michigan, which eked past the first cut. He then went 71-67 Friday to reach the prestigious Sweet Sixteen, itself enough of an accomplishment to make most players' summers. Saturday morning he defeated Len Mattiace (who would lose a 2003 Masters playoff to Mike Weir) and in the afternoon he topped Doug Martin, who had won the qualifying medal against one of the summer's strongest fields by an eye-popping nine shots.

Sunday morning's semifinal was the kind of match that would make anyone pray for a day where everything went perfect. Sutherland would face Greg Lesher, low amateur in that year's U.S. Open. The previous day Lesher advanced past the quarterfinals by eliminating Phil Mickelson (who in a few months would win the PGA Tour's Northern Telecom Open as an amateur).

As is still the case with many Western Amateur competitors, Sutherland and a friend were guests of a local family. The family lived in Kalamazoo, about thirty miles east on Interstate 94. The family loaned them one of their cars for the week, so when the pair returned to the house Saturday night they naturally left David's clubs in the trunk.

Which wouldn't have been a problem if Sutherland and his friend hadn't discovered early Sunday that the family had taken that car, most likely by force of habit, to attend church services. Imagine for a moment the panic. You have no idea where the family worships, no way to reach them (there weren't too many cell phones floating around in 1989) and the match of a lifetime fast approaching.

With Sutherland's friend driving the family's other car, the pair began crisscrossing the city looking for the car with the clubs. Remarkably, they found it in fairly short order. The only remaining hurdle was getting to the first tee by the starting time.

Remember that scene in *The Blues Brothers* where Jake and Elwood drive like mad in a police car to reach the tax assessor's office before the deadline? It was a lot like that. At one point Sutherland and his friend had the car doing 110 miles per hour.

"We had a radar detector, and about a mile before we were caught my friend started hitting the brakes," Sutherland admitted later that day. The officer clocked the car doing 87 in a 65-mph zone. "As we were pulling away from the trooper, my friend said, 'If we get caught again, they're not going to stop us until we get to the parking lot.'"

Meanwhile, the gallery at The Point's first tee milled nervously, scrutinizing any car rolling up the long entrance drive. Lesher was "visualizing how it would be to play alone" because The Rules of Golf call not for disqualification of the absent party but require the one present to play for his victory. In the closing seconds, literally, Sutherland's car came onto the property at breakneck speed and screeched to a stop in the parking lot. Sutherland scrambled out, wearing one untied shoe and carrying the other. Once on the tee, he mumbled a quick apology, put on his other shoe, took a few practice swings and ripped his first drive.

Sutherland was so consumed by the morning's adventures that he barely caught his breath all day. Lesher, thrown off his rhythm by the surprise appearance, began the match 6-5-5 and was 5 down after seven holes. Sutherland won, 3 and 2. After a brief lunch break Sutherland went back out and captured the title by defeating Tony Mollica, a six-time Western competitor and that year's qualifying runner-up, 2 and 1.

"You know, that's the way we play a lot of our golf in college," Lesher recalled later that day. "You just get out of the van, take a practice swing and rip it down the middle, like there's nothing to it."

And that may be worth a try. Whenever you find your head is stuffed to bursting with tips and suggestions and lessons and sayings, try going straight from the parking lot to the first tee with a golf shoe tucked under your arm. No practice balls, no putts, nothing.

Of course, the speeding ticket is optional.

~Brett Avery

Oliver Twist Hits the Links

They call it golf because all of the other four-letter words were taken.
~Raymond Floyd

The last round of golf I ever played was hardly better than my first, thirty years prior. Both were an orgy of whiffs, skulls, chunks, grounders and four-putts. I could blame it on having never taken a lesson, or on an absence of athletic prowess that's almost worthy of medical study, or the fact that I've been bullied through equipment convenience into playing right-handed clubs even though I'm a southpaw. But the truth is that the roots of my golfing life were poisoned beyond recovery long before I ever swung a club.

My golf-addict father, who returned on summer weekends to our hometown from his job in faraway Toronto, always promptly fled the bosom of his family at eight in the morning on both Saturdays and Sundays. I was eleven years old when he first invited me to be his caddy. An invitation from my father, as is the case with some fathers, was indistinguishable from a command.

"Golf" often conjures a Cheever-ish country club setting, but this tale requires a step down to a humbler spread. My father, an underpaid civil servant with six kids and finances so strapped that he couldn't afford a car, was actually a charter member of our nine-hole course that charged just three dollars a round. Like most of my father's interests, golf excluded family participation. If anything, it served as the perfect escape from his ill-fitting paternal role. The golf course was one place he could be certain we'd never be, as home was one place we could equally be certain he'd never be.

Back then, before the popularity of carts, the serious golfer required a caddy much in the same vein the serious boulevardier required spats. Why my father chose me over someone else's kid, I'll never know, but I wonder if the reason dealt with something more than just saving a few precious coins. Maybe he thought commandeering me to lug his bag around while following at a respectful distance represented a wholesome dad-and-lad outing. Or perhaps it was all about healthy outdoor exercise for a growing boy. Or possibly about introducing me to a nobler pastime I would embrace myself in due time.

Even little kids can have big egos. Seldom enamored of serving somebody else's needs and whims for four or five hours at a stretch, and particularly not while staying mute and invisible, to me caddying was a humiliating erasure of self, like being paid not to exist. Plus I had two older, stronger, more pliant brothers my father could easily have nominated. The implicit sadism of his choosing me did not go unrecorded in my book of grudges. At eleven I didn't want to collect stamps, I didn't want to dance ballet and I didn't want to caddy.

My father was a jock in his youth, and so far as I could tell, this defined his life in high school and afterward. He'd been a pretty good semi-pro catcher, as well as the county badminton champ. Entering his forties, golf offered him a last living link with competitive sport.

The luminary golfer of the time was Byron Nelson, a name I knew because it freakishly packed Lord Byron and Admiral Nelson into the same place at the same time. Other than this I was perfectly ignorant of the game. But, despite this ignorance, I could sense the change in barometric pressure when my father sliced or hooked or otherwise botched a shot. There would be this pregnant moment of perfect quiet, as just before the Big Bang, and then would come his acting out the drama of the good man betrayed by the cosmos. Disbelief, rage, expression of rage in the form of an inanimate steel club suddenly lurched with every erg of energy the betrayed can summon against the betrayer—which in these cases was the sum total of gravity, time and space, rotation of the earth and astrophysics. I was far too junior, and in my station too humble, to open my mouth. A wisecrack would ensure the town's only recorded filicide.

My father had a graceful swing and usually belled tee shots like home runs. Alas, he was also a man living on the edge of his nerves, even in repose. He was easily frustrated by life's little insults, each of which he took as personal: a cat underfoot, a lardy waiter, a lipped putt. It was like my father had been born without a filter to absorb and dampen shocks to his system.

Faced with an errant golf shot, the poor bastard had no choice but to explode. And it wasn't the club spiraling up into the blue or the expletives that seemed to keep it aloft, so much as the lingering aftermath that truly roiled my guts. For the next two or three holes after an outburst, nobody in the group would feel free to speak or even look at the smoldering ogre who used to be "Dad." He would retreat into a silence that was more powerful than even the loudest noise, nursing his fractured pride while boiling at Fate's inexplicable treachery in breaking the agreement to exempt him from all mortal pain. Eventually he would wrestle his demons enough to return to the game, but it took something out of everyone in vicinity, and this glimpse of the sulfurous being within served to redouble my already entrenched terror of crossing him. Or even merely approaching him.

My self-pity reached its climax after the day's play. I would rest my sore haunches on the bumper of a car in the parking lot, too timid to go and ask for a Coke while he and his pals lingered over Molsons in the clubhouse. (The 19th hole was always the longest of them all.) When my father appeared he was weary, as well as a little tipsy. Our short drives home in the borrowed government Plymouth were never chatty. I was too relieved at gaining my freedom for this last withholding of intimate communication to irk me. And I was also too grateful for getting back my freedom to ask for any money I was owed for my services. More often than not, the money never was forthcoming.

I don't remember exactly when or why my caddying career petered out. My father kept on playing for the rest of his (tragically short) life, but after about age fifteen I was no longer required to be a part of it. By then we'd moved to the city. He'd risen in the world and joined a posh club, where perhaps it would have been seen as déclassé to dragoon your own kid as your caddy.

In retrospect, that abiding resentment at lugging a bag of clubs over several hilly miles, in a pursuit that had nothing to do with me, does seem a mite hysterical. It wasn't slavery, for god's sake. I suffered no lasting harm. Only decades afterward did I grasp the truth; my caddying agonies weren't and never had been about golf at all. It was an effort without reward as chopping rocks in a Georgia chain gang—and without the one particular reward that would have made it worthwhile.

Because not even there, in his personal, private world, at play on his beloved golf course within a club-length's touch, did my father and I draw one inch closer, even manage to connect. Such a chance for sustained proximity to that all-powerful figure was pitifully rare away from the golf course. And indeed, no other such opportunity would ever be granted again.

~Bruce McCall

A Ray of Hope

Give your stress wings and let it fly away.
~Carin Hartness

Hockey Hall of Famer Raymond Bourque is no different than Nirvana. Some get it and some do not. Some understand the unique and revolutionary artistry; some do not. I've always understood Bourque's art more than Nirvana's, and after spending three and a half hours on a golf course with the man, I understand him even more.

It was during his guest broadcasting stay at ESPN that Bourque inquired around the office about playing some golf. I quickly offered my course, Wampanoag Country Club in West Hartford, Connecticut, which is a Donald Ross gem. From the moment he accepted the invitation I began thinking how cool it would be to shoot a 77, Bourque's jersey number for most of his career. I always identify golf rounds with players' uniforms. It's just the way I think. For this round, playing with arguably one of the ten greatest hockey players of all time, a 77 would be way cooler than a 67.

I was thirteen when Raymond Bourque entered the NHL as the mystical defenseman who was going to help bereaving Boston Bruins fans get over the early death of Bobby Orr's career. There was no ESPN in the summer of 1979. The most important sports figures to me then were Willie Stargell, Terry Bradshaw, Jack Nicklaus, Larry Bird, Jimmy Connors and Gerry Cheevers' goalie mask. Any athlete coming on to the scene from this point in my life onward would pretty much be a part of my consciousness forever, as this was the time I really began remembering a lot of detail. It's also about the time my parents gave me a tape recorder and I started playing broadcaster by turning down the sound on the TV and calling my own play-by-play.

And now here he was, #77, an icon, on the first hole about to tee it up with yours truly. Moments like this are, at first, very strange. How did all the breaks, all the luck, all the joy, all the sports passion come together to the point where I was now standing on the tee with one of my boyhood idols? I knew if I thought about it too much my ears would bleed.

To avoid playing the wrong ball, most golfers use a Sharpie to mark dots or lines. I, however, always identify mine with hockey players' names. Today, I decided, "Cashman" would be on the side of my golf ball, in honor of former Boston Bruin and Bourque teammate, Wayne Cashman. Cash Man Money, Yo. I hit the tee shot well, which was a major relief. First impressions are important.

I'm normally a pretty good putter, but as I brought the putter back on the first green, the nerves hit. I kept thinking "my goodness, Ray Bourque is watching me putt." Suddenly, I had the touch of Judge Smails on the 18th at Bushwood. The birdie-putt was about twenty-five feet. My dead-hand crush stopped about ten feet past the hole and I missed that one coming back, too.

I was able to settle down and par the 2nd hole. Meanwhile, Bourque displayed a golf game similar to his hockey. Powerful and technically sound, a great set-up and a solid swing. He hit his short irons very far, could jack his 8-iron up to 170 yards if he had to. His putting stroke was straight back and straight through, tour quality.

On the 4th hole, Bourque reached into his golf bag and pulled out a Titleist 77 and handed it to me. This might qualify as the coolest thing I've ever seen. When you're Ray Bourque, Titleist will do such things for you. I was so inspired by Bourque's gift that I birdied the hole.

Bourque is an ideal playing partner. A good player, not slow, quick with a "nice shot" comment, and extremely complimentary of the golf course I called home. Nothing makes a golfer feel better than when a guest raves about his course. It's the greatest assist a guest can make. As usual, Bourque's assist was right on the lead tape of my Mizuno irons.

When we reached the 17th tee-box I was 4-over par. If I finished with two pars, I'd card a 76. A Rosy Grier, or an Orlando Pace. A par-birdie finish would be a Mean Joe Greene. Birdie-birdie would card me a Merlin Olsen or a "Father Murphy." But I wasn't here to shoot an Orlando Pace or even a Joe Greene. I wanted to shoot a Ray Bourque. And I informed Bourque of my intentions as I teed up.

I made a tough two putt at the 17th to stay at 4-over. This was key because the 18th at Wampanoag is a tough 420-yard par 4 to an elevated green with a severe back to front slope. Having to make par would be a challenge, but a bogey—and a 77—would be a piece of cake.

Bourque hit his best tee ball of the day and I hit my best. His approach came up short and left. Mine landed on the green about twenty feet past the hole. Bourque chipped to two feet and tapped in for par to shoot 79. I had a very difficult downhill left-to-righter, a tough two-putt but a perfect three-putt scenario to shoot my 77 with Ray Bourque. The plan was to cozy it down to three to five feet, miss on purpose to about twelve inches, and then tap in for a 77. Frame me and hang me on the wall.

My stroke was smooth and perfect, which is how someone with high enthusiasm and low expectations hits the ball. I was, after all, trying to miss. As the putt trickled down the slippery slope of the 18th green, I got that feeling that players of all levels sometimes get when a putt is halfway to the hole. It's a feeling akin to Christmas Eve.

But instead of hopeful anticipation, I screamed, "Don't go in! Don't go in!"

Bourque smiled as he watched the red lettered "Cashman" Titleist slowly tumble over itself, over and over down the green. There was no way this putt could go in. But it did.

My Ray Bourque became a Mean Joe Greene.

After the round, thinking of that putt over a beverage, I theorized to Bourque a true and great secret of golf: That less is more. I'd noticed in our round that he sometimes tried to force the ball to where he wanted it to go, instead of relying on his talent. Golf is a counterintuitive game. To hit the ball up, you have to swing down. To curve it right, you have to swing left. To curve it left, you have to swing right. The harder you try, the more tense you become and the more you fail. I tried to make a bogey on the 18th and had made a birdie.

From the moment Bourque first stepped on professional ice as an eighteen-year-old, most people knew he was destined to be a legend. But it wasn't until 2001, forty years old and playing in his final NHL game, that Bourque first raised the Stanley Cup.

During this Stanley Cup run, teammate Patrick Roy seemed tense as he played poorly in the first round of the playoffs against the Vancouver Canucks. As Roy's French-speaking companion for much of the year, Bourque told the goalie to relax, *relâcher*, have fun. So Roy relaxed, let go, and in the weeks to come helped lead the Avalanche to the Stanley Cup. You see, when Roy and Bourque and the Avalanche stopped trying to win the Stanley Cup, they won it. For good players like Bourque and Roy, when you have game, all you need to do is relax and play.

So if Ray Bourque is looking for a golf lesson, he just has to look at the picture of himself holding up the Stanley Cup and remember how he and his teammates won the championship.

Relâcher.

~John Buccigross

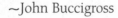

Inside the
U.S. Open Contest

A wife, three kids, a good job and stage four lung cancer. This is what I have. I've never smoked. I was thirty-eight years old when I was diagnosed, completely out of the blue. Now I'm thirty-nine.

Sixty percent of all people with lung cancer are either non-smokers or haven't smoked in a decade. If you picked strangers off the street and told them this they wouldn't believe it. But it's true.

And if you tuned in early to the Sunday broadcast of the 2008 U.S. Open at Torrey Pines, you might recognize my name. I'm the guy who won *Golf Digest's* contest to play there with Justin Timberlake, Tony Romo and Matt Lauer the Friday before the tournament. The rough was thick, the pins were tucked, the greens were lightning and the ubiquitous cameras didn't let me forget for even a moment that my shots (and blunders) would be televised. The goal was to break 100, but the idea was to connect the professional game with the every-man. Golf is unique in that this connection is possible. People get the opportunity to play championship courses, often in championship conditions, regularly. I shot 114, but don't look back on my effort with any regret. I gave it my best.

I remember when I first saw the blurb in my December issue. It jumped off the page. Right away it hit me that if I was lucky enough to win I could do two things: raise awareness about lung cancer and show the world that someone diagnosed with it fifteen months prior could play the toughest course in America.

I worked with my wife and my brother to make my hundred-word essay really sing before I e-mailed it. The magazine responded that I'd be contacted by February 14th if I advanced. They got something like 56,000 entries. When February 13th came, I accepted that I hadn't made it, but felt good for having at least tried. But that evening Craig Bestrom, an editor at *Golf Digest*, called to tell me I'd made it to the top five percent.

They did interviews all over the country. In March they flew eleven "semi-finalists" to Dallas for another session of interviews as well as to watch us play. There were camera crews. I guess the editors wanted to get a preview of how well our swings might hold up under pressure.

Man was I nervous. On the range I shanked my first half-bucket *Tin Cup* style—twenty-five consecutive hosel-squirters off to the right. But somehow my first tee shot on the course was right down the middle. And after that I was fine.

I couldn't stay for dinner that night because I had to fly back to Omaha for chemotherapy early the next morning. The other contestants stayed, and were treated to dinner with Hank Haney and others from the *Golf Digest* staff. Though from what I later heard "treated" might not be the best term. Truer words were probably never spoken, but apparently Hank was pretty harsh. He got up and categorized every reason, from psychological inexperience to handicap statistics, why none of us had a flying pig's chance of breaking 100 on a U.S. Open course set-up.

Looking back I guess I'm glad I wasn't there to hear it.

From those eleven the magazine culled five finalists. I was out to lunch with friends when I got the call. Since the magazine was planning to make a big announcement to promote the online election, where the public would vote for which person they wanted to play, à la *American Idol*, I was instructed not to tell anyone I had made the finals for a month. I kept a pretty good lid on it. The only people who knew were my family and the friends I was out to lunch with that day.

You get that far along in something as big as this and you just want to follow the rules.

It's a funny thing to suddenly become famous. To suddenly receive stacks of letters and e-mails from complete strangers. People would track down my number and call to tell me they were praying for me. Some people mailed me crosses and others radon kits (radon is a natural gas emitted from the ground believed to be a cause of non-smoker lung cancer—my house did not test positive for high levels). One fellow, Brent Johnson, who lives in San Francisco but who like me is from Nebraska, arranged for he and I to fly on his course's private plane and play eighteen holes.

You read bad stories in the news every day. You get caught up in your busy life. It's easy to become hardened. But the one thing a little fame let me discover is that the great majority of people are so good-hearted, so caring. I didn't realize this before I got sick.

Human beings care about other human beings, regardless of fame. Greg Norman, who caddied in our foursome for his friend Matt Lauer, called me the day after the British Open. He'd nearly become the oldest player ever to win a major. Plus he was on his honeymoon with bride Chris Evert. Yet, part of him was thinking of me. He reached me in the hospital, just to say hi, to ask how I was doing.

And speaking of Matt Lauer, he actually called the other day to invite me to play golf. I had to decline. I've had some setbacks with the cancer and I'm not strong enough right now. But we've rescheduled a round a few months from now, when I'll be doing better.

~John Atkinson

Perpetual Promise

I may not be there yet, but I'm closer than I was yesterday.
~Author Unknown

Mort Lachman, in the tradition of those for whom humor is a livelihood, often relies on self-deprecation, notably when discussing his golf game. Once Bob Hope's head writer and the executive producer of the legendary television sitcom *All in the Family*, Lachman also lays claim to being the world's worst golfer.

Yet his pursuit of a remedy is neither trivial nor funny. Books are his passion, and the office of his home in Hollywood is cluttered with them, a preponderance dedicated to golf instruction.

When I was ushered into Lachman's office one summer morning, I interrupted him as he was reading from one of them, certain that he had discovered a cure for the topped tee shot. It should be noted here that Lachman's age at the time was ninety.

He said he began each day by picking up a golf club and standing in front of a mirror.

"To stretch?" I presumed.

"No," he said, "to check my swing."

It was his daily mission to improve golf skills that probably peaked during the Nixon administration. He continued to play a daily nine holes, unbridled optimism accompanying him always to the first tee.

The notion that someone at ninety-something (or eighty- or

seventy- or sixty-) is going to find a cure that will improve the curb appeal of their scorecard is absurd. It also is beside the point. Golf at its core might be a vile game, but it is not without its charms, among them the shelf life of hope. It has no expiration date.

And so, against odds that we tend not even to consider, we embrace the possibility that today will be the day that golf ceases to qualify as an unsolved mystery. Even the man whose last name evoked such optimism was not immune. Bob Hope once said he intended to shoot his age even if he had to live to be a hundred to do so.

I once had the privilege of playing with Tony Penna, the old pro and legendary club maker, who was in his eighties at the time. His passion for the game had long outlasted his skills. Nonetheless, Penna was unperturbed. He'd take a Penna-model persimmon driver and hit a slinging hook in an attempt to squeeze a few extra yards from the tee. He'd then use the same club from the fairway as well.

Even Arnold Palmer, long after age had deprived him of the ability to compete, was hopelessly hopeful. The 12th hole at his Latrobe Country Club in Latrobe, Pennsylvania, features a creek that crosses the fairway about 240 yards from the tee. Palmer once vowed he would quit playing when he no longer could carry the creek with his driver.

Years after he last carried the creek, he is still at it, stubbornly pulling driver with a degree of certainty that the creek is navigable. Inevitably, he hits his ball into the creek, takes a drop, and perhaps more often than not still salvages par.

Not long ago Palmer completed a round there and repaired to the 19th hole. A television was tuned to The Golf Channel, which at the moment was airing an instructional segment. He intently watched for a few minutes, then turned to a friend.

"That's what I need to work on," Palmer said, blissfully clinging to golf's perpetual promise. That tomorrow will be better than today.

~John Strege

10

Tour Pros Worry About the Chunk Too

Golfers just love punishment. And that's where I come in.
~Pete Dye

I've been a PGA Tour caddy for twenty years, with Fred Funk the last eight. I've been inside the ropes and up close with a lot of top players.

It might surprise you to hear that tour pros go through a lot of the same mental anguish as the average weekend golfer. Yep, they sometimes worry about snapping a shot in the water or chunking a little chip. They simply have a lot more physical ability and mental discipline to get over it quickly.

They've learned to handle it.

I remember Billy Andrade, a tour veteran, talking about his tee shot in Las Vegas when he came to the final hole with the lead. He had won three tournaments in his career by then. The 18th fairway there is pretty big, but all he could see was trouble.

There was wild desert to the left. If he yanked it, he thought, he would lose the tournament. So he juked around and looked to the right, and noticed an out-of-bounds fence he hadn't noticed in fourteen years playing there. It had to be a hundred yards right, but he was now worried about blowing it OB.

He backed off and somehow refocused. Then he drove it down the middle and won the tournament. But he had to overcome the same demons the rest of us do.

What's that old saying? No man is a hero to his valet? My experience is that the pros are just normal people with abnormal skills. Their confidence level can go up and down like the stock market.

It was 2003, we were on the range at the International waiting for a rain delay to end. Fred had made over $1.5 million for the year and had made nineteen birdies the week before—but he now he's just lost it. Hittin' it awful.

No big deal, right? Some weeks you have it, some you don't, right? Not for Fred. He was CERTAIN his career was OVER. No way he'd ever make another cut. Couldn't play the game anymore. It was so sad, I almost was crying myself. But then I remembered a pledge I made... never feel too sorry for anyone who owns his own jet.

The next week at the PGA Championship at Oak Hill, Friday afternoon after his second round, we're back on the range, and Fred is still in deep swing depression. Up walks Rick Martino, PGA Master professional, fellow Maryland Terp (Fred was my coach at Maryland). Nice guy. But I'm thinking... oh, here we go... all we need, another cook in the kitchen.

But Rick doesn't say a thing for a long time. Then asks, almost apologizing, if he can offer a thought. "You can't swing your right arm down fast enough," he says. Fred hits one shot—and BOOM! That was it. After a couple more swings, he was ready to run to the first tee.

But he had to sleep first. The next morning he hits his first warm-up wedge, turns and announces, "I got it!" He stripes it about 300 dead center off the first tee and sprints to the next shot. He could have won that week, but finished tied for seventh and made the Presidents Cup team. Like I said, never feel too sorry for anyone who owns...

Think about that the next time you're down about your game. No matter how good you are, some weeks you just don't have it. Heck, even Tiger finishes second once in a while.

Another time a fellow pro was saying he was excited and had a great attitude about the start of a new season in Hawaii because he'd won a tournament and had a two-year exemption. Said it was a beautiful setting. Said he could finally relax and free-wheel it and have more fun out here now. He bogeyed his first hole, double-bogeyed the second and flung his putter about sixty feet, and hit his bag.

It was a nice toss, but hey, it's the SECOND HOLE OF THE YEAR... and he's ALREADY LOST IT!

This game can be really brutal, no matter how good or bad you play it or for how long. The word "shank" is just as unwelcome on tour as it is anywhere else in golf. Once we were playing with Bobby Wadkins (that's the team "we" as in Fred and I—you know—we birdied one and two, then he three putted three) and weren't paying attention when he hit his second shot from the middle of the fairway. We saw him playing his third from well short of the green and way right.

I see him over there and I'm thinking, "Well, there is only one possible thing that happened here, and I'm not going to bring it up." So Fred has a delicate little chip confronting him, and he looks over at Bobby and says to me, "What did he do, shank it?" I almost dropped the bag. I said I didn't see Wadkins' shot, just hoping the word wouldn't get in his head the way things can out here. Thankfully it didn't. I guess Fred's comment should have told me his mindset was OK.

The 17th hole at the Players Championship always messes with the pros' minds. It's only a short par 3, but the island green and unpredictable wind cause a lot of bad scores.

Every year on that hole we caddies have our own closest-to-the-pin contest the Wednesday before the tournament. The players come out and caddy and mostly heckle. A few years ago, Doug Barron's caddy hit a horrendous shot on Wednesday.

On Friday in the tournament (not even Thursday but Friday) Doug hits a shot in the water at 17. As the group is walking off the green Doug turns to his caddy and says, "You know, I couldn't get your shot on Wednesday out of my head."

That might be a sign, you know? There's a caddy who needs to get himself another player. Immediately.

Sometimes the 17th brings good memories. We're on the tee Wednesday a couple years ago, and somebody says that Michael Campbell offered to double his caddy's salary for the week if the caddy hit the green. So I have the ball teed up and am just about to swing when Fred says, "Double or nothing on your salary?"

I say right back, "Absolutely."

I hit the shot right on the green—a 9-iron I think it was—and that about ruined Fred's week knowing he was going to have to pay me double. His mistake was challenging me when I didn't have time to think about it. If he'd said it on the 14th hole I would have had no chance.

Players are thinking about the 17th long before they ever get there. Everybody dreads that hole. You can't help it. As you play the 16th you can hear the big crowd whooping and hollering. They love to gamble on that hole. You look over there from the 16th fairway to see if a train wreck is in progress. OK, plane crash. You might recover from a train wreck. We were finishing the rain-delayed third round on Monday morning in 2005, the year Fred won, and saw all of Bob Tway's record 12 on the hole. In a fierce wind, he hit four balls in the water, and went from 10th place to 72nd! This is a man who's won eight tournaments including the PGA Championship, and is considered pretty even-keeled temperamentally.

You couldn't say that about the late Tommy Bolt, whose nicknames included "Tempestuous" and "Thunder" and "Terrible." He was a wonderful shotmaker with marvelous control of the ball, but his temper always seemed to obscure his talent. He once said, "This here's a game the Pope would get mad at."

I heard a Bolt story that he went to the caddymaster at a tournament back in the days before the pros had full-time caddies, and said he wanted a caddy who wouldn't talk. Wouldn't say a word. So at the 14th hole of the first round his man hasn't said a word and Bolt is near the lead, but he drives it into the trees on the right.

Bolt's addressing the ball, and gestures and says to the caddy,

"Watch this shot. I'm gonna fade it under this tree and around that one." He knocks it on the green, turns to the caddy and says, "Man, wasn't that the best shot you've ever seen?"

The caddy doesn't say a word. And Bolt says, "I'm giving you permission to speak now. Isn't that the best shot you've ever seen?"

And the caddy says, "Mr. Bolt, that was not your golf ball."

~Mark Long

Apexes

It is almost impossible to remember how tragic a place the world is when one is playing golf.

~Robert Lynd

11

My Guilty Ace

Golf is a game that is played on a five-inch course—
the distance between your ears.
~Bobby Jones

The 5th hole at Hotchkiss—a lovely, hilly, tough course that winds its way through the campus of the prep school of the same name—looks as if it should be the easiest par 3 in the history of the game: 140 yards, sloping straight downhill. The huge green, fronted by a thin strand of sand, beckons like some enormous, comfortable throw rug. From the tee-box it seems as if you could spray your shot anywhere and this green would still gather the ball in. My friends all routinely birdie the 5th.

I, on the other hand, routinely mess it up. The 5th has me psyched. A short iron shot off a tee ought to be the easiest shot in golf, right? Not for me. Of course, for me, no shot is easy. If I had a handicap, it'd probably be in the high twenties, so it's not as if I've mastered any part of the game. I took it up seven years ago, at the age of forty-eight, and my backswing still looks like some flickering, spasmodic image you'd have seen on a wind-up nickelodeon machine in 1905. All of which makes what happened on that afternoon two summers ago all the more bizarre.

I was playing by myself, as I often like to do, because playing alone lessens the pressure. It had been raining on and off for a couple of days, and a fine mist creased a steady drizzle as I hiked up the hill toward the 5th tee-box. I'd played the first four holes decently, and had a legitimate chance to break 50 for the nine (always my ultimate goal). For some reason I'd decided to keep score that day, which I seldom do.

I teed the ball a little higher than usual, to ensure I'd get it in the air and have a chance at bogey to keep my good round going. I swung my 7-iron. When I looked up, I saw the ball describing an abnormally high parabola through the gray sky. My shot was not only straight, but seemed to have the right distance as well. Could I land close enough for a legitimate birdie putt?

I watched the ball descend through the mist until I lost sight of it against a backdrop of trees. Then I heard the distant but delightfully unmistakable sound of a golf ball plonking onto a green. My eye caught the ball, just briefly. It looked to have hit just a few feet behind the cup. Then I lost it again. Then, a fraction of second later, I heard a loud "clank."

A clank? Like a ball hitting a flagstick? That can't be bad, I thought. If it hit the flagstick, on a slow green, how far away could it have bounded? On the other hand, I thought, what if...? But the thought of an ace seemed absurd. I've amassed maybe one birdie a year since I took the game up. No way could I have just made a hole-in-one.

But the closer I got to the green, the more excited I grew. I could see no ball. But as I neared the hole, my heart sank. There was no sign of white.

But wait! The cup was full of murky brown water, and there, bobbing just beneath its surface, was my ball. I felt nothing but shock.

I quickly looked around to see if I'd had any witnesses. Not a soul. I fixed my ball's plug mark about six feet behind the hole. I took my scorecard out of my back pocket and, with hands trembling, scrawled a "1."

And then I went on to shoot 25-over the last four holes. I was a mental mess. Instead of doing a two-step down the fairways, I was slogging, hitting desultory shots, laden with guilt. As much as I love the game of golf, I am supremely terrible at it, and my fluky ace had left me feeling the way a kid who's stolen a candy bar from the drugstore can't enjoy the taste of it. After all, if my ball hadn't hit the flag, it probably would have spun back another thirty feet. This ace had involved a whole lot of luck. I hadn't really earned it.

Back home, I tacked my scorecard to the bulletin board. But I couldn't look at it. I was not worthy. And over the next few months, the guilt just worsened—especially when I played with a friend, a few weeks later, a very good lifelong golfer, a very sweet guy. When I mentioned my ace when we reached the 5th his face clouded over. "I never got one," he said. I felt terrible.

So I decided to stop mentioning my ace, except to my philosophical Irish golfing buddy Michael, an even-headed native of County Clare, who, having served as my psychotherapeutic sounding board ever since I'd told him about my guilt-ridden hole-in-one, finally set my head on straight one day.

"Look, the whole stupid game is luck," he said, after sinking an improbably long putt. "If you hit a drive into a tree and it bounces back into the fairway, you don't question that, right? If a great drive finds its way into the sand, you don't question that, right? The golf gods give, the golf gods taketh away. And aces? Show me a single ace that didn't need some luck, at some point. You shot a hole-in-one. The golf gods were smiling on you that day. Enjoy it."

He was right, of course. I now allow myself to glance at my tacked-up scorecard, and savor that amazing little pencil-scrawled "1." Now I'm fine to tell the story of my ace in mixed company (guys who've gotten one, guys who haven't). Maybe it was supernatural. Maybe the golf gods, watching me hack and duff my way through round after round, knowing I'll probably never break 95 in my life, decided to give me one moment to savor. Or maybe it was pure, blind luck.

Either way, I am finally at peace with my ace. Hey, any way you figure it, it was a hell of a shot. And it'll always be mine.

~Peter Richmond

You're Away

Sometimes the poorest man leaves his children the richest inheritance.
~Ruth E. Renkel

When I was twelve years old, my father abandoned me, my mother and my two younger siblings, condemning us to several years of welfare checks, heatless winters, evictions, hunger pains and public ridicule. I never thought I would forgive him, but over the years we established a tenuous relationship. The connection was our love for golf. Ultimately, after a few martinis at the 19th hole one night, Dad confessed that he had been a terrible father and that he hoped to somehow make it up to me some day. I still harbored ill feelings towards him, but over time I learned a little more about why he had left us. No good excuses, but some were rational.

In 1990, as he approached his sixtieth birthday, I was cognizant more than ever of how the male members of our family had a history of dying young. It hit me that my father, a seriously overweight smoker, might be pushing that envelope. With that ominous thought in mind, I decided to take a leap of faith.

On June 23, 1990, we had a small birthday party for Dad. Towards the evening's end, I handed him his birthday card. He skipped past the Hallmark greeting and focused on the note inside. It read:

"Dear Dad, congratulations on your sixtieth birthday. To commemorate this occasion, we invite you to join us for five days at Pebble Beach—all expenses paid."

He read it several times, occasionally glancing up at me. Then his hands started trembling and he left the room quickly, lest he display any emotion.

Several weeks earlier, I had talked to my brother Robert and step-brother Sean about my plan and they quickly bought in. My wife, although conscious of the incredible cost, understood why I needed to give this gift. I paid for the week, a bill I am probably still paying off, but it was worth every dime.

We flew into Monterey Airport in February, 1991, grabbed a cab and headed for Pebble Beach via the breathtaking 17 Mile Drive. After checking in, we walked up to Room 5 and gasped in unison as we looked out the big picture windows overlooking Pebble's famous 18th fairway. Later on, after being joined by my brother-in-law from San Luis Obispo, we went into town for dinner and, on a lark, rented a video camera that practically took two people to carry.

The next morning, sweating bullets despite the cool Pacific air, we all managed to get off the first tee with at least fifty sets of eyes watching us. We leapt into our electric carts to escape the gawkers and, once in the clear, started passing the camera around to record the day's events.

The day was pristine, the sky crystal blue, which matched the color of my father's newly purchased Pebble Beach visor. We made our way through the first six holes, then lost our collective breaths as we arrived at the tee of the short, par-3 7th and saw the waves of the Pacific crashing behind the green. The next few holes along the coast were a magnificent blur, but the camera kept running, to remind us later on that we had actually played them.

At the tee-box on 18, we paused to soak it all in. Sean walked behind and filmed Dad and me as we smoked our drives down the middle of the famous finishing hole. When my ball landed 40 yards past my dad's, I couldn't help but gloat "Hey, Dad, you're away!"

Sean pushed his drive to the right. After locating his ball, he grabbed the camera and started filming again. With a steady hand, he captured my father and I walking side by side up the fairway. Unable to resist the camera, we removed our visors and waved to the imaginary crowd that was roaring in our heads. It's an image for a lifetime. Every year in early February, I sneak downstairs to watch that film and privately allow the tears to flow.

At week's end, my father and Sean had to fly to New York. I sensed that the goodbyes were going to be awkward. Sean and I exchanged firm, manly handshakes. I then turned to my father, still wearing his new Pebble Beach visor. I reached out my hand and could see his eyes welling up. He ignored my hand and put his arms around me. "I'll never forget this, Ronnie. I love you very much."

It was the first time my father had ever told me that.

"I love you too, Dad."

In his few remaining years, we said it a lot more to each other. Before he died in 1997, he tried hard to make up for lost time with me and actually became a good grandfather to my two sons. We enjoyed the occasional round of golf over those years. His Pebble Beach visor now has an honored place in my study.

Today, I play golf with my two teenage sons at our local club. It's not Pebble Beach, but I've learned that it's not the venue that makes golfing with your sons so special. It's slapping the ball around in all sorts of directions, laughing at a three-putt from ten feet, high-fiving after a birdie and having them tell me, "Hey, Dad, you're away."

~Ron Fitzsimmons

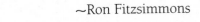

You Can't Bring a Baseball Swing to the Golf Course

If I can hit a curveball, why can't I hit a ball that is standing still on a course?
~Larry Nelson

can't get rid of my baseball player's swing no matter how hard I try. I draw the club back slow like I'm cocking a bat, pause at the top like I'm waiting to read the pitch, then fire down with my hips, releasing way too early, finishing tilted back with all my weight on my right side, my left toe extended as if toward center field. A regular Sammy Sosa on the driving range I must look like. More often than not I strike the turf several inches behind the ball and unearth a divot half the size of home plate.

This isn't a great source of misery for me. I golf only sporadically for fun, usually taking a cart and a few beers along for the ride. As for baseball, it ended up taking me to a university where I got to pitch for four years.

One of my closest friends growing up quit baseball for golf when we were both thirteen. He was small, always looked about three years younger than anyone on the field, but played a handy shortstop and ran fast enough to turn a lot of weak contact hits into doubles. I tried to convince him to come back to the team but he was resolute in his decision. Golf, he told me, was the sport for a little guy. If everyone else was hitting 8-iron he could still stick a 5-iron. If he couldn't reach a par 5 in two he could still wedge on and make the putt for birdie.

The spring of our junior year in high school this friend qualified for the men's state amateur. He was psyched—at the time it was the biggest event he'd ever been in. I remember him coming up to me at my locker.

"Hey Jared, you want to caddy?"

I smiled, a little perplexed. The few times we'd gone golfing had been pretty disastrous. I'd displayed a pretty loose grasp of the rules, like not setting the bag down on the greens and not walking between the player's ball and the cup. No doubt there were lots of other weird rules I had broken unknowingly. Surely I'd screw up and ruin this tournament for him. "I don't know anything about golf," I said. "You've seen me in action."

"You don't have to do anything," my friend said. "Just carry the bag and follow me around. I'll read all my own putts and figure all the yardages."

I still wasn't convinced. "What's the date?"

He told me and it didn't conflict with any of my baseball games.

"Come on," he kept on. "I get a practice round at the course the day before the tournament. You can say you're my caddy and we'll both play for free."

What the heck, free anything meant a lot to a teenager without cash flow. Actually, now that I think about it, that's probably half the reason he asked me. So he wouldn't have to pay a real caddy.

As promised, when we showed up for the practice round my friend was on some list and we didn't have to pay a thing. We even got a free bucket for the range.

I'd brought my own clubs; a rusty set of Spaldings with sweet spots the size of a nickel and cracked rubber grips that had been baking in our garage since whenever whatever relative last left them there. The woods were equally pathetic, some toyish-looking things from Kmart.

I stretched. Made some practice swings. Sliced a few, topped a few, duffed a few. Back in those days it never took me too long to figure out why my curve ball wasn't breaking, but the mechanics of the golf swing have always escaped me. My friend offered me some ridiculously vague tips, like pretending my arms were a pendulum attached to a barrel or some equally useless nonsense. I was just trying to get the ball in the air. So as I swatted away, growing more and more disillusioned as I tried to uncover the causes and effects from different ways of rotating my shoulders, I started glancing over at my friend's bag. Every club was shiny and top of the line. His driver was the size of a grapefruit and made an awesome sound like an Easton hit hard down the third base line.

"Let me try your driver," I said, convinced that at least some of my problems were equipment related.

He shook his head no.

"Oh, come on," I said. "What's the big deal? You won't let anyone touch your precious clubs."

He sighed and handed it over. "One shot," he said, holding up his index finger. "Then I've got to practice with it."

I got in my stance and waggled the club. Despite the big black head that dwarfed the ball it felt much lighter than mine. It looked impossible to miss with. Though I felt like I was bending down lower than usual to address the ball. "It seems shorter than mine," I said.

"The shaft's cut an inch," my friend responded, irritably. I'd inadvertently touched a nerve. My 5'1" friend was a tad sensitive about his height. I knew for a fact he had lied at the DMV and had them print 5'2" on his first license. As if that were much better.

"Tee it lower," he said. "I don't want you putting a sky mark on it."

I pushed the ball a little lower to quiet him, then got back into my stance. I reared back, confident that with this fancy club the ball was going to soar on a straight line to the far reaches of the range.

Instead of the sharp strike of metal on Surlyn, the soft dead feel of dirt shuddered up my arms—I'd hit way behind the ball. Next there came a terrible "whoop-whoop-whoop" sound like a boomerang, and as I wrapped around to my Sosa-like finish the club felt strangely light and whippy, like a fishing pole without a fish. In the corner of my eye I saw the black head tumbling 40 yards or so down the range.

Oops.

My friend grabbed the club, or what was left of it, straight from my hands. He examined the end of the shaft, which was jagged and splintered with graphite fibers. He looked like he was about to cry.

I told him how incredibly sorry I was, that I'd buy him a new one. After a period of muteness he said not to worry about it, that he could send it back to the manufacturer and have it re-shafted for free. Though it would take weeks, he added.

That afternoon we walked around the course fairly quietly. My friend hit 3-wood off every tee and cursed each time his "longer-than-they-would-have-been" approach shots missed the green.

I don't remember exactly how the subject was broached, but I do remember not being asked to caddy the following day. My friend borrowed an unfamiliar driver from some guy he knew and played badly and missed the cut.

This was all ten years ago. We're still the closest of friends. We live on opposite sides of the country, yet still make the effort to hang out at least twice a year. We're now actually the same height, though I've still got a few pounds on him. He still loves the game and plays in all sorts of amateur events, says distance is no longer an issue. When we get together, reminisce over a few cold ones, we often laugh about the time I ruined his first big tournament. Last time we saw each other he brought me a brand new 460cc driver as a gift. "Now you can break your own," he said. He's still trying to get me to take this game seriously.

Even with my ugly baseball swing, every once in a while, when by chance I catch it just right, I can drive it past the little guy. Though he'd probably tell you different.

~Jared Slater

"Age, nothing—I'd be satisfied to play my weight."

Anything Can Happen

There is no type of miracle that can't happen at least once in golf.
~Grantland Rice

Playing in front of crowds is an experience that takes getting used to, and I've been pretty lucky that I've had a lot of this kind of experience, but playing in the final group on Sunday in a PGA Tour event is something else entirely. I can't say my familiarity with this is exactly firsthand, but it's about as close as anyone can get.

It was the 2001 AT&T Pebble Beach National Pro-Am. This is, in my opinion, the "Masters" for amateur golfers who don't compete regularly. My partner, Phil Mickelson, had lit it up on Friday and Saturday to put himself in a position to win the individual pro title, worth $720,000. On the team format, which is net best ball, we were right in the mix as well. I had been doing my part with my then 6-handicap (I've worked my way to scratch now) to rack up some net-birdies and net-eagles. I'd even canned a 70-footer for a net-eagle at Pebble Beach on Saturday that made the tournament highlights on CNN.

It was my third time playing in the tournament, but that Sunday was unlike any other day previous. I felt like I was in an elite club when we teed off on Sunday afternoon in the last group. Peter Kostis was following us with a microphone, there were television cameras everywhere, and the immediate, tangible importance of every shot made the atmosphere electric. Phil, understandably, wasn't paying much attention to what I was doing. He'd gotten off to a frustrating start, missing a lot of make-able birdies, and wasn't overly engrossed in our "team" charge. He was in his own zone. It was of course amazing just to be there in the presence of it all, drinking it up. Talk about "inside the ropes" access.

When we got to the 14th hole, a long par 5, we were four strokes behind the team leaders, Tiger Woods and Jerry Chang (Tiger's former college teammate at Stanford). With five holes to go, it seemed unlikely that we were going to challenge the lead. I hit a great drive, and I had a 3-wood in my hands for the second shot. It was a stroke hole for me, so if I could make a natural birdie it would alter the scope of our chances. I wouldn't say I was too nervous, but man, was I excited. My heart thumped in my chest.

I hit the worst shot I've ever hit. It came out of nowhere. I skank-pulled that 3-wood so bad the ball almost hit my left shoe. I'm talking almost a 90-degree yank. My ball split the crowd and rolled over the cart path into some weeds. Right then, at that horrifyingly low moment, a spectator yelled, "My grandmother hits better shots than that!"

This guy was obviously oblivious to my play that week, but still, there was nothing I could do. I couldn't explain to him and the rest of the snickering crowd that I had been playing pretty decently, that this shot had been the aberration. I just had to take the abuse. As the marshals cleared the crowd so I could take a stance my head spun. I was embarrassed. I had that feeling that every golfer has experienced when you feel that you have thrown your chances away.

Well, I pitched out to the fairway, knocked a pitching wedge to seven feet, and made the par putt for a net-birdie! I birdied the next hole with a miraculous 6-iron under a tree and over bunker that rolled onto the green to six feet. Phil bogeyed that hole, so he got very focused on 16 and 17 and birdied those two. Just like that, four birdies in a row and with one hole left, we had a one stroke lead in the team event.

I wish I could say we carried it home. Anyone who watched the coverage probably doesn't remember my bogey on 18 but they might remember Phil famously attempting to hit driver off the deck to reach the par 5 in two. It was gutsy, exactly the play he had to try to steal the title away from Davis Love III, already sitting comfortably in the clubhouse. But alas, Phil's shot cannonballed into the Pacific. Though it's cool to think I was standing right next to him when he hit it.

So in the end we ended up tying for first place with Woods/Chang. Now my name's on a trophy next to the greatest player ever. Not bad!

This all happened eight years ago, but to this day I replay the moment of the grandmother comment whenever I get into trouble on the golf course. It reminds me that anything can happen. After I yanked that 3-wood, I thought there was no chance of getting a piece of first place. I would've bet my career album sales on it.

Absolutely anything can happen in golf. You can shoot your best score after starting out with three bogies in a row. Every golfer should have one on-course memory to gather strength from in times of trouble. The 14th at Pebble is mine.

~Kenny G

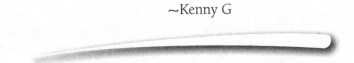

An Iowa Steamer

The uglier a man's legs are, the better he plays golf. It's almost a law.
~H.G. Wells

The skies opened, and by the time the storm was done our town had been deluged with nine inches of rain. I know it sounds unbelievable, but trust me, it was nine inches if it was a drop.

Our club course closed so the grounds crew could sort things out. But a phone call to a local public course, on a more elevated property suited to quicker drainage, found us a place to play. It was ninety-five degrees and the sun was out in force. It was a frightful day, a real steam bath. One of those days when you reach for one tee in your pocket, but the cloth is so damp and sticky that all your tees, ball markers, pivot tools and what have you come peeling out as well.

One member of our foursome was my then aged father-in-law, Mr. Louis Walker, who in his prime had played to a 3-handicap. He had been a player of statewide renown, a champion of tournaments at many levels. He was a very large man, not only in the physical sense but also ethically. Mr. Walker was one who played by the rules completely, in golf and life. He was a successful businessman, a prominent civic leader, a devoted father, and a pillar of the church.

Even as his skills declined with age, Mr. Walker's competitive edge never left him. His golf that hot day was frightful and he grew very upset about it. He played a losing front nine, the thick, suppressive air bringing out the worst in him. Uncharacteristically, his mood was down, and each hole he complained vocally about the conditions, his swing, and the world in general.

We stopped for liquids at the turn. After two lackluster shots on the par-5 10th, Mr. Walker was still not in range of the green. His son and I had just hit our second shots, when his son, speechless and with a flabbergasted look, mutely pointed across the fairway with his gloved left hand. I turned to see what was shocking him so.

Mr. Walker, ever the model of propriety, there stood in his boxers. We watched as the old man then carefully folded his trousers and placed them in the basket of the cart.

His son and I rushed over to see what his intentions were. "Simple," Mr. Walker said. "I've figured out the trouble with my swing. My trousers are too damp from the humidity so I can't pivot properly."

So there he stood, a man known to everyone in the city, in red and white boxer underwear, a blue polo shirt, a white cap, black shoes and black socks, and with very, very white legs.

His son and I proffered that several problems could arise; other women golfers on the course could be offended, possibly the police would arrive with charges ranging from indecent exposure to lunacy. None of our warnings fazed him, however, and we played on. At one point Mr. Walker was so bold as to cross another fairway to point out to a female golfer where he'd seen her ball enter a hazard. Her thank you was perfunctory, nervous, careful, and while backing away.

And you know what? Mr. Walker managed those last eight holes in 1-over par. He took all the money and left me with a day of golf I remember with awe, comedy, and perhaps reverence.

~Dr. Sam Christensen

16

Chicken Soup for the Soul

Shopping to Buy Woods on a Snowy Evening

Whose woods these are I think I know.
His handicap is very low;
He will not see me shopping here
To see his woods fill me with woe.

My little wife must think it queer
To shop without a club pro near
Between the woods and bunker rakes
The darkest evening of the year.

She gives her earring bells a shake
To ask if there is some mistake.
The only other sound's the sweep
Of many practice swings I take.

The woods are lovely, taut and cheap.
But I've a handicap to keep,
And smiles to give so I won't weep,
And smiles to give so I won't weep.

~Harris Green

17

Ernie's Last Game

*As you walk down the fairway of life you must smell the roses,
for you only get to play one round.*
~Ben Hogan

My husband used to say that when he died he wanted to be cremated and have his ashes sprinkled over Marilyn Monroe. Recently our friend, Ernie, was diagnosed with a very aggressive cancer and given only three weeks to live. Ernie's dying wish wasn't as vulgar. He simply wanted to be cremated and have his ashes sprinkled over the green at the local public course where he had got his most treasured hole-in-one.

Ernie requested that his three golf buddies who filled the regular foursome each week and his best friend, Jim, be the ones to accompany his wife Maggie to carry out the secret ceremony. Knowing city officials would not take kindly to this plan, Ernie plotted with his wife and these four friends as though it were one last mischievous game. The whole idea of it put a twinkle in his eye.

In order that no one would spill the beans prematurely, Maggie was to wait several days after the cremation. Then, on the spur of the moment, she would call the others and give the simple instructions, "Tonight's the night!"

And so it was. The five of them lingered until dark in the parking lot across the street from the golf course. When there were no lights from oncoming vehicles, they quickly hustled out of their car and dashed across the street to the sturdy, white, wooden fence that surrounded the course. Then, flashlights pointed to the ground, they crept over the fence and onto the 6th green where the roguish deed was to be done.

Reggie, Mike and Jim held flashlights. Paul held the box of ashes as Maggie sprinkled them over the green. "There's so much left, what will we do with the rest?" Jim asked.

"You know," Reggie said with a grin, "Ernie was lucky to get that hole-in-one. He did hit an awful lot more balls into that sand trap. What do you say we sprinkle some of the ashes into the sand there, too?"

And so they did. But there were still more ashes left.

Paul smiled and reminded everyone, "Actually, a lot of Ernie's balls are sitting at the bottom of that pond over there, too. Maybe we could sprinkle the rest in there."

With a lump in their throats and a prayer in their hearts, by that pond's edge they said their final goodbye to a friend who had in death, as in life, shown them a joyful and humorous spirit.

Mission accomplished, they snuck off the course the same way they entered, hightailed it back to the car.

Now when Reggie, Mike and Paul are on the 6th green, they say they can almost feel Ernie's spirit with them. They figure he's laughing along with them when one of their balls goes into the sand trap or into the pond. It's a private joke that only five people understand.

~Kay Connor Pliszka

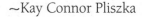

18

Playing Augusta National

Growing up on the Jersey Shore, I didn't play much golf, but my dad was always so excited when The Masters came on every April. He would darken the den as best he could to bring out the brilliant colors of Augusta National on our Zenith television. Like it does for so many, I think the tournament and the club represented an array of wonderful things to him; the end of winter and the start of another golf season, the renewal of spring and the chance to watch some of his sporting idols. So what if he fell asleep an hour into the telecast?

After graduating college in 1982, I started playing a bit more, often with my dad, who was stricken with an inoperable brain tumor that same year. As a physician, he clearly knew the prognosis when he received the news. Looking at his brain scan, he once told me, was like reading his own obituary.

When he passed away five years later, golf started to become an obsession of mine, partly because playing was a way to stay connected with him. This obsession led me to becoming a golf writer and, eventually, an editor at *Links* magazine.

My dad never made it to the Masters in person, but I finally did in 1999. When I first walked out of the press building and onto the first fairway, I felt a little bit like Dorothy in *The Wizard of Oz* when she walks out of her house after it crashes into Munchkinland, the moment when the film goes from black and white to color. There is a hyper reality to the place. The grass is greener, the azaleas brighter and the sand whiter than you can possibly imagine.

As eye opening as it was to see the course for the first time, I was even more flabbergasted when I got to actually play it in 2008. The Monday after the tournament is the media-day lottery, and I was lucky enough to win a spot. To finally play the holes I'd always dreamed of playing, to be faced with the same shots I first knew from watching on television with my dad, was surreal. Of course, my round went by way too fast.

Each year at The Masters there are more than a thousand credentialed journalists, but only a couple of hundred are eligible for the lottery. Up until a few years ago, there was a "one-and-done" policy for journalists when it came to playing the course following the tournament. But this was changed to once every seven years after Gary D'Amato of the *Milwaukee Journal-Sentinel* wrote a letter to former Augusta National chairman Hootie Johnson asking him to rethink the policy given all the course changes over the years.

How my lucky ticket got punched my first year in the lottery is still a mystery to me.

I remember turning onto Magnolia Lane, driving as slow as my car would go so that I might savor the moment just that bit longer. I rode past the logo of yellow flowers in the Founder's Circle to the club drop area where a line of caddies in their trademark white jumpsuits were waiting. My caddy, Todd, introduced himself and told me he'd meet me at the range. I was so excited I passed on the free Danish and coffee.

Included in my 8:02 foursome was my good friend Mike Arkush, the golf editor from *Yahoo! Sports*. The fact that Mike and I both got selected and then got paired together was pure luck (we think), but it made the day only that much better to have an old friend with whom to share the round.

They started the media on both nines. With a chill in the air and the sun just coming up over the tall pine trees that line the 10th hole, I had first-tee jitters times ten, not because of the small crowd that had gathered but because Augusta National is a living link with my dad. I wanted to see my ball catch the severe down-slope on the 450-yard hole just like I had seen Arnie, Jack and Tiger's balls do countless times. Alas, I pushed my drive right into the trees.

The Member tees measure just 6,365 yards, almost 1,100 hundred yards less than The Masters tees. Strangely, there are no intermediate tees in the 6,800-yard range. Also, atypically, there are no ball washers or plaques by the tees with hole layouts and yardages.

The small, white scorecard is a wonderfully succinct statement to the club's less-is-more philosophy. It doesn't even contain the course's rating and slope, but, then again, there aren't any. Hole handicaps are based on length, so the 145-yard 12th is rated as the 16th hardest hole, which is clearly not the case, even on the calm morning like I had. (It played the second most difficult hole during the 2008 tournament with a 3.30 stroke average.)

How fast are the greens, you ask? They hadn't been cut before our round, but they still had to Stimp around twelve or thirteen by my guess. With the pin placements in their same Sunday locations, I felt like I was putting on newly waxed gymnasium floors. I was so tentative, even on uphill putts, that I couldn't apply my normal stroke on the ball. My putting suffered; by day's end I had thirty-six total waves of the wand. Though I'm happy to say I didn't have any four-putts.

As we walked off the back of the last green, longtime CBS announcer Jim Nantz, a friend of Mike's, was there to greet us and ask about our round. The only way the day could have been any better was if my dad were playing with me. But in a way, he was. I don't think I've ever felt his presence as strongly since his passing as I did that Monday. I'm sure he was watching.

He might have even stayed awake for the entire round.

~Tom Cunneff

19

Hot Dogs and Sansabelts

Never drive faster than your guardian angel can fly.
~Author Unknown

We'd just stocked up on sodas and hotdogs at the turn. The 10th is a 160-yard, severely downhill par 3 with a fifty-foot drop from tee to green. My Pops, my two brothers and I all teed off and as usual, had the green surrounded but the putting surface vacant. Pops hopped into the lead cart driven by my older brother. My younger brother and I followed as we hurried off to our hopeful pars. This particular cart path plummets steeply down the right side of the fairway before making an abrupt ninety-degree left turn at the bottom, where it then gradually continues down to the green.

Rather than wait until the longer 11th hole (as many have often elected), Pops decided to eat his hot dog right then on the way to the green. As he sized up his first bite he leaned to his right, over the side of the cart, lest he dribble any mustard or pickle relish on his new Sansabelt slacks. At that unfortunate moment, my brother took the hard left turn without pumping the brake. (Sansabrake, if you will.) Close on their tail, my younger brother and I were at the proper vantage point to watch it unfold.

Pops was jettisoned from the cart like a human cannonball. Somehow, in some miraculous display of seventy-year-old man agility, he landed on his feet. But having flown 10 or so yards through the air à la Carl Lewis, the harsh rules of physics made it so Pops couldn't help but be running faster than a man of seventy should be running. Way faster! To his credit, I'll say he was on the verge of regaining his inertial balance when he came upon a small collection of course maintenance debris. Upon this he tripped, rolling head over FootJoys several times before coming to a stop. Flat on his back with his arms outstretched as if preparing to ascend to the heavens, completely motionless.

We were horrified. I screeched our cart to a halt on the slope and we jumped out. We raced towards him, praying that he wasn't hurt (or worse).

Pops sat up slowly, looked around. We inspected him for injuries but aside from a sore shoulder, the only damage we could find was to his severely squeezed hot dog, still firmly locked in his fist. I told him he must have wanted it pretty darn bad. But he wasn't quite ready to laugh.

After a few minutes to rest and regain his composure, pick the grass from his hair and dust off the Sansabelts, he hopped back into the cart, finished his hot dog. Then he proceeded to make a fantastic up and down to par the hole. My brothers and I, relieved he wasn't injured, yet simultaneously reeling with laughter, all made bogey. Pops won the skins. Again.

~Brian Amos Fox

20

Low and Left

> *In youth we learn; in age we understand.*
> ~Marie Ebner-Eschenbach

"Do you think I should wait or go ahead and hit?" I asked my friend Mike.

"I don't know," Mike said. "He's pretty close."

"Yeah," I answered. "But he's on the left side of the fairway. I never hit it left."

Just ten years old, my golf skills were still in their embryonic stages—as was my knowledge of etiquette. My drives all tended to drift weakly high and right. My occasional well-struck tee shot would start straight, but then always fade to the right edge of the fairway.

Low and left? Never.

So as those last heedless words left my lips, I started my backswing. A brief turn of the hips, a subtle rotation of the shoulders, and the ball rocketed off the clubface—low and left.

Rarely in life are we afforded the divine power of foretelling the future, seeing events unfold before they occur. Like maybe when the car ahead on the freeway abruptly stops, and no amount of brake pressure would have avoided the impending collision.

So as my small, white missile streaked down the left side of the fairway, I saw the future for an instant. I no longer hoped the ball wouldn't hit the fellow golfer in front of me—that was a foregone conclusion. No, instead, I hoped it would merely hit him in the thigh, the butt, or at least the upper arm, someplace fleshy with some padding. Just, please, not directly on bone, I thought. And not on the head.

I would like to believe I heartily yelled "Fore!" But, in reality, I barely mustered a weak and reluctant "Hey." Mike heard me, but the fellow 170 yards down the fairway certainly did not.

Maybe if I just closed my eyes and prayed, I could pretend this never happened, that I never hit a golf ball with this man — possibly a husband, a father, a favorite son — just down the fairway.

But no such luck. The ball continued the seemingly eternal flight toward its human destination. Now just yards away, I realized that my Pinnacle was on a beeline toward the center of the man's back, as if his shoulder blades were goalposts for a descending football.

In a matter of milliseconds, my mind feverishly raced through dozens of potential outcomes, each more horrid and life altering than the former: broken bones, newspaper headlines, prison time, a funeral. What will Dad say? Will I be banned from the course? Will I ever play again? Do juvenile detention centers have golf courses?

Then, with a dull and horrid thump, the ball struck right in the middle of his back. Dead center. The lump in my throat grew two-fold. Though I tried to swallow, every ounce of moisture in my mouth relocated to the palms of my hands. I simply thought, "I'm screwed."

The man's stride halted mid-step. He never fell down. He never slumped over. He hardly even flinched. As if superhuman, some sort of mythical golfing god, he slowly turned around with his head slightly tilted toward his right shoulder. He stared at me with eyes that seemed to judge my entire brief life.

I wanted to run. I wanted to point at Mike. He's the one who hit you! I wanted to take some practice swings and nonchalantly act as if nothing happened, as if I were simply warming up for my drive, that the reckless offender must have been playing from some other hole.

But, instead, I waved. "Sorry about that," I sheepishly hollered, waiting for the man to bolt into a sprint back up the hill.

But the brute never said a word. He just continued to stare.

"Is he OK?" Mike asked. "That had to hurt."

"I think so. What should I do?"

"I don't know," Mike said, turning toward his golf bag, as if washing his hands of any guilt by association.

"Sorry," I yelled again, hoping a second apology would render the matter resolved.

We waited a few more seconds, still expecting him to charge back up the fairway, crazily waving a pitching wedge in his hand. You stupid kids! What do you think you are doing! But, stunningly, he turned back around and began a slow gait toward the green, leaving my ball lying in the sparsely mown rough behind him. In silence, I lowered my head and stared at the ground.

The man hadn't shouted. He hadn't thrown my ball into the woods. He hadn't offered any animated hand gestures. And after his round he didn't report my actions to the pro shop. He just walked away and continued his round, leaving me to wallow in my guilt and idiocy.

Twenty years later, I have no idea why that man walked away. Maybe he just dismissed me as a stupid kid, a ten-year-old not worth wasting his time on. Or perhaps the ball just hadn't hurt that much. Although I can't imagine how a line-drive tee shot from 170 yards wouldn't bring pain. Whatever the reason, I learned a fundamental rule of golf etiquette that day: don't dare hit into the group ahead.

And, on the rare occasion when someone hits into me, I don't yell or throw a fit. I simply stare.

~Robert Bruce

America's Course

Laundry is the only thing that should be separated by color.
~Author Unknown

She all but threw herself at the ball, all seventy pounds of her. The small driver accented with a bright pink grip sent her golf ball, also pink, some 120 yards down the fairway, a mighty blow for a girl of nine. She then promptly ran after it with excited abandon, as if the ball might disappear if she did not hasten to strike her next shot.

Off some distance, standing outside the door of the modest clubhouse on this sunny and hot afternoon, was the proprietor of the club and his daughter. They watched with knowing wonder and genuine appreciation—not only for the girl's preternatural talent, but also for her enthusiasm for a game that had been their life's work. Later, they would tell the little girl's father how much they enjoyed taking in the simple innocence and joy of her tee shot.

"That little girl loves the game," said the elderly proprietor, ninety years old but still effusing boyish passion for golf. In his voice there was wistfulness and a trace of melancholy, as if he were recalling in his mind's eye the little girl in his now grown daughter next to him. "You can tell. You can see it the way she went after that ball and went scurrying down that fairway. Stay on it with her. Keep encouraging her."

The elderly man, Dr. William Powell, had built that fairway and the rest of the par-71 golf course not just with his bare hands, but his bared soul, his sweat, his tears, his blood, and his dignity. Clearview Golf Club in East Canton, Ohio, is the only golf club in the world designed, built, owned and operated by an African-American citizen. It proclaims itself "America's Course."

Powell, the great-grandson of Alabama slaves, began building his dream course in 1946 after fighting for America in World War II. He had learned the game as a pre-teen from a white doctor, becoming a standout player, captaining both his high school and college teams before serving in the Army. Overseas, he had the opportunity to play some of the United Kingdom's great layouts. But after the war, he encountered retrenchments of prejudice, and was denied access to courses at home. Undaunted, he decided to build his own place, one that would afford access to all golfers.

Even little ones.

That young girl swinging the pink driver was my daughter, Ellie. She and my son, Alex, and I played eighteen holes that day at Mr. Powell's Clearview Golf Club in July of 2006. That year, the historic club celebrated its sixtieth anniversary. Our visit represented the third of six trips I made there that summer from my home near Columbus to visit with Dr. P (as he is known), his daughter, Renee, a former LPGA golfer, and his son, Larry, the course superintendent, to gather information for a feature story I was writing for *Golf World* magazine. I learned how the family had poured their lives and fortunes into the golf course, and though they barely earned a living from it, had managed to create a place that fulfilled its mission — to welcome golfers from all walks of life.

Even if financial success has been elusive, Clearview has been celebrated as one of America's most important golf courses, attracting television and newspaper coverage from around the world. A marker from the Ohio Historical Society has been erected behind the first tee. The course is listed among a dozen courses on the National Registry of Historic Places.

Clearly, its legacy is secure, but not because of markers or official proclamations of recognition or the mountains of well-deserved print publicity.

No, not in the least. The legacy is secure because my children remember that day and why we were there—to enjoy the game together and to also learn about an important piece of American history in their home state. And especially my daughter, who remembers the few words Dr. P said to her after our round over Cokes in the pre-Civil War farmhouse that still serves as the clubhouse.

"I can tell you're a golfer," Dr. P said to her, seeing my daughter in a way that so many people over the years had refused to look at him. His words denoted an acceptance of her with what one would describe as fraternal pride augmented by genuine enthusiasm. He accepted her without blinders or prejudice or hesitation.

~David Shedloski

The Golf Book

Working the Ball

My only fear is that I may have to go out and get a real job.

~Fuzzy Zoeller

Never Ever Say Never

He conquers who endures.

~Persius

Let me open with one of the best statements I've ever heard. While practicing after an early round at Memphis, in ninety-degree heat with matching humidity, Kirk Triplett yelled over to a bunch of sweaty pros, "There has to be something really screwed up with us to excel at this game."

I think Kirk's little quip explains how this game can really mess with you. When things are going well, life is good. The life of the road, with its bad food, bad hotels and lonely downtime, is okay. But play poorly and everything gets magnified. Negative vibes seem to have a ripple effect into every aspect of life.

I don't believe there is such a thing as a natural golfer. Can you imagine someone picking up a club for the first time and making a magnificent swing, sending the ball on a beautiful flight and on target? Maybe in the movies. I do believe that every player who has made it on tour has worked extremely hard to learn what it takes to score.

It baffles me to see some guys, who have professional talent beyond what I could ever imagine, struggle or never make it. At the same time, others make it with less talent, and go on to have great careers. I'm not sure where I fit in this scenario, but you can judge for yourself.

My childhood years were the best. I cannot imagine anyone having better times than me and my friends shared from age seven through college. We all had jobs, we had sports, we had good homes, good schools, but most of all, good times.

From age eight until sixteen, I had a paper route. Each year my route grew until I had about one hundred customers. When I turned sixteen, I started driving the delivery truck on weekends, making eight dollars per hour, a lot of money back then. I did this through college. At age twelve, I also started working at the U of Maryland golf course. I started as a cart boy, then range maintenance, then pro shop.

My athletic background was typical of most kids back then. I played nearly every sport at the boys club level. Baseball, football, basketball, not really excelling in any one of them. I was a very good athlete, but I didn't really believe in my skills. One sport I did do outside the norm was boxing. From age eight to sixteen I fought in the Junior Golden Gloves. We trained hard, fought hard, even bled hard, but it was fun if you can believe that.

All this and I haven't mentioned golf. Well, at age ten I went with my dad to caddie for him, and I decided to try the game. I loved it and really got into it, except I never gave anything else up. My responsibilities with work and other sports, let alone school, meant my time for actually playing golf was limited early on. I believe to this day, my dedication to being a good employee, a decent student, and to do the best I could at any sport, molded me for my drive to get to the tour.

I've said that I was a good athlete, but I was small and not very fast. Bad combo to stand out in most sports except boxing and golf. In boxing you always fought someone the same size, and I liked that, except there were some pretty tough guys my size. Does Sugar Ray Leonard ring a bell? Well, he rang many a bell, and I witnessed most, because he grew up in the same county I did. He was one of those "can't miss" kids.

Me, I was never a "can't miss" kid; I just kind of blended in. I was average as a junior golfer, but I became one of the best in the county in high school. My freshman year at U of Maryland I did not make the team, then transferred to PGCC (Prince George's Community College) for two years, then went back to Maryland and was team captain my last two years. Following graduation, I headed south to a Florida mini tour in 1981 and went "belly up."

My future in golf looked bleak, until my coach at Maryland offered me his job because he got promoted to Athletic Director. From 1982 to 1988, I was Coach Funk, when hired the youngest Division I head coach in history. It was through this time period my game picked up. I worked hard on my game, harder than any of the players. I was determined to see if I had what it took to make it. In 1984, I won the National Assistant Pro Championship. This allowed me to go to Q-School, but I failed. Failing in '85 led me to '86 Q-School.

Having had my best summer, I tore a rotator in my left shoulder and failed again. Skipping '87 Q-School, I showed up with no expectations and what happened? I made it.

Failing my rookie year sent me back to Q-School but I easily qualified and made it back to the Tour. I never went to Q-School again. My career was a long progression, many highs, seemingly even more lows, but the triumphs did come and my career as a whole was a great success.

I believe my childhood experience helped mold me, even drove me to have the successes I have had. I've had one goal this whole time: "How good can I get?" I believe I can't answer this yet; I can still improve, still learn. Stay tuned for the sequel to my story because of my belief, "Never Ever Say Never."

~Fred Funk
as seen in the DVD *Chicken Soup Conversations for the Golfer's Soul*

23

Chalas's Chance Encounter

Bruce Chalas knew that changing careers at age fifty-seven was unconventional at best, risky at worst. But he offered a smile, said he trusted the road he was now going down. The two of us were in line for coffee during a break in festivities of an annual banquet saluting the Francis Ouimet Scholarship Fund. "Golf has never failed me," Chalas said. "It won't this time, either."

This decision to end his business career and embark on a life of golf instruction was wild, Chalas conceded. But he explained that the seed had been planted four decades earlier, the day one of golf's greatest names came to his rescue.

"I told you that story, didn't I?"

When I told him he had not, Chalas shook his head. He then recounted a trip to West Palm Beach in the winter of 1972, that of a young man in pursuit of employment.

Chalas had never exactly dreamed of a career in glue, but this wasn't exactly like Dustin Hoffman being told about plastics in *The Graduate*. Permatex was a leading glue manufacturer and the chance to talk to company officials about a possible job opportunity was something this twenty-year-old college senior couldn't turn down.

It was just that, well, Chalas was a college senior and felt there was no need to spend every minute of his whirlwind trip to Florida pondering work. Having handled the interview, Chalas surveyed the brilliant Florida weather and decided golf was in order.

No rental car? No worries. Chalas had a thumb, so standing outside the Holiday Inn on the corner of PGA Boulevard and Military Trail, the young man from Babson College in Wellesley, Massachusetts waited for a ride, golf clubs by his side. Oh, if he really had to, Chalas could have walked, for the PGA of America's 54-hole facility is not much more than a mile away. But within minutes, a car pulled over. Young Chalas tossed his clubs in the back and hopped in the front passenger seat.

At which time he cast his eyes on an American icon. None other than Byron Nelson was sitting behind the wheel.

"I'm a golfer, too," said Nelson. "Where are you going?"

Dumbfounded, Chalas could only stare. All through his youth Chalas had read about the game's legends and studied what had made them so great. Chalas knew that Nelson had done unthinkable things on the golf course—eleven straight wins, eighteen in a season, five major titles—and now, he sat not four feet away. Searching for some sort of response, Chalas could only come up with, "I know you're a golfer, and you're quite a good one."

A chili-dip of comments, thought Chalas, but Nelson laughed. The great man was a few weeks shy of his sixtieth birthday and more than twenty years removed from his 52nd and final PGA Tour win, but the dignity for which he was renowned shined through.

Nelson asked again where he was going. Chalas explained his situation, how he felt a slight interruption in his job search to play some golf was not being irresponsible. Nelson smiled and told him that it was a very short ride to the PGA of America's facility, John D. MacArthur's monument to himself and a safe haven for professional golfers looking to escape a winter's embrace. He was pleased to be able to assist.

The close proximity between the hotel and the golf course had at first seemed ideal, but Chalas now wished it were a twenty-mile ride. Two hundred, even. He had inhaled the Ben Hogan books, but Ben Hogan never would have picked him up thumbing and offered a ride to the golf course. Chalas told himself to act quickly, to think of something to say because this opportunity surely would never cross his way again.

"Mister Nelson," said Chalas, "when we get to the golf course, would you mind watching me hit a few balls?"

Chalas had learned the game as a young boy in the country town of Millis, thirty miles west of Boston. And while he harbored no thoughts of a professional career, he loved the game and wanted to be as competitive an amateur golfer as he could. Charlie Shephard, the longtime club pro at Glen Ellen Country Club in Millis, had been Chalas' mentor for many years, telling the young boy on countless occasions that golf would deliver great joy. But after putting forth such a bold request of Lord Byron, Chalas wondered if he wasn't in line to be embarrassed or disappointed.

"Well, I'm not playing today. I'm just must meeting some friends," said Nelson. "So, I'd love to take a look."

The sun never felt warmer, the game never so rewarding as it did that January day in 1972. With a joy that he had never quite experienced, Chalas took hold of his clubs and sent a half-dozen golf balls soaring into the Florida air. After each one he stole a quick glance to the side, just to be sure that the great Byron Nelson was watching. He was, too, quiet at first, until finally he suggested that Chalas think about a slight change in the way he held the club.

"The grip," he told Chalas. "Put some strength in that grip."

More balls were struck under the watchful eye of Nelson, more suggestions were offered to the wide-eyed Chalas. For nearly thirty minutes, two strangers separated by nearly forty years in age — one of them a gentleman farmer who had lived through the Great Depression, the other a college student living at the tail-end of the hippie generation — were joined together by their love of a game. Chalas had developed his passion for golf years earlier, but says that this chance meeting cemented forever his love affair with golf.

"He was such a simple man, a consummate gentleman," said Chalas. "He told me stories that day, of his years on the PGA Tour and his trips to Massachusetts where his pal, Jug McSpaden was a club pro. The tips he offered were basic stuff, but even now, all these years later, I fall back on them."

Chalas returned to his native Massachusetts after that trip to Florida, graduated from Babson, and set off on a career in sales as an independent manufacturer's representative. It provided some wonderful means and afforded him the opportunity to marry and raise two children, but he wouldn't deny that an added bonus to his independence was the ability to maintain an avid golf schedule. Chalas was the Massachusetts Golf Association's Player of the Year in 1980, a two-time winner of the State Four-Ball Championship, the 1985 New England Amateur champion, and fourteen times a competitor in a United States Golf Association event, including the 1980 U.S. Open at Baltusrol. The mix of work and golf always worked well, but in the winter of 2008, some thirty-six years after his chance lesson with Nelson, Chalas made a decision.

"I love to teach and I love golf," he told me. "So I told my wife, Lorraine, I'm going to teach golf."

Just like that, Chalas was a professional golfer. No, not the one you'll see stalking million-dollar purses on network TV, but the kind who'll stand quietly to the side and watch players from ages eight to eighty-eight swing a club, then offer advice to make it easier. An unconventional career move, yes, but to his delight, Chalas has had students come his way at one of Boston's true blue-collar munis, Fresh Pond Golf Course in Cambridge, right there in the shadows of that bastion of education, Harvard University.

"Of course, you'll advertise yourself as one of Byron Nelson's former students, right?" I asked.

"No," he said, laughing, "but I'll always remember how I pleaded with him to take a look and how one of the greatest players ever was kind enough to do so. He was so sincere, so willing to help, and things he told me I find myself telling my students."

A one-mile ride turned into thirty minutes, "but it has carried over forty years," Chalas said.

~Jim McCabe

24

Chicken Soup
for the *Soul*

A Rough Start
in the Business

Go find some stimulating, fulfilling, challenging human endeavor that,
unlike golf, does not require a commitment of time and effort to realize
maximum enjoyment. And call me when you find it.
~Jim Flick

I wasn't a great player, but a connected friend's father vouched for my work ethic and managed to land me the job of second assistant professional at the vaulted Mohawk Club in Schenectady, New York. The head professional there, John Maurycy, had played the PGA Tour, held countless course records in our local area and beyond all that had played in U.S. Opens and PGA Championships. I was terrified to play with him. The first time I did, his wife, Bonnie, accompanied us for nine holes. Despite my extraordinarily strong grip and hyperactive knee action, I scraped it around in 40 shots and figured that would pass and I could keep my job.

Two days later John called me into his office. "You are the worst player I have ever seen in my life that thought they were going to be a golf professional!" he started. "I understand that the PGA of America thinks that we are going to be businessmen in the next generation, but at the end of the day the only real credibility we have is our ability to play and teach. You seem like a nice kid and the members seem to like you and it would appear you're a hard worker but you are so bad a player that I don't know if I could help you. I'll try but I don't even know where to start."

As I walked out of that office, feeling a foot shorter than when I walked in, I couldn't help but reflect on the decisions that had led to this moment. It had all started in high school when my friends told me that if I could shoot 45 I could make the team and play for free at the Schenectady muni. I had never really played golf at that point in my life but I embraced it right away. It was honest. The other sports I had played had been so encumbered by coaches' and parents' opinions of your ability that golf seemed perfectly straightforward by comparison. You shot the score you shot, and that was that.

And I figured out how to do it. If I hit two balls in the air and could find them both, then I just had to chip onto the green and two-putt and that added up to 45 for nine holes. That summer before tryouts I was washing dishes nights at the Steak and Ale, and every morning went to the muni to work out my homegrown technique. They had some impractical rule that you could only play eighteen holes a day with the $1 junior fee. So I quickly figured out the 17th green was very close to the 2nd tee, and that it was not hard to scoot across and "start over." Bob Haggerty was the golf professional and while he knew what I was doing, he let it go. Over the next few years Bob would try to reel me in a bit, but he never tried too hard. I had my way at the muni and so did an entire cadre of other kids. Bob died last year and they had a service for him at the course. I counted at least ten golf professionals amongst the attendees. There would have been none had it not been for Bob nurturing our love of the game.

After high school, sitting in a class at Albany State, bored, reading the *Albany Times Union*, I noticed an ad for an assistant golf professional at Pinehaven Country Club. I got up from my seat, went out to the parking lot, hopped in my car and drove straight to the course. I didn't get the job. But certain of my career choice, I talked to the pro at the Town of Colonie Golf Course, Mr. Gunning. Mr. Gunning was willing to give me a try.

It was early spring. I showed up on the opening day of the course at 5:30 A.M. I tried to understand the taking of tee times, greens fees, cart charges, shop sales, everything. I was clearly over my head but I parked carts, picked the driving range, ran around the shop and tried my best to help. At 8:00 P.M. I crept into the clubhouse bar after closing the shop and asked for a beer. I sat in the corner, sipped my Miller Lite, contemplated my future in the golf business.

There were fifteen to twenty guys at the big table, still playing cards and drinking. They were all hammered and content to enjoy the fact that the golf season had begun and they were back into the days that gave them so much pleasure. That was until one of them stood up, tipped the whole table over, cards, bottles, cash and ashtrays, and said, "Sumbody gunna die." (Now it might be me and it might be you but "Sumbody gunna die.") And with that he dove into the pile and started throwing punches. It was on but I took a pass. By the time I hit Consul Road the squad cars were rolling in.

Two weeks in Mr. Gunning fired me. Now when someone is asking you to work eighty hours a week for $170 and you are showing up and doing it with a smile on your face, you got to wonder if this is your best career opportunity. Meanwhile I had advanced to the lofty position of bartender at the Steak and Ale, where a typical Saturday night equaled a week in the golf business.

Now it would seem unlikely that someone who had lasted a mere two weeks at a local public course would be hired at the fanciest private club in the Capital District. But as I said, a friend's father had put in the good word for me.

The Mohawk Golf Club had a far different attitude. I was blown away by the fact that people actually left their bags at the club. Why didn't they just drive around with them in the trunk of their car? On my first day, I remember the first group was Mr. Pump, Mr. Pump, Mr. Gill, and Mr. Leader.

I raced into the bag room and quickly found their bags according to their "member numbers" and strapped them on two carts. Mr. Pump came out of the locker room and I stood proud of my work. Mr. Pump looked at the carts, and then at me, and said, "I'm driving." I did not know how to respond, so I said, "Yes, Mr. Pump that will be fine." He stared at me some more. "I'm driving," he reiterated. I did not know what to say. We did this dance for a few more minutes until John strolled around.

Mr. Pump erupted. "Maurycy, where the hell do you find these kids? They don't know what they're doing. When are we going to get some halfway decent help around here?"

I of course then learned that the driver's bag goes on the left hand side of the cart and the rider on the right. I almost burst out laughing. So you guys can't be bothered to carry your clubs in your trunk and now you're telling me it's too much to get out of the left side of a golf cart and pull your club out of a bag on the right of the cart? I mean, you're in a golf cart to begin with.

In spite of my naivety John came through on his pledge to try to help me, even though he wasn't sure where to start. He showed me how to properly grip the club, explained how the swing was meant to be. Every night I went to the local driving range, often using the headlights from my car so I could practice deep into the night. With my new weaker grip and the remnants of my non-releasing swing, I was hitting shanks the likes of which many have never seen. Also unfortunate was the fact that there was a Holiday Inn just to right of the range. It was not too many nights into my project that the owner suggested I move to the far left of the range. It was not too many nights more until I had to build a little portable barrier to protect the cars in the Holiday Inn parking lot.

Often on these nights other patrons would ask the owner what exactly was going on at the far end of the range. I would overhear him explaining that that was the assistant golf professional at the Mohawk Golf Club practicing shanking balls into a barrier. The barrier, which was nothing more than plywood I propped up with golf clubs, was about four feet long and three feet tall. It did a fine job of blocking any ball I shanked off the hosel or double-hit with the face.

I kept at it all summer and in the fall went to Florida with $200 in my pocket and the makeshift barrier. Though I had to cut the plywood a little to fit it in the trunk of my car.

When I returned to Mohawk the next spring, I still hadn't found a swing. I hoped John would understand that while I had taken his advice very seriously for the past twelve months, I was not getting it and currently could not break 100. I not only couldn't do it his way, I now I couldn't do it my old way either. It was odd. He didn't seem concerned at all. "You'll get it. Don't worry," was all he said.

I was too embarrassed to say, "I don't think you understand. I have hit five million balls over the past twelve months and only about eight of them went in the air."

We worked on my game more that spring. It was not uncommon for John and I to play a fast nine (and I'm talking forty-five minutes walking) while Bonnie watched the shop. Every minute I spent on a golf course with him alone was an amazing privilege. One day, when we got to the 6th hole, I had hit some kind of half-shank drive and had about 135 yards to the green. Then, for the first time ever, I hit a good golf shot. I remember it so distinctly. It all felt so right. The ball flew high and it hooked just that little bit, landed on the green and spun back next to the hole. John didn't really notice. But having now hit one good shot, I figured maybe there would be another if I kept after it.

All that was twenty-eight years ago, but I remember it like it was yesterday. Eventually I became a Member of the PGA and for a time even had a fairly good game. John taught me how to hit balls but even he couldn't solve my nervousness, which hit home one year when I qualified for a PGA Tour event, the B.C. Open. When I showed up on the first day, I found it was a very small range where you had to hit in a staggered arrangement, leaving a player standing exactly where I would've set up my old plywood barrier. Since the player standing by the one available spot was Johnny Miller, I thought perhaps I would be better served to go practice my putting rather than risk a sudden regression that would take out my idol.

And it was through John Maurycy that I got the job as the head professional at the Dorset Field Club in southern Vermont, established 1886. I've been there twenty-one years. I still laugh on the inside when I pick up bags and the member or guest tells me who will be driving the cart. To look out my golf shop window and see the fall foliage on this wonderful golf course, I have to thank my friend

John for being so patient with me all those years ago, which has allowed me the opportunity to spend my life in golf.

~Craig McLean

25

Being Put in One's Place

I am always ready to learn although I do not always like being taught.
~Winston Churchill

When the U.S. Open was held at Shinnecock Hills Golf Club in 1986, I showed up expecting to serve as the USGA's player liaison. For a field of 156 players, this would mean dealing mostly with their issues surrounding complimentary tickets, hotel rooms, parking at the tournament, even finding babysitters. I had been doing this kind of tournament administration for the USGA for the past few years and had managed to build up a rapport with many of the players.

But that year the USGA gave me a different job. I was the starter on the first tee.

I was of course surprised when executive director Frank Hannigan came to me with the prestigious assignment. The first tee starter the years prior had been David Fay. However, that spring, David was taking longer than expected to recover from a surgery. They needed someone to fill in. My only USGA starting experience up to that point in time had been at the 1981 U.S. Amateur at The Olympic Club. I figured I hadn't impressed anyone as I had been on the bench the last five years.

But there I was, standing on the first tee at the U.S. Open. Weather-wise, the first round at Shinnecock Hills that year was one of the worst opening days in U.S. Open history. Winds gusted and rain poured. Though a former Boy Scout, I had forgotten to "Be Prepared." I had no rain gear and no clipboard to anchor the starting sheets, local rules or scorecards. Everything was drenched within the first hour of my eight-hour shift. I did have an umbrella, but early on it inverted in the gale-like winds. When I disposed of the useless umbrella, even the trash receptacle I threw it in blew away.

For the three days I toiled as starter, rather unceremoniously, we all held hope that David would be released from the hospital in time for the final round. Nobody wished for that more than Hannigan and me, but it was not to be. At breakfast prior to Sunday's round, Hannigan informed me that I would again be handling the first tee starting responsibilities. "Welcome to show biz," his only advice, as the start of Sunday's round was the only one of the week broadcast live.

I guess I didn't screw up too badly. Healthy, David returned as the starter for the 1987 and 1988 U.S. Opens, and for these two years I was asked to fill in whenever David needed a break. Then in 1989 I was asked to be the starter, and it's a job I've held ever since.

And now, every year, I admit to the surprise of a child on Christmas morning when I arrive at the U.S. Open and see my name on the assignment sheet as first tee starter. It is an incredible honor, and one I cherish. It gives me chills to think that my voice is being broadcast around the globe. Like most people, I think my voice sounds weird when I hear a recording of it. No one knows better than I that it has been a long way from my beginning in golf at the Chevron Driving Range on Route 66 near Chicago to the first tee of the United States Open.

Occasionally, I am invited to start players at other events. Most recently, two weeks after Tiger's remarkable victory at Torrey Pines, I was asked to handle the first tee duties at a USGA Junior qualifier at The Los Angeles Country Club. When a young man from San Diego arrived at the first tee with time to chat, I initiated conversation by inquiring if he'd attended the U.S. Open near his home.

"Yes," he said, "I was there for Saturday's round."

"Did you go near the first tee?" I asked.

The boy nodded he had.

"How well was the starter doing the introductions?" I asked.

The boy thought about it. "He was... hmm... pretty good," he offered with little enthusiasm.

"Pretty good!" I (probably) shouted, "How could he have done better?"

"He said some names, like Tiger's, LOUDER than the others," the boy said, upping slightly the volume of his voice on the word.

"I'll work on that," I told him.

Sure enough, upon revisiting the reels, the boy was right. I had said some names a little louder than others. Even though I've been doing this for twenty-two years, I can still get nervous and my voice can still get jumpy. My goal is to treat every player exactly the same, so I'll remember the boy's advice when I'm on the tee next year at Bethpage Black.

~Ronald Read

26

The Compliment

t has been years since the PGA Tour last came to Pleasant Valley Country Club in Sutton, Massachusetts, but in its day, the annual arrival of the game's best players was a major social and athletic event in that little town about fifty miles southwest of Boston.

Actually, the game's very best players didn't play there with any regularity. Although Ben Hogan, Jack Nicklaus, Sam Snead, Gary Player and Arnold Palmer (winner of the Kemper Open when it debuted in Sutton) all competed at Pleasant Valley, the venue didn't get a lot of repeat business from Hall of Famers. But that didn't diminish the area's enthusiasm for the tournament, nor the amount of coverage it received from the *Worcester Telegram & Gazette*, the hometown paper.

When I took over the *Telegram's* golf beat in 1989, the event, which had had twelve different names in thirty-two years, was known as the Bank of Boston Classic. That summer the tour and Pleasant Valley owner Ted Mingolla had announced that the event, typically held a week or two after Labor Day, would move to mid-summer the following year. Summer dates, in theory, would raise the tournament's prospects for television coverage and, in turn, its profile and revenues.

During tournament week my job was to write the game story, a short feature or two, and several notes each day. In addition, I was responsible for writing the golf column that would appear the Sunday of the championship. Needing a topic, I chose to write about how I was going to miss Pleasant Valley as a September staple in the fall sports scene.

I used a couple of personal anecdotes—caddying in the '68 Kemper Classic and the '69 AVCO Classic—as part of the story. The AVCO had not been a pleasant experience. I drew a pro from Cape Cod named Dan Keefe who went oh-for-three when viewed through the eyes of this twenty-year-old caddy. Keefe missed the cut, was uncommunicative and/or miserable for the better part of our time together, and didn't pay very well.

At least that's the story I would have written had I not been encouraged to speak with Brad Faxon before typing the piece.

Faxon, whom I hadn't met before the '89 Bank of Boston, knew a different Keefe. His Keefe was the head professional at Eastward Ho!, where the Faxons were members and friends. As a pre-teen, Brad had learned the game under Keefe's tutelage.

Faxon told me about a patient, caring man who before becoming one of the best golfers in New England had played Ivy League hockey at Brown. The temperamental Keefe I'd glimpsed was, in fact, a man who had battled depression throughout his life. Faxon was fourteen when he last saw Keefe. They had played a few holes together at Eastward Ho! A bit later that same evening, Keefe and Faxon's dad chatted a bit by phone. It turned out to be a goodbye call. Keefe was found dead the next day in the pro shop, hung by his own hand.

When my Sunday column appeared, Faxon was in contention. With most of the back nine left to play, he was one of six players tied for the lead. As he and his caddy made their way from Pleasant Valley's 11th green to the 12th tee, splitting the throng of spectators near the clubhouse, our paths crossed. To my surprise, Faxon stopped and said, "Hey, Tim, good column this morning."

That a player in contention for his first PGA Tour victory would take a moment and acknowledge something other than his task at hand at hand impresses me to this day. I'd like to report that I had the presence to thank Faxon for allowing me to write a better story, but I confess the circumstances of the most memorable compliment I've received in thirty years as a sports journalist left me at a loss for words. I don't recall coming up with anything better than a generic "thanks."

Faxon didn't win that day—Blaine McCallister did when Faxon couldn't convert a 12-foot birdie putt on the final hole—but he has gone on to record eight tour victories. In 2006 Faxon received the Payne Stewart Award, which annually acknowledges the player who shows respect for golf's traditions by the way he handles himself and his charity work.

The award came as no surprise to this reporter.

~Tim Murphy

27

Just About Perfect

Donald Ross wrote the book *Golf Has Never Failed Me*, a title that has appealed to me greatly and one that I'll refer to often throughout this story. I received Ross's book as a gift many years ago, at the height of my interest in course design—which was, some might think odd, when I was fourteen. There aren't too many eighth graders interested in Donald Ross green complexes, as far as I know.

I started playing golf at ten, played my first tournament at thirteen, got my handicap into the single digits at sixteen, and hit my peak by dropping to a 0.8 Index at seventeen. The wheels slowly started to fall off from there. I played golf all throughout high school and wanted to get the attention of Division I coaches to play on scholarship in college, but to no avail. I gladly opted to attend the small, liberal arts college that my dad and brother attended.

I transitioned to collegiate athletics pretty well during my freshman year, playing every tournament and averaging just under 78. Sophomore year was another story. My game started to unravel; I showed just enough flashes of my old form now and then to keep the coach interested. This wasn't just me having a rough patch in terms of my game. Slowly but surely, my love for the game was diminishing and being replaced by feelings of requirement and necessity. After seven years of hard work and tournament golf and not reaching the level I wanted, practicing became a chore and playing lost its enjoyment. I decided not to continue after my sophomore year.

I essentially put the clubs in the closet for a year, taking them out maybe half a dozen times to play a goof-off nine holes with friends. Funnily enough, after my game went south and I took this self-imposed time off, my passion reignited. I just loved being out there again, even if I didn't come close to breaking 80. However, this resurgent passion didn't manifest itself through a renewed desire to play competitively; rather, it was through the realization of how significant the game of golf had been in my life, how many people I had met through it, and how much the game had shaped my character for the better.

With this passion fully realized, the stars seemed to start to align. During the fall of my senior year in college, I learned about the USGA Fellowship in Leadership and Service. As an English major with no real idea (or for that matter prospects) of what to do after graduation, this sounded perfect. I spent hours upon hours perfecting my application, reworking my cover letter, making contacts with people of significance related to the USGA, and more. My networking led me to the Director of one of the USGA's regions, whose son was a classmate of mine in college. His son and I had become great friends earlier in our senior year thanks to our mutual love of golf, and his father was tremendously supportive of my application. With the personal endorsement of a USGA "big hitter," I thought I was a shoe-in for the Fellowship.

I passed the first round of phone interviews and the USGA flew me to Colorado Springs for another interview. The wheels were turning and all was going beautifully. In the evening there was a formal dinner for the applicants and I was even seated next to one of the women who had interviewed me earlier in the day. How propitious! I was sure I'd aced the morning interview, I didn't lodge lettuce in my teeth, and I thought I'd receive an offer within weeks. I waited... and waited... and waited... but no phone call, no e-mail. You know where this is going from here. Finally, after the USGA's official deadline for giving applicants an answer had significantly passed, I called and asked about the status of my application. Long story short, I didn't get it. I had failed. Or had golf failed me? I must admit, I thought the latter.

That was a big blow. I had put everything, *everything*, into that application. I became disillusioned with my desire to work in golf, and even with the game itself. This anchor of my life had lost its hold and now I felt like I was drifting aimlessly.

It was back to the drawing board regarding what to do after graduation. Feeling adventurous, I decided to commit to a previous application for graduate school I'd made earlier in the year, throw caution to the wind, and pursue a Masters degree in Australia. Being born "Down Under," this would be the perfect way to enhance my resumé and be adventurous before I had to get serious.

While Down Under, my passion for golf renewed, but this time due to serious misfortune. While I was living thousands of miles away, my mother was unexpectedly diagnosed with cancer. At age fifty-five and in seemingly great health, this diagnosis was completely out of the blue. I flew back and forth from Australia to the Midwest numerous times to be with her during treatment, and I even wanted to stay at home permanently while she was in and out of the hospital. But, being the mom that she was, she demanded, literally, that I continue with school and finish my degree. It was tough, mentally and emotionally, but while in Australia, golf provided a cathartic outlet for me to cope with the challenges my mother was facing. My great friend Elliot, also a student in my Masters program and who is from Melbourne, the city where I was born, became my weekly golfing buddy. He didn't know it at the time, but the friendship and companionship he and his wife provided was huge in helping me cope with my mom's illness.

After finishing grad school six months after her diagnosis, I came back to the Midwest and resumed my pursuit of a job in golf. My passion was back after the USGA hiccup. I applied for a business development job with Kemper Sports Management in Chicago, again utilizing my great network and contacts. I took the same approach as with the USGA—hone that resumé, network with people related to Kemper, and do all you can to ensure success. I came to Chicago and interviewed with five different people in the organization and, again, thought I'd nailed it. Wait a few weeks and they'll have a decision,

I was told. I waited... and waited. Finally I e-mailed the human resources director. Again, you know where this is going. No dice.

Strike Two for golf—it had failed me a second time! I was confused, a bit embittered, and unsure about this game that I loved so much. What had I done wrong?

I didn't think there would be a strike three for golf applications, but there was. I applied for a job with Renaissance Golf Design in Traverse City, Michigan. I applied quite on a whim, only two weeks after my mom passed away from cancer, under the thinking that life is too short not to pursue your dreams.

This job would've been too much fun—literally working on-site, digging irrigation ditches or doing sculpting work in either Colorado or Oregon on one of Tom Doak's construction projects. After the trauma of losing my mom, I wanted to do something very different and personally enriching, and for someone in his early twenties with a passion for golf and a sense of travel and adventure, this would have been ideal. Plus, I knew scores about course design. I had even played four courses designed by Doak, including two in the southern hemisphere. However, by this time I'd learned my lesson about expectations. I didn't get too hopeful. And in case you're not following the theme here, I didn't get this one either.

After getting the rejection from them less than a month after my mom passed away (on my birthday, no less), I wrote off the possibility of working in golf. All those years of playing and competing and learning and dissecting the game hadn't resulted in a job for me, and the third strike, coupled with my personal challenges, left me feeling lost. Forget working in golf, I thought.

However, I quickly realized that perhaps my attitude of entitlement was the problem. Rather than feeling bitter or vindictive about not getting a job in golf, which I had done after the USGA and Kemper failures, I decided to turn the problem on its head. Rather than thinking about what I had done in golf and why I "should" get a job, I considered what golf had done for me. I asked myself the following question, thinking of Donald Ross's book:

Had golf *really* failed me?

The answer was simple: No, not at all.

Golf has never failed me, because it's taken me to all corners of Michigan and the Midwest, and much of the American south, during travel for tournaments as a junior amateur with my mom. She was my travel planner, my granola bar and Gatorade retriever, my statistical scorecard keeper, and my absolute number one fan. I learned more about Mom and shared so many wonderful experiences with her in seven short years of tournament golf that it's impossible to put into words. Losing her to cancer earlier this year makes me cherish all the wonderful memories we shared on the course.

Golf has never failed me, because it strengthened my bond with my family, as we shared the game on a weekly basis growing up. Our twilight rounds of nine holes on Sunday afternoon (followed by a hot dog, of course) brought my brother and me closer together and let my mom and dad share time with us in a sport we loved, rather than requiring them to spectate from the sidelines of a baseball field or a basketball court.

Golf has never failed me, because it allowed our family to see some of the most beautiful parts of the world. Mom and I played our last round of golf together at Kauri Cliffs on the North Island of New Zealand in January 2007, just a month before she was diagnosed. I have a picture of us standing on the 17th tee looking out over the ocean, both of us beaming, even though the day was gray and cloudy. I think the Golf Gods were watching, too — it's no coincidence I birdied the 15th and 16th holes and made a thirty-foot eagle putt on the 18th hole in our last round together. It was a special way to finish. I had no idea that'd be the last time we'd play together.

Golf has never failed me, because I've met more amazing people through the sport than I could even begin to name in this story. Barrett, my best of friends who I played 73 holes with in one day at St. Andrews, Scotland (and 300 holes over the course of eight days) is just one example. And of course, there's my friend and mentor who delivered the eulogy at my mother's funeral. Burr is not only the chaplain of the university I attended, but he was also my assistant golf coach. My mom traveled to watch many of my college tournaments, and she and Burr got to know each other very well by watching our team play throughout the course of the day. A few months after my mom was diagnosed and her treatment was progressing very well, she said to me, "If I pass away, I want Burr to speak at my funeral." At the time, I didn't think there was any chance that would become a reality, but after she passed I honored her wishes and Burr delivered the most touching eulogy.

As if these reasons weren't enough, I most recently realized that golf has never failed me because of a wedding I attended in October 2008. Ryan, the son of the USGA director who earlier supported my Fellowship application, was the groom. He asked me to be a grooms-man, and I was honored to be there for him and his bride. During the nuptials I stood alongside Ryan and his father on the very campus where I'd once put so much time and effort into golf, whether through a job application or through my role on the team. Being there made me realize that I was so wrong to be upset about any employment setbacks that occurred in the realm of golf. I couldn't hold an ounce of ill will towards the game.

At this wedding I again remembered Donald Ross's book title, *Golf Has Never Failed Me*. He was right. If anything, looking back, *I failed it*. I felt entitled to a job at times, and failed to realize that golf has positively influenced my life in ways that cannot be measured. In the immediacy after not earning the employment positions I so wanted, I took that for granted. Even though I wasn't able to work with the USGA, Kemper Sports, or Renaissance Golf Design, I've had the opportunity to interview with them and meet many great people, and those are experiences that must be treasured.

When I look back at my life in golf—the successes and failures, the achievements and disappointments, but much more so the experiences I've had with my mother and family, and the bonds of friendship I've forged with wonderful people close to my heart—I realize that my relationship with the game has been just about perfect.

Thank you, Donald Ross, you were right. Golf really, truly has never failed me.

~Tom Borda

28

Bearer's Eye View

A Standard Bearer should have some knowledge of golf, should be able to walk eighteen holes and present a professional demeanor...
Standard Bearers are a useful tool in keeping spectators informed as to how the players are performing.
~*Volunteer form, USGA 2007 event*

There is a reason I have size thirteen feet, a permanent hat crease in the back of my hair, an indelible Jack Nicklaus tan on my forearms, twelve pairs of khaki shorts, a closetful of club logo golf shirts (two of each), and an enviable collection of autographed Pro V1's. For three consecutive summers, or roughly for 450 holes, I have served my sport as a standard bearer, leading PGA and LPGA players and their caddies through their paces on some of the most challenging courses in existence. I've been the lynchpin between spectator and player, the ever present, out in front "useful tool."

Through all of my sign pole parading I've witnessed up close what sports commentators often dub "the agony and the ecstasy." I've seen a gallery favorite frozen from a bunker faux pas at Winged Foot that led to a triple-bogey. I've seen a veteran who was desperate to make the cut repeat chipping once, twice and then a third time through a haze of cigar smoke at Oakmont as though the ball were on a yo-yo string being pulled back towards him. I saw the original girl wonder, during her LPGA reentry at Pine Needles, torpedo a ringer into the grandstands at the 10th and then give ear burns to a full row of spectators as she passed. I've watched "mature golfers" throw grass-spitting tantrums worthy of two-year-olds, heard a portfolio of cuss words in a slew of languages from Korean to Spanish to Aussie, and been privy to tears, smashed clubs and prayers for guidance through the back nine.

On the other hand, there've been days when I've seen such amazing skill and beauty that I've had to bite my tongue to keep from yelling out. There's nothing quite like being up close when Furyk sticks it to a foot from a bazillion yards away in the rough. Or watching Vijay's chip rotate a little up, a little forward, then fall into the hole like a baby bird that's been rocked out of the nest; you simply can't get over how easy these guys can make it look when you're standing right behind them. I've even seen a player kiss a dirty towel stuffed in his bag for luck and then drop a deep fescue shot close by brushing the flag. It's so phenomenal to watch players pull off bewildering scores and saves, that sometimes I'm convinced there is a higher being playing the course with us.

After several rounds, a standard bearer quickly figures out that there is more to the job than just parading the players and carrying the sign with the scores. At the 2007 Wyndham Open, I came to the rescue of a caddy who almost passed out in the 105-degree weather. I took the bag, he picked up my sign duty, and I swear it was so hot no one noticed except his player. My respect for hornet bees was put to the test once when I had to reach into a cooler where they were swarming and grab allergy medicine for a Park—or was it a Kim—who had been stung and was swelling quickly. Once I had to sacrifice my standard bearer apron to help cover a pair of seriously split pants. I've shooed gophers, chipmunks and snakes from on-course Port-a-Potties. I once endured a weather delay trapped in a luxury Lexus SUV player transport car with three of the hottest (figuratively and literally) LPGA stars on the circuit (here's a hint, think pink). I've helped pick up toothbrushes, combs, mouthwash, car keys, money clips, chewing gum, and crayons that have tumbled out of unzipped side bag pockets. It's all in a day's work.

From a historical perspective, it's important to note that standard bearers in time of war have been specifically chosen, revered leaders.

The term goes back to the Roman Era when each brigade of Roman soldiers was identified by the colors and insignia carried throughout battle by the handpicked standard bearer. When the "standard" fell, someone had won. I've often thought that having the standard bearer throw down his sign on the 18th green to signify the true moment of victory might be a dramatic historical plug for the USGA to consider adding to their championship rituals. I'm still waiting to hear back from them on my suggestion.

When I first started, I was told by a senior scorer that the seriousness of carrying the standard is comparable to being the altar boy in church who carries the lit candles in the procession. Except in golf there are potentially tens of millions of television viewers watching you hoist the ten-pound metal billboard, not just a small congregation hoping the candle wax doesn't spill onto your angelic sleeves. I don't want to belittle this comparison; carrying the standard is part of the "religion" of golf. When your arms have to be aligned with your hips and your fingers are cemented to a metal pole for as long as six hours in order to keep to the sign at the proper angle, when you can't twist your body because it will in turn twist the sign so as to make it illegible to the crowd, when you can't sneeze because the scores will jiggle, you do look to a higher being for self-control. Add to that 100-degree temperatures or pelting rain, and you're praying to make it through.

There are certain protocols we learn to anticipate. Besides having to sport the color coordinated polo and logo hats, we're outfitted with this belt-like contraption that looks somewhat like what a sumo wrestler wears. This belt has a deep front pocket that the sign pole ostensibly fits into to provide extra support—except this isn't the case and you end up carrying it instead with all the weight in your palms. It also has pockets that serve to carry the clunky metal score numbers. You get a stack of black "over" numbers zero to twenty, a stack of red "unders" zero to twenty, and three "evens."

Having once endured the humiliation of a pro and his caddy smirking as they helped pick up my stash of numbers as they spilled out on the 14th green at Winged Foot, early on I learned it's all about how well you get your numbering system in place before the 1st hole. Black left, red right, sequential, straight up. A polished standard bearer can simultaneously eyeball the official walking scorer for updates, shuffle what's in his apron almost by feel in order to find the right numbers, and keep marching his players forward to the next hole, making the sign changes before play resumes. Even par does, however, make life a lot easier.

If we do the job right, and this is where the "professional demeanor" part comes in, a polished standard bearer can set the tone for his group of players. If I am composed and looking confident, I like to think the players pick up my unspoken vibes and tend to do better.

The quintessential standard bearer sees all, tells little, and keeps on leading, hoping that one day his will be one of the names on that sign out there in front. It's not a bad dream at all, you just have to show up and take it one step at a time.

~Kaameran Stenberg

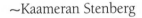

29

No Complaints

Golf writers might whine about a lousy roast beef sandwich or poor Internet access in the press room, but there's really no such thing as a bad day in our business. We get paid to cover the biggest tournaments at the best courses in the world. All in all, it's a pretty sweet deal. Some assignments, though, prove better than others.

It was the Saturday of the 1997 Ryder Cup at Valderrama in Andalucia, Spain. The course has a stunning view of the Rock of Gibraltar. While gazing at the Mediterranean, I heard from the BBC radio coverage that Michael Jordan was on the course. As the golf reporter for the *Chicago Tribune*, the fact that city's No. 1 star, the king of basketball, was among the spectators meant I had better go find him.

I was walking the holes scanning the crowds, when it hit me that Jordan was probably following Tiger. The scuttlebutt was they had recently become buddies. Sure enough, I found Tiger's match and located His Airness riding on the back of U.S. captain Tom Kite's cart. I watched Jordan react to the shots. He exulted when a birdie putt fell and winced when the Americans lost a hole.

"Man, this is great," Jordan kept saying. The Ryder Cup pressure, he told me later, where there is a verdict for every hole, really appealed to him. I learned that Jordan was on a family vacation in Monaco, but had pried himself away to spend a day watching golf. On the 12th hole, somebody came up to him and said it was time to go. It was time to catch the flight back to Monaco. It was clear from the look on Jordan's face that he wanted to stay. Another reporter and I advised Jordan to take a later flight.

"You're Michael Jordan," we said with the strong implication he has the power to do what he wants.

"No, you don't understand," he said. "My wife will kill me if I don't get back."

It was heartening to see Jordan was just like us, at least on the domestic front. Alas, he departed. Or so we thought. A hole later, we saw him again, but only briefly. Finally, he was whisked away.

Jordan's day was done, but there was plenty of golf on the agenda. I wandered over to the 17th hole. It was then that I noticed George Bush sitting on a hill overlooking the green.

First Jordan, now Bush. I thought, "How many times do you get to talk to a former President?" As I stepped towards him, I saw a Secret Service man (the earpiece gave him away despite his polo shirt) but he made no move to thwart my advancement. I thought it a bit strange that you could just walk up to a former president in a foreign country. Apparently, I looked trustworthy.

Bush, though, hardly looked like the one-time leader of the free world. There was no large entourage. He was casually chatting with a small group of photographers and one reporter.

I introduced myself and soon found myself sitting along with the group. Bush told us he had perched himself on the 17th hole so he could congratulate the American team if they won a match. Since the next match was on the 14th hole, and since Bush didn't seem anxious to go anywhere, our small group had him all to ourselves.

I noticed Bush was wearing pair of socks with the Masters logo. The socks were pretty dirty, which meant he had been walking the course. Not bad for a man who was seventy-three years old at the time.

Naturally, the conversation turned to golf. He talked about a recent round he had with three-time U.S. Open champion Hale Irwin. However, with Bush, it never was about score. Known for being a speed golfer, he boasted, "We played eighteen holes in two hours."

Of course, with the Ryder Cup on the line, the pace of the golf we were watching was much, much slower. Bush told us about the last time he saw Ronald Reagan. Due to his Alzheimer's, Bush said he wasn't sure if Reagan recognized his vice president.

Feeling a bit bold, I asked Bush how the *Chicago Tribune* had treated him while he was in office. Bush said, "Well, I can't think of anything bad, so it must have been OK." No surprise there, considering the *Tribune* is a staunch Republican paper. As a lifelong Democrat, I didn't have the heart to tell Bush I didn't vote for him.

Tom Lehman and Phil Mickelson were the next group to come to the 17th. Their wives, Melissa and Amy, noticed Bush and sat down next to us. Somehow I managed to get in the group picture that would run in David Feherty's book about the Ryder Cup.

I remember vividly Bush leaning forward on the grass, holding Amy's and Melissa's hands, ready to jump out onto the green to congratulate a winning American pairing. But the big moment didn't happen. Mickelson and Lehman didn't win the hole, and would go on to halve their match. In fact, Bush never got to greet a victorious American twosome that day. The Americans were shut out en route to eventually losing the Ryder Cup to the Europeans on Sunday, 14 1/2 to 13 1/2.

After the last group came through, Bush dejectedly lifted himself from the grass and made his way to the clubhouse. Meanwhile, Jordan surely received the bad news en route to Monaco. But the day was a victory for me. I got to spend it with a king and a president.

~Ed Sherman

30

The 16th Tee

An American living in Scotland, the frequent subject in long-distance calls back to friends and family, dialed in wool-socked feet at the hallway payphone of my dormitory, was the weather. I told horror stories. Summer rain could be like a shower nozzle set to straight cold. Once, after a night at the pubs, I returned to my room to discover that a wind so violent had blown open my window and deposited a dusting of sidewalk gravel on my bed (and I lived on the fourth floor). Getting dressed to play golf was like getting ready to go skiing: long underwear, fleece, waterproofs, a winter hat, mittens to wear between shots.

So when I invited my friend Ged to fly over for the 2005 British Open, to work as a grandstand marshal along with me and the other university golf team guys, I told him to pack some sweaters even though it was July. With a puffed chest told him he didn't know what he was in store for.

As meteorological fate would have it, the weather at St. Andrews that week was the most benign possible, high 80s and sunny with barely a trace of breeze, making my calls home look like a pile of bull. The week provided the only occasion in my two years there that I went swimming in the adjacent North Sea for actual pleasure, not as a lark. Under the scoring conditions, history watched as Tiger Woods shot under par every day and led every round to win at -14.

Many a purist (sadist) would've liked the professionals to battle the elements and the winner to finish at some stoic figure like +8. But that week the weather came exactly one day late.

That Monday after, I awoke to the harsh whistling of wind squeezing through the alley beneath my window. I pulled back the lone curtain. The sky was steel.

I saw Ged off at the bus station, then made the short walk to the Old Course to resume my summer of job of caddying. The cobble streets were not in their usual quaint perfection. Tumbling in the wind, or else trembling in a corner, were wine-stained plastic cups, damp cigarette butts, scrapped signage and other traces of the post-tournament revelry of some 50,000 attendees (at least that had been the figure getting thrown around). I was in fact feeling a bit bleary myself.

I was lucky to get the caddying job. With the exchange rate at 2:1, it was good to be earning some pounds to augment my stipend. I had been able to get my foot in the caddyshack door early that spring because my postgraduate class hours were minimal and the boosted tourism of an Open year made the demand for caddies great enough they'd take an American. Out of the perhaps ninety regular caddies, there was only one other American, also a student.

As a thank you for being a major sponsor of the championship, that Monday Lexus had exclusive access to the Old Course. All the Sunday hole-locations were left in place so that the company's employees might experience a greater tie with history.

The St. Andrews Links Trust has a policy that no man with more than a 24-handicap, or a woman with a 30-handicap, is allowed to play the Old Course. And this is a policy that is enforced strictly. When I had come over in September to start classes, then twenty-two years old, I wasn't a member of a club in America and so didn't keep an official Index anywhere. To get my permit to play, I had first tried printing out my NCAA scoring record (which in the high 70s wasn't stellar but at least demonstrated a certain level) from the Internet and personally delivering it with my application. But the powers that be did not accept this. In time, the pro at my father's club in the States, where I had played under his membership through my teenage years, concocted a handicap card for me and mailed it over.

I arrived at the caddyshack, and there paid into caddymaster Rick Mackenzie's weathered hand the daily £5 "work-permit fee" and took my place on the outdoor benches with the other caddies. Most were sitting with their hands in their pockets and their collars up against the cold. The chat that morning was that handicap cards were not being checked. A special waive of policy. Apparently a lot of awkward swings had been witnessed going off the 1st tee.

I can't remember the name of the fellow I caddied for that day, but I remember him as being likely worse than a 24-handicap. Sure, he was a cheerful and bright guy who didn't get mad at his blunders and wasn't afraid to poke fun at himself, which was always good. I tried to help him as best I could and I think he had an enjoyable day at my service. However, when we got to the 7th tee and there were four foursomes and their caddies, thirty-two people altogether, waiting for the 7th fairway to clear like a stuck drain, dread overcame me.

When our turn finally came, forty minutes later, my player nailed, predictably, a low hard top 50 yards into the thorny gorse bushes directly in front of the tee. He was already running low on ammunition at that point, and so I had to go in to retrieve.

The round wore on. And on and on and on. Obviously there are worse gigs, and I would hate to be perceived as a complainer, but caddying for beginners on a dehydrated, wind-trampled major championship course with Sunday pin locations on a cold day is no fun. Non-stop raking of bunkers, crossing fairways in zig-zags, searching for lost balls on every shot, constantly hoping against hope for anything straight and airborne, all while remaining outwardly positive, takes a psychological toll. When I checked my watch at the turn, three hours and seven minutes had expired since our tee time. On pace for a six hour and fourteen minute round—unheard of. The three other caddies and I commiserated silently, glancing at our golfers as if our captors.

But when we reached the 16th tee these bad feelings faded. A genuine smile came across my face. In two years living in St. Andrews, I estimate I went around the Old Course about 120 times, equal parts playing and caddying. And every single time I got to the 16th tee, without fail, the mood of the round changed. Whether I was scoring awful or looping for somebody miserable, or rain had soaked my grips to the steel, or the wind was bitter cold and I'd neglected to bring even a cracker for my body to burn like kindling, always when I got to the 16th my mind brightened. To me it's the stretch when the Old Course really becomes the Old Course. The town comes back into focus—the Rusacks Hotel, red Hamilton Hall, the fortress of the Royal & Ancient clubhouse. The 16th tee is the point where the quality and history of each shot left to be played is overwhelming.

Now people are always attempting to wax poetically about the Old Course and it gets tiresome, but hear me out.

Even if the remaining shots on these last three holes are all botched, there's still a special feeling over each one. The maddeningly placed Principal's Nose bunker makes how to play the 16th tee shot a painfully arrived at decision for a player of any caliber, no matter the wind direction. And the approach there is delicate wherever the flag is or how short an iron you have in your hands. Then there's the blind Road Hole tee shot, a blast over the railroad shed that skirts alongside the Old Course Hotel windows. A thrill whenever the ball hits, or doesn't hit, building. Then comes the long approach into the front bank of the green with the famous stonewall lurking behind. As you come to the green you'll more than likely pass someone heading to the range on the shell walkway or be waved hello by patrons standing outside the Jigger Inn.

Then at the 18th there's the final drive, the let-it-all-hang-loose ripper down the 110-yard-wide fairway, that with a draw may get the green, or with a slice, ricochet off a car parked in front of the New Club. If your heart doesn't skip as you then walk over the legend-worn stones of the ancient Swilcan Bridge, you're not a golfer, perhaps not even human. And to end it, the final putt dropping, even if it's just a tap-in, on the tilted surface sculpted by Old Tom Morris himself. If four feet or more, the usual gallery of milling townsfolk is reliable to applaud.

And as my Lexus employee played these last three that post-Open Monday, I could tell from his body language he recognized them as the most special part of the course, too. I snapped his camera as he and his colleagues stood on the bridge. I think he tripled 16 and quadrupled 17, but as I remember, squeaked a par on 18, miraculously (accidentally) judging a putt from the Valley of Sin to within two feet. We high-fived.

As we walked off the 18th green, Rick Mackenzie the caddymaster, was standing waiting for me. Our eyes locked as he waved his index finger toward the 1st tee. My stomach growled; I had been thinking about a Tesco's chicken and bacon sandwich since the 4th hole. But I knew that if I didn't head directly to the first tee, I'd be "up the road"—Mackenzie's brogue colloquialism for "fired."

There were four people standing on the 1st tee, stretching and loosening up their swings like hula-hoop dancers. It was OK, I told myself. I'd be on the 16th tee again in five hours.

~Max Adler

Gamesmanship

*Splosh! One of the finest sights in the world:
the other man's ball dropping in the water—
preferably so that he can see it but cannot quite reach it
and has therefore to leave it there,
thus rendering himself so mad that he loses the next hole as well.*

~Henry Longhurst

Girls Will Be Girls

It's not whether you win or lose—but whether I win or lose.

~Sandy Lyle

We're competitive. And we can be downright mean. Much to Cyndi Lauper's chagrin, girls don't just want to have fun. In fact, many of us scheme and manipulate more than members of the opposite sex.

Until you compete against us, girls are seen as sweet and unimposing. But take us on and you'll probably use two words to describe our behavior: passive aggressive.

I've played against girls in junior and amateur golf tournaments for ten years and counting. Sure, not all are diehard competitors. But the majority want nothing more than to beat you to the ground. We'll never say it, but our actions will prove it.

When I started playing golf a decade ago, I didn't have a competitive bone in me. Growing up in New York City, my athletic world was ballet, long walks and occasional weekend escapes north to ski. There was no need to pirouette faster than the girl next to me, walk more blocks than other New Yorkers, or ski at breakneck speed.

Then came golf.

I played in my first golf tournament when I was fourteen, right after my family moved to Miami. As my handicap decreased, my competitors turned from being helpful and encouraging to masters of slick manipulation. Passive aggressiveness, to me, is silent yet obvious resentment, and includes repeated behaviors done with intent to sabotage. Junior golfers didn't have such manners. But once I got to college and top-tier amateur events, I noticed the girls with good track records often exhibited such subtle, though clear, hostility.

Now I'm the first to admit that I'm a short knocker. A good drive for me goes 230 yards (with roll). I played for the University of Virginia's women's golf team, and so was routinely paired with some pretty top-shelf Division I players who could really hit it. Needless to say, I was usually the shortest hitter in my group. I had no problem being paired with the long drivers, but here's what ticked me off.

As all three of us would approach our tee balls, the big hitter would repeatedly walk across the fairway to check that my ball wasn't hers. Now she knows she's the one lying 40 yards ahead of me. It's obviously a subliminal message that screams, "I'm so much farther than you off the tee, you pathetic wimp." If she did it once, fine. But checking that my ball is truly mine more than ten times in eighteen holes? Come on.

More often than not, I didn't have the honors on the tee. And teeing off first is the perfect opportunity to get into your opponent's head. I came across lots of girls who would hit their tee shots safely down the middle and then say, "Thank goodness I didn't hit my ball into that fairway bunker. I was there yesterday. It's death." So what do I think about as I set up on the tee? That dreaded fairway bunker. Thanks. Thanks a lot.

Match play tournaments are perhaps the perfect stage to show-case passive aggressive skills. I consider myself a generous person. If a three-foot putt is straight and clear-cut, I automatically give it and consider it in. Make it a three-foot slider, however, and I'm going to have to see you make it. Should I feel bad if my opponent doesn't make a short breaking putt to keep the match square? No. But once when it happened, I got the silent treatment for the rest of the match and was forced to tap in every putt, even inchers, from thereon in. Her missed putt made for a sour three hours, and I ultimately kept thinking about it far more than I did the shot at hand.

I'm not saying all girls are passive aggressive. Some mean well and want nothing more than to watch you succeed. I'm a positive, go-lucky girl in the office. Get me on a golf course and I'll still seem like that optimistic person.

Just don't let me fool you.

~Ashley Mayo

"YOU'VE GOT THE CUTEST DIMPLES."

32

The Golf War

Golf, he replied, was much too serious a matter to be called a sport.
~John Pearson, James Bond: The Authorized Biography

It's not that Jimmy and I were warmongers bent on finding trouble. We were just two typical forthright Scots who didn't put up with nonsense on the golf course. If a slow foursome didn't let us play through, or a group perpetually took too long to hunt for lost balls, we got vocal. Jimmy, especially, received a typical Scottish pleasure in confrontation. Being of a similar nature, this never put me up or down. But the return to golf of a chap named Gordon Angus made us reexamine our ways.

After an absence from the game that lasted years, Gordon turned up one Saturday morning with a set of old clubs to play a round on his own. Gordon had gone to junior school with Jimmy, some forty years earlier, and despite being opposite personalities (Gordon was studious and serious while Jimmy most definitely was not) the two were good friends. Jimmy and I wouldn't hear of him playing alone. So we invited Gordon to join us that Saturday, and from then on the three of us started playing regularly.

The behavior of Jimmy and I was no doubt a shock to Gordon. Once, when someone hit a ball that just missed my head without shouting "Fore!" and Jimmy and I waited for the culprit to ignite a loud verbal battle, Gordon nearly fainted. After it was over, Gordon meekly suggested, "I'm sure he didn't do it on purpose. Maybe you should just have had a quiet word of advice with him later in the clubhouse."

"What?" Jimmy demanded, as if he couldn't believe what he was hearing. I didn't give Gordon's suggestion much credence either.

So it went on. And if Jimmy and I didn't have any problems, we would instead take up arms on Gordon's behalf. Why was his entry into the golf club taking so long? Why couldn't he get a locker when we knew someone else who had got one? And so forth.

For these battles, Gordon always had a much more peaceful solution, but we never listened. "It's Gordon's way," Jimmy explained to me. "He always was a bookworm. Very quiet and never spoke up for himself."

One morning, there was a single playing in front of the three of us. On one hole, the man left his caddy cart with his golf clubs just off the edge of the green and disappeared.

We waited and waited, Jimmy in particular growing more and more irate. Finally, we all played our shots and began to walk up to the hole.

As we neared the hole, we saw the man sitting in a small old pavilion near the 12th green. Jimmy roared over at him full throttle, "What the... what do you think you're doing... who do you think you... why didn't you waive us through..." And so forth.

It was Gordon who said, "Jimmy, wait, I think he's in trouble."

We walked nearer. The man was grey in the face and clasping at his chest, barely conscious. I realized right away the man was having a heart attack. I had once served as a medic, and so proceeded to do everything I could for him while Jimmy used his mobile to call an ambulance. By good luck, the 12th hole was not far from the main road and within fifteen minutes, the man was off in the ambulance.

All three of us were silent. Jimmy sighed, "I hope my shouts of abuse are not the last words he ever hears on this earth." We called the golf to a halt and went back to the clubhouse, where Jimmy remained much quieter than usual.

A few days later, we heard that the man had "died" in the ambulance but that the doctors had miraculously managed to bring him back again. He was in intensive care for a week, but finally made a complete recovery.

Once he was out the old man lost no time in contacting us to give his thanks. As we spoke of the day, it was obvious that the man had not been aware of Jimmy's shouting.

The next week, we were halfway around the golf course when Jimmy turned to Gordon and said, "There is some sense to what you say, about always giving people a chance to explain before you tear into them." Gordon and I stared at Jimmy, and then at each other, in amazement. Jimmy shrugged, "I've been thinking about my roaring at the guy having the heart attack."

Two weeks later, a man and his dog walked straight in front of the 4th tee just as Jimmy was about to drive. "What the he..." Jimmy cut himself off on mid-sentence, "He... have a nice day."

The man smiled back. "Hi Jimmy. I thought I recognized you. Say, I have some golf balls for you. The dog picks them up all the time."

Jimmy turned to Gordon, "You are definitely right, and this proves it."

Jimmy has passed away now, and it would be fine to say that from that time onwards he took a calmer approach to golf and to life. But in fact, his change of heart only lasted until a remarkably lethargic foursome playing in front of us did not wave us through. When Jimmy discovered two of them were men he had never liked since his teenage days, he ran ahead and gave them a verbal blast and a lecture on the etiquette of golf in his own special terminology.

Years after Jimmy had passed, Gordon and I were reminiscing. "You know, I was glad his transformation of character didn't last long." Gordon said. "It was his volatile outbursts that made me like him so much. You knew exactly where you stood with Jimmy. He was the most honest man I ever met. Sure, I got on him about being nicer to people, but really I admired his courage."

~Eric Stark

33

Getting Sacked by #56

As players, we always have a way to get back at you.
~Lawrence Taylor

During the off-season I play golf two or three times a week. I'll even sneak in a round here and there during the season. But I never play with any of my Colts teammates. I couldn't take it. Football guys talk more trash than anybody. I don't want to show up at practice and get ragged about missing a four-footer or losing a press. It'd get bad in the locker room. I mean real bad. I play golf to relax. That's why I have my local group of guys to beat up on me. They're not going to tell anybody what I shot.

Of course, it can't always be low profile. A few years back I got asked to play in Michael Jordan's Celebrity Invitational in the Bahamas. I was just getting into golf then, but could typically shoot in the 90s if I kept my act together. I remember I had been playing pretty well leading up to it, and so was pretty psyched to fly down there. I had my people called Michael's people to let him know I would play.

It's a best-ball format tournament, and they pair you into two-man teams. Wouldn't you know it, I got paired with Lawrence Taylor, the former star linebacker for the New York Giants, as if I even need to tell anybody who he is.

L.T. was my favorite player growing up, without question. I grew up in Connecticut and so the Giants were my team. In my bedroom I had L.T. posters and stickers plastered all over my walls. I mean #56 was my idol.

Now imagine how nervous you'd be meeting your boyhood idol for the first time. Combine that with the fact that there are television cameras all around. Now I'm fine with millions of people watching me rush a quarterback, but my golf swing, that's a different story. I was shaking in my spikes as I teed up my ball.

Since retiring, Lawrence Taylor eats, sleeps and breathes golf. He's a scratch player, plays thirty-six holes a day and thinks nothing of it. *Sports Illustrated* subscribers will remember the cover story that ran in July 2006, about how his addiction to golf saved him from another worse type of addiction. That story also talked about how competitive L.T. is on the golf course. All I can say is you better believe it. I could tell by the look in his eye on the 1st tee that he was there with one purpose: to win the tournament.

I actually whiffed shots that day. Swung at the ball and missed with cameras rolling. And when I didn't whiff I would top the ball or squirt it off the hosel. I couldn't believe how bad I played. L.T. couldn't believe it either. He kept giving me the evil eye after each one of my meltdowns. I only needed to help him a little, but I didn't help him at all, not even on one hole. I was apologizing to him up and down the fairways the whole weekend. I even tried to talk some football with him to break the ice, but L.T. wouldn't have any of it. He was there to play golf. First time ever meeting my idol and I piss him off.

I've gotten better since. I can even throw up some scores in the 80s when I get it going. I've actually run into Laurence a few times, at other celebrity golf outings and such, and each time he's introduced me as the worst golfer who ever lived. Busted my chops hard. I mean, L.T. and I are friends now, but he had no qualms taking me out in front of everyone. I still haven't played with him again, so I'm awaiting the chance to redeem myself.

But like I was saying at the beginning, the only thing harder than golf is playing golf with other football players. They're professionals at getting in your head.

~Dwight Freeney

Living With the Yips

Why am I using a new putter? Because the last one didn't float too well.
~Craig Stadler

My husband has the yips. He tells me it's a disease, a physical malady, something only slightly worse than cancer. There is no treatment, no cure, and it can slowly drive you insane, at least that's the way he moans about it after his regular Saturday morning golf game. He tells me not to worry, and that it's not contagious. I wouldn't know; I don't play golf. What I do know is that it's turned my normally well-adjusted husband into an obsessive, babbling facsimile of his former self.

I tell him that it's nothing to be concerned about, that he's played and enjoyed golf all of his life, and that the yips will fade just as rapidly as they came. "Remember that nasty slice you developed during the club championship last year? Well, that's gone now. Just the other day you told me how well you're driving the ball."

"It's not the same thing," he answers. "My new super game-improvement, offset driver took care of my slice. There is no equipment fix for the yips."

I'll agree with that. He's spent a fortune on putters. He's too embarrassed to buy them from his club pro so he travels across town to anonymously purchase them from one of those golf discount places. He has long ones, short ones, and middle length belly putters;

he has mallets, blades, and putters with two balls and three balls on them; he has one he calls the spider, and one that looks like it's more suited to Batman's utility belt than a golfing green. None of them seems to work.

"I must have done something," he says. "I don't know what it is, but I've done something to anger the gods of golf, and now they're taking their revenge."

"That's ridiculous!" I answer. "Have you touched the sand with your sand wedge before blasting out of a bunker without penalizing yourself?"

"No."

"Have you improved your lie out of one of those fairway divots you're always complaining about?"

"No."

"What about accidently moving your ball without telling your golfing partners?"

"No."

"Well then, it's not the golf gods. It's a psychological problem, something in your head. Try not to think about it. You'll get over it."

"You don't understand," he said. "I've tried everything. Left hand high, left hand low, left hand only, no left hand, it doesn't make any difference."

"What are you talking about?"

"My grip, my putter grip. I've even tried the claw."

"Sounds sinister."

"Doc Bauermeister says my fast twitch muscles are out of control. It's something to do with peripheral nerves and neurotransmitters. He's a pathologist. He studies these things. He should know."

"He's your golfing buddy and he's yanking your chain. You need a psychiatrist, not a pathologist."

And so it goes.

Three weeks ago, we sat on the couch as he told me about his game, searching for answers. I tried not to look him in the eye. He'd hit fourteen of eighteen greens in regulation, which is very good, but he'd three-putted eight times and four-putted twice, which is very bad. It was so bad his friends started giving him three and four-footers. "Take it away," they'd say. "That's close enough." It was humiliating. Something had to be done.

Dave Pelz says that anyone can learn to putt well if they work at it. All they need to do is practice. He's some kind of a short game putting and chipping guru, a scientist of sorts, and he applies the scientific method to the game of golf.

My husband bought Pelz's books—all of them. He studied them religiously. He took them to work along with his putter so that he could practice in his office in his spare time. He even slept with Pelz's *Short Game Bible* under his pillow, presumably to better absorb its contained wisdom.

He worked on his game and practiced every day, the Dave Pelz way. He practiced at the club before and after work, and all day on Saturdays and Sundays. He even skipped meals to practice. I was starting to worry about him. Then, after two weeks of this obsessive madness, he announced that he was once again ready to face his three golfing buddies in the fabled Saturday morning game.

The appointed hour came; the game started at eight. He parred the 1st hole and then the 2nd. He pushed his drive on the third into the trees, chipped out, and settled for a two-putt bogey with no sign of the yips. He parred the 4th and 5th, and flew a 6-iron to within four feet of the cup on the par-3 6th. Then he sunk the pressure putt. He sunk another on the par-5 17th for a birdie, making him and his partner one up with one to go. Things were going his way. He was relaxed and at ease. And then as he was approaching the 18th tee someone said, "Press."

My husband yipped. Now my husband is a rational man. He knows that one bad hole doesn't ruin an entire season. It could have happened to anybody.

"You'll be all right," I said to him, sounding as supportive as I could. I held his hand.

He tentatively answered with an uncertain voice, "I hope you're right."

"Of course I'm right. You yourself said that you played seventeen great holes without a yip. That's better than you've played in months. You're getting better. You'll get through this. I know you will."

After a self-reflective pause he questioned, "Do you really think so?"

"I more than think so, I know so. You're my man." I moved a little closer and smiled my most comforting smile. "And after all, things could have been worse."

With a touch of sadness he asked, "How could they have been worse?"

"Well, you could have had the shanks."

The room suddenly became quiet. The birds stopped chirping, the sun went behind a cloud, our dog hid under the bed, the Earth seemingly stood still. My kind and gentle husband looked at me with a look of horror in his eyes and said, "Now you've done it."

~Vicki Griffin

No Chance at the Course Record

I met a young man at work who was a terrific golfer. He wanted to impress his fiancée, so one day he brought her along to the course to watch him play. It was just the three of us. The young man went birdie, birdie, par, birdie, eagle, eagle, par, par, par.

For the first eagle, he canned a 45-foot snake. When it went in, the woman said, "Is that good?"

I picked up the ball and threw it back to him and said, "You cannot do that again." He did.

He shot a 29 (-7) on the front side. And this was no pitch-n-putt course. The back tees, from where we were playing, measured 3,637 yards. After he made his par on the 9th and I announced his score, again the woman said, "Is that good?" Our eyes rolled. I have never seen that kind of golf played up close since. But she did not want to keep riding around. So the young man stopped playing at the turn and left the course to drive her home, or wherever they were going.

He never married her.

~Nelson Bayne

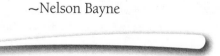

Golf Widow

In case you don't know very much about the game of golf,
a good 1-iron shot is about as easy to come by as an understanding wife.
~Dan Jenkins

I am not a golfer. I find it boring, monotonous and if you ask me, I think the clothes some of the guys wear are pretty silly. The black and white saddle shoes remind of the horrid style from my early days in Catholic school.

But I am the wife of a golfer. Society has dubbed women like me "Golf Widows." You know us, our husbands never forget a tee time but always forget our birthdays and anniversaries. Dog-eared *Golf Digest* magazines are on the floor of every bathroom in the house. Talk of Big Bertha makes their faces light up.

So even though I don't play golf, the sport is a fundamental part of my life. Because of this sport I know what my husband is doing and who he is doing it with. Because of this sport the love of my life enjoys a few hours every week in the North Carolina sunshine. It's a guy's world when Al, Jim, Greg and Steve walk onto the fairways Sunday morning. I imagine them laughing at their bad shots, praising the occasional good ones, and never once saying to the other, "Do these green plaid pants make my butt look big?"

Golf's perk for me is that I get the whole bed to myself on Sunday morning, as he's always tip-toeing out the door no later than 7:00 A.M. I don't have to get up and cook bacon and eggs with a side order of pancakes as is my lot in the winter months of life. I don't have to lay there and pretend that I am enjoying him reading the sports section of the newspaper to me. I get to be the first in the shower and use up all the hot water. I get to prop up the pillows, eat toast, and lie in bed watching movies on Lifetime and cry without worrying that I'm making a fool of myself.

So even thought I don't play golf, don't really like anything about golf, I guess you could say that in my own weird way, I love golf. But don't tell my husband. I prefer to make him feel a little guilty about leaving me alone on Sunday morning. And a little guilt can mean a nice piece of jewelry later on!

~Trish Bonsall

Chicken Soup for the **Soul**

11/22/33

Call it a clan, call it a network, call it a tribe, call it a family.
Whatever you call it, whoever you are, you need one.
~Jane Howard

With the best of intentions, but not without hesitation, I coordinated a recent family golf trip. For the first time the Ginella boys: my dad, two older brothers and I, would get away for a few days of small ball, banter, good food and cards. In the weeks leading up to our departure, according to my mom, my dad was three degrees north of excited. He told his San Diego neighbors that his three sons had arranged for two rooms at La Quinta Resort and Spa, three rounds of golf, a two-hour private group lesson at the Jim Mclean School of Golf at PGA West and a dinner at Palmer's, part steakhouse and part Arnold Palmer memorabilia museum. He's my dad's all-time favorite.

My dad boxed growing up and then taught boxing at his alma mater, the University of Santa Clara. He has had multiple broken noses (you should see the other guy) and limps on a pair of bad knees (never had surgery) and holds the golf club with nine fingers (lost a pinky to a whirling car engine). He's a lifetime 20-something handicap. If he misses a short putt, plug your ears, he's swearing. If he makes a bogey on a par 4, it's not a five, it's a "Fever in the f&$#! house." A double-bogey on a par 4 is never a six, it's a "sexxx."

My father, John Ginella, was born on Nov. 22, 1933. I've always loved the symmetry of his birth date — 11/22/33. This trip was in honor of his 75th birthday. The King signed and sent a print, "To John, Happy 75th Birthday—Arnold Palmer." Our plan was to give it to my dad the night we were out to dinner at his restaurant.

I'm the youngest of five kids by nine years. We all had the same set of parents, who've been miraculously married for fifty-one years. My brothers, Sean and Mark, are separated by two years, (Sean is fifty and Mark is forty-eight), and it's a good thing they're separated by 2,500 miles because if they're ever in the same zip code, they'll argue and fight over *anything*. One year, which ruined a Christmas, they fought over what they thought was the last piece of pumpkin pie. There was pushing and threats. We found out later, after half the house left in a driving snowstorm and hauling heavy hearts, that there were two more pumpkin pies in the extra refrigerator in my parent's garage.

Unfortunately there's more. The police were once called to a Thanksgiving not long after we all held hands and said grace. In a post-meal game of dominoes, Mark indicated Dad was cheating. Ginellas are a lot of things, but not cheats. Mark's declaration, "Dad, you're cheating," was followed shortly by the sheriff's lights flashing in the driveway.

There's even more than that, but you get the idea. Life as a Ginella, especially when surrounded by other Ginellas, is flammable. The interesting thing, especially to friends and onlookers of Ginella dust-ups, is that after a period of time has passed, apologies are passed around and we move on.

It should also be noted, because the worst of who we are is pretty twisted, we would also all take bullets, lay ourselves in front of locomotives and wrestle hungry sharks for one another. Some of us might even survive all three. We can call each other names, but if you call us a name, we have to fight. You know the drill.

Because I'm so much younger than the rest of my siblings, and have fewer barnacles of past altercations on my boat, I am, by default, the peacekeeper of the family. I can't say I'm always successful.

So before this special golf trip, I worked both corners of the ring. I called Mark and explained that we needed to all get along for three days. We needed to do this for Dad because it was his birthday and we could never know how much longer he would be around. Mark agreed to no fights. Then I called Sean. I was confident we were all on the same page.

As we loaded up the bags and clubs, just getting my dad out of the driver's seat was a small miracle. Triple-teamed, he finally allowed that Mark should drive. Even Dad seemed to be trying to compromise for the good of the group. "I don't know who died and made Mark in charge of everything," Dad said, as he climbed into the passenger seat—*of Mark's car!* But just the fact that he wasn't driving was an early 1-up.

It's a two-and-a-half-hour drive from San Diego to La Quinta. Even with the early lead, all the pep talks and the sense that we were on the same page, I knew this was a ticking bomb.

During the drive, Sean kept the conversation on Dad and off two of the likely pressure points—politics and religion. Sean led the reflections on Dad's forty-one-year career as an engineer for his one and only employer, Bechtel Power Corp. Mark and I did a lot of listening.

As we came down the hill into Palm Springs, we stopped at a popular turnout to admire the view. We handed the camera to another onlooker and posed for some group pictures. With interlocking arms and sincere smiles, I thought, "We're doing this. We're actually on a family golf trip." I also couldn't help but wonder, was this the saying of grace right before the game of dominoes?

Our first tee time was that afternoon at the Mountain Course at La Quinta. When Mark plays golf, he drinks. And when Mark, who's a lawyer, does anything, he does it with a gallop. Needless to say, by the back nine, he was three degrees north of sober. And when Mark drinks it puts Dad, who doesn't drink, on edge. I found myself drinking just to deflect some of the attention. Sean, who also doesn't drink, and who has been working hard at trying to break 90, was consumed by his own golf game.

Mark and Sean are within a shot of each other in terms of handicaps (I'd say both are about a 20). In a preemptive attempt to defuse that portion of their rivalry, I had made them partners for the trip in a 54-hole match against Dad and me. My Index is an 8 and my dad is currently a 28. Peacemaker that I am, I dolled out the shots.

All the way to the last putt on the last hole, where we all made a par, the first eighteen holes were close and we had a good time. Mark and Sean were only up ten bucks. A layer of tension was brewing below the surface, but I remember thinking, no matter what happens, at the very least, we'll always have the memory of this round together.

That night, the first meal was at Adobe, a Mexican restaurant "on the campus" of La Quinta. It was good food, good conversation and then back to our room for Sunday night football on a living room flat screen. Men being men, the scene was lifted straight off the Serengeti. A small pack of male lions, some grunts and some groans, licking and resting away the events of the day. We were one with several sofas. That is, until Bernard Berrian, a wide receiver for the Minnesota Vikings, was on the back end of a 99-yard touchdown pass.

Sean remarked with delight, "Oh no, Bernard Berrian!"

Mark, ruffled, yelled back, "Shut up, Sean. Yelling Bernard Berrian. You know that's my whole season."

Another family pressure point is fantasy football. I've been the commissioner of "GinellaFFL" for eighteen years. We have twelve teams, twenty participants from various stages of life, and annually we throw in monetary value and live and die by how our teams score each week. Mark's team was dying right before our eyes. Yelling the name of a lightning fast man in a tight purple suit, well, that act put a picture of Sean's head in the middle of Mark's proverbial dartboard.

The next day, on the 27th hole of the trip, Sean received a phone call from a good friend in Hawaii. I was in the cart with my dad and only caught the end of the conversation. Mark filled in the gaps. With his palms up in disbelief, and visibly annoyed, Mark said, "Sean is giving a Hawaii surf report to Bob Fram from his golf car—*in Palm Springs!*"

I can kick myself now. I should've switched cart partners after round one. At the turn my dad and I stopped to buy refreshments. By the time I pulled up to the next tee, our 28th hole, a brotherly brawl had erupted. Apparently while they waited for my dad and me to return with the drinks, Sean had started to check his messages. "You know that's my pet peeve," said Mark. "I'm on vacation and we're trying to play golf. Get off your damn cell phone."

"OK, Mark, you're right. I'm sorry," said Sean, in a condescending tone.

"You don't mean that," said Mark. "You can take that 'sorry' and shove it up your...!"

We all hit. A half a hole later, Mark questioned my dad about a drop he was taking from a lake running along the fairway. I tried to explain the situation because, if anything, when I'm playing golf with any portion of this group, I'm the rulebook. Mark didn't understand. I explained again. Mark argued. I explained again and asked, "Are you messing with me?" Now *I* was mad. Like I said, I don't always succeed at keeping the peace.

Remember, any indication of calling a Ginella a cheat means trouble. Before I knew it, Mark and I had a screaming match going across the fairway that escalated to a place Mark and I don't usually go. "Do you want to get in the last word?" he asked. "Yes," I said. Expletives ensued.

"Mark," my Dad hammered, "quit arguing."

Now it was Mark who was being triple-teamed, and if you factor in the fantasy football from the night before, in an unlikely scenario, he was ready to tap out of this ultimate fighting championship. We managed to finish a very quiet eight remaining holes, but our foursome only carded one meal. After we got home, and unbeknownst to the rest of us, Mark went to his room, showered, packed and drove home.

It might've been inevitable, but it was also necessary. For my dad's sake, we had to give a trip like this a shot. We finished the trip as a threesome and after insisting to keep the topic of conversation off of what had transpired with Mark, we had a great time. The steak and the mac-and-cheese at Palmer's—all perfect. And my dad loved the signed print.

A few days after the trip Mark sent an e-mail explaining why he left. He said he was dealing with financial pressures back at home, wasn't having fun, felt he was bringing the group down, and so this time opted to make a subtle exit. The last line of his e-mail was, "I'M SORRY." Which couldn't have been an easy send for a right wing and righteous lawyer. Not to mention a rather proud soul.

We all followed his lead; Sean covered Mark's portion of the trip. I apologized for putting us in that position that set us up for failure. I indicated in my e-mail that maybe we should try again on 11/22/13, when Dad turns eighty.

And then came Dad's perspective. For an engineer and a guy who made a living working with numbers, he sure is good with words. This is the bulk of his e-mail:

Because we're all passionate about whatever we feel is important at the time, sometimes the passion takes over for reason. We've all been guilty of unreasonable passion to various degrees at one time or another. So let's let the past go out with the tide. And let's resolve to do a better job of harnessing our passions and directing them to the purpose for which we come together the next time. I hope we don't wait until I'm eighty to do it again. This was too much fun to let that much time lapse. It doesn't have to be on as grand a scale as this one, seventy-five is a special number. But it can be when the families are gathering for any other occasion, and "the boys" can get away for a few rounds of great golf again.

You all make Mom and me so very proud of your accomplishments and for the love you have for family. Stay close because, as Mom says, "When we're gone, you must know that the greatest gift we could give you, is each other."

Love and gratitude, Dad

So there you have it. In a weird and twisted way, the mission was still accomplished—we just did it Ginella style.

~Matt Ginella

Never Let a Big Gun Bring You Down

Competing in the Bing Crosby National Pro-Am, now the AT&T Pebble Beach Pro-Am, is about the biggest thrill any amateur can imagine. A week of playing Pebble Beach Golf Links, Cypress Point Club and Spyglass Hill, rubbing elbows with the biggest names in golf, sports, Hollywood and business—it simply doesn't get any better.

I should know: I've participated five times.

Each was memorable in its own way, but one experience stands out. It was 1983 and I was paired in the event with co-host Nathaniel Crosby, son of late tournament founder Bing Crosby. We became good pals prior to Nathaniel pulling off his surprise victory at the 1981 U.S. Amateur Championship at The Olympic Club. For some unknown reason, he invited me to be his partner for the Pro-Am. I couldn't accept fast enough.

At the time I was a San Francisco sportswriter pretty much in charge of my schedule, and so was able to find enough time to maintain a 2-handicap. But as anyone who has played in the tournament will attest, it's difficult to play to your handicap for many reasons.

1. The courses are long, challenging and usually damp in mid-January or early February when the event is played.

2. Many amateurs—especially first-timers—burn out by playing three practice rounds and are exhausted by the time the tournament starts on Thursday.

3. There are parties every night.

4. The pressure of performing in front of spectators and possibly television cameras can be terrifying. Truthfully, unless you are paired in the celebrity rotation, meaning potential TV time in front of large galleries, nobody much cares how you play except your family and friends. That said, every shot seems important and you try so hard, you are drained after each round.

Crosby being Crosby, we drew the celebrity rotation in the first round Thursday at Cypress Point, or as former USGA President Sandy Tatum calls the course, "The Sistine Chapel of Golf." This is no exaggeration. It is a magical meeting of sand, surf and turf, truly one of the prettiest places on earth, where deer usually outnumber members. The membership is small and well heeled. As comedian Bob Hope once cracked, "They had a membership drive at Cypress Point and drove out fifteen members."

Crosby, a young professional trying to make his way to the PGA Tour, hung tough for most of the round. His ink-stained partner had his moments, too. In fact, we were among the team leaders when we arrived at the famous 230-yard par-3 16th hole, which requires a heroic carry over ocean and jagged rocks.

As is usually the case, there was a backup on the tee; the hole is as demanding as it is breathtaking, and triple-bogeys do tend to take a while to hole out. As we stood there behind two groups, I had plenty of time—too much, frankly—to consider my options, which were to play safe to the left of the green or go for broke.

When it was our turn to hit, Crosby played safe, not wanting to jeopardize his good round. He asked me to do the same, but I politely declined. My logic was simple: how many opportunities would I have to knock my tee shot onto the 16th green in front of several thousand spectators? I had to try.

With stomach churning, I chose a 3-wood and told myself to swing smooth. Somehow, my body obeyed, and the ball came off sweet to carry the water and cliff, finishing fifteen feet from the hole. The crowd roared; Crosby rolled his eyes.

As I floated off the tee, grinning from ear to ear, I walked by the group waiting behind us, which included Lanny Wadkins and Ben Crenshaw. I glanced at Wadkins, who was sitting on the end of his golf bag, hoping to snag a compliment. Having just produced the shot of my life, I figured he had to be impressed.

He wasn't.

Wadkins stared at the ground, not even bothering to look me in the eye, then uttered three words I will never forget. "Routine, huh pal?"

I almost fell into the ice plant. It was just his way of letting me know I had overachieved, gotten lucky. There were still comments like "Great shot, Mark!" and "Way to go, kid!" popping from the gallery but I barely heard them. All good feelings drained from by body like water down a sink, the plug pulled by Wadkins.

As I made the left-to-right loop to the green around the ocean, I thought about Wadkins and how badly I wanted to sink the birdie putt. "I'll show him," I thought. But I didn't. In the end I was lucky to two-putt.

I reminded Wadkins of this story four years later during a friendly round at San Francisco Golf Club arranged by another former USGA President, Grant Spaeth. Wadkins said he didn't remember, but semi-apologized for shattering my world. Then he shot the easiest 64 I've ever seen.

Moral of the story: never let a big gun bring you down.

~Mark Soltau

The Golf Book

Fathers

*Often the deepest relationships can be developed
during the simplest activities.*

~Gary Smalley

Appreciating Bad Golf

L
ike so many of my golf problems, this one began at address: I've never known how to address my father-in-law. After my wedding in 2003, I couldn't bring myself to call him "Dennis" and I already had a "Dad." So we eventually came to address each other as "Hey" and "Hey There." As in...

HIM: "Hey, you gonna let me in?"

ME: "Hey There. Thanks for the unannounced visit."

One morning, in the first year of my marriage, Hey There drew me aside on the second tee of our local municipal goat track. "Hey," he said, putting his hand on my shoulder in the manner of someone about to share a deep confidence. "I've given this a lot of thought and..."—he paused while a 737 screamed to a landing at the adjacent international airport—"I want you to start calling me Pop."

"Pop?" I said, suddenly feeling eight years old. "And what should I call your wife, Snap or Crackle?"

Hey There was not amused by this remark, and never again raised the subject. This was just the beginning of our excruciating efforts to bond on the golf course.

It didn't help that we came from different golf traditions. I had grown accustomed, in twenty years as a sportswriter, to playing the world's finest courses. Hey There played courses whose signs, with suggestions like "Shirts Preferred," depressed me on arrival.

I'm used to signs that ask, "Leave Rakes in Bunker." Hey There is more used to reading, "Rake Leaves in Bunker."

Worse, my sixty-seven-year-old father-in-law only ever plays nine holes. Seniors may like to believe that sixty is the new forty. But in golf, nine will never be the new eighteen. It's an abomination, a crime against nature. And so Hey There talks of "making the turn" on the fifth fairway. He hopes to someday "break 45." And he refers to the clubhouse bar as the 10th hole

And yet these ninety-minute lightning rounds have become "the thing we do together." Golf is our "shared interest," though his enthusiasm for his brand of golf is not something I am always able to reciprocate.

One morning Hey There called me from Dick's Sporting Goods.

"What are you buying?" I asked.

"Golf hats," Hey There said.

This answer rendered me momentarily incapable of speech. I didn't know, until then, that anybody actually *bought* golf hats. Rather, I thought they reproduced in my hall closet, where at least a hundred giveaway lids have come to life only to die without ever being worn.

But then we are radically different men, of radically different temperaments. I often begin cursing on my downswing. If I am playing poorly, and I almost always am, I fall mute for several holes, and silently brood in the shotgun seat of our cart. I take pleasure, I'm afraid, in the on-course misfortunes of my playing partner, an unbecoming trait that I inherited from my own father. (On every errant tee shot of mine, my dad still belts out the chorus to "Goodbye, My Coney Island Baby.")

Whereas my father-in-law is the gentlest soul I have ever met. My wife claims to have never seen him lose his temper. He hugs everyone by way of greeting, holds hands with the people seated on either side of him while saying grace at dinner, and ends every telephone conversation with "I love you," even, I suspect, when bidding farewell to a telemarketer.

And so it was with fascination that I watched him come to a slow boil on the golf course one recent fall day. On the eighth and penultimate hole of our round, he was bent over a three-foot putt for par. But I was away, and made a point of preemptively draining my five-footer for par. "No pressure," I said, and Hey There abruptly backed away from his ball.

There followed from Hey There an eternity of sighing, plumb-bobbing, line-reading and grass-sweeping. Then he calmly stepped up to his ball and ran it eleven feet past the hole.

What happened next filled me with a kind of fatherly pride for my father-in-law: He flung his putter thirty feet into the air.

The club went windmilling in a parabola that was positively majestic, though one that he instantly regretted. And so Hey There began trying to wave the club away from the green, like Carlton Fisk waving at his home run in Game Six of the 1975 World Series.

But alas, like most of his drives, his putter had too much height and not enough distance. It kamikazed down to the green headfirst, leaving an L-shaped gash like a surgical scar.

My anger had scarred him, and he in turn had scarred the green. I was proud.

But you know what? His patience has left its own mark on me. I no longer mind playing nine holes, my new goal is to break 40, and the tire fire burning just off the third fairway is no longer an eyesore to me, rather a benefit: It plays as a lateral-hazard.

In the first five years of my marriage, Hey There has taught me to appreciate bad golf. And the three children I've blessed him with within that time have given me another gift, a new name for my father-in-law.

Grandpa.

~Steve Rushin

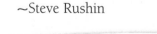

My Gift to My Son

Success in this game depends less on strength of body than strength of mind and character.

~Arnold Palmer

Taking my teenage son out on our weekly Sunday golf adventure is sometimes like pulling teeth without Novacaine. It's difficult for golf's pastoral qualities to compete with friends, girls, iPods and text messaging. Frankly, there are times when I'd prefer to golf alone than listen to him complain about his slice and the crucial events with his friends that he is missing by walking the same old course with the same old man.

Yet, for reasons I have only now come to comprehend, I've always insisted he come along with me.

It came to me as I saw him wading oppressively toward the green on the ninth fairway. It was the final hole after a particularly dismal half-round for both of us. With gray thunderclouds gathering above, the darkness floating ominously, threatening to descend and spirit my son away, I began to realize why this game was so crucial to his development into manhood. As I watched him disappear over a hilly rise, flanked by heavy milkweed and light clover, it occurred to me that he no longer resembled the person I knew in my dreams. When I thought of him in my sleep, he was still a child, young and vulnerable and innocent. Here, walking sullenly in the distance, was a much taller lad, tanned and lean, with growing and impressive muscle development in his arms and shoulders. I could almost see the frame of the man he would become. Why hadn't I recognized such a startling change before? When exactly did he begin to out-drive me with regularity and where did this newfound physical power come from? Who was this young man and why did I insist that this game play such an important role in his life? What was it I expected him to learn?

The picture, of course, was not complete. Like an artist molding clay on a muddy potter's wheel, the vase was not yet ready for flowers and water. There was still more child than man in the mindset of the person who was marching up ahead toward the clubhouse and into adulthood. It was my hope that golf would work its magic here too.

I knew what to expect on the drive home. The same excuses would ring throughout the cab of my old red truck, drowning out the rattling of the clubs tossed haphazardly in the bed.

"I can't play this game," and "I'll never get rid of this slice," and "I don't want to do this anymore. It isn't fair."

And there it was.

Golf can be many things. Some say it is a microcosm of life itself but I choose to see it as an antidote to life. If golf has taught me anything, it is that the game, unlike life, is completely and unequivocally fair. Inherently fair. Always fair. It is one of those few, magical things in our lives that we can actually control. Time spent on the driving range working on a nasty hook can be rewarded with a pristine tee shot, the ball cutting through the blue skies of a Sunday morning like a white bullet. It takes some of us longer than others to realize the universal truth that while the ball rarely goes where we want it, it always goes exactly where we put it.

One day, hopefully soon, my son will understand this concept. Excuses for a bad round will fall away naturally as did his interest in Etch A Sketch and Tinkertoys. The brutal, honest truth of the inherent unfairness of life and the total, complete fairness of golf will take hold. Perhaps he will use these lessons in other areas of his life. Perhaps not. But golf will at least give him the opportunity to understand the concept that we should make every effort to master those few things in life that are truly under our control. It's the greatest gift I could ever give him. Golf is the venue that allows me to give it.

~Mark Spangler

Dreamer

Hope is but the dream of those who wake.
~Matthew Prior

Golf illuminates the essential character of those who play. It has a knack for enhancing the positive attributes of some people as well as shining a light on the character defects that we all struggle with from time to time (some, I'm afraid, more than others). We've all played with the guy who gives himself five-footers without the faintest indication of guilt or remorse. That says something important, I think, about the golfer in question.

My dad was a dreamer whose optimistic streak far surpassed the reality of his life. For more than twenty-five years, he never ceased to wax enthusiastically about the coming business triumph he was just on the cusp of achieving. He chased that mirage from the moment he left the last of a series of jobs on Wall Street in the mid-70s, until his death from a stroke at age sixty-six in 2002.

During that span my sister and I heard about oil leases in West Texas, consulting opportunities with Fortune 500 companies that my dad cold-called with hand-written notes scratched out on yellow legal pads, and other fantastic opportunities too numerous to mention. Until just before the end of his days, I felt an obligation to nod my assent and say banal things like, "That sounds great, Dad," to nearly every moneymaking proposition he mentioned, every potential ownership stake he floated to us.

The gulf between my dad's hopes and the reality of his business career was reflected in his approach to golf as well. I took up the sport in college after laying the tennis rackets aside, falling in love with the contrasting simplicity and devilish nature of the game. I was hooked. In those early days I would even memorize course layouts in my head and replay rounds shot-by-shot when I tried to fall asleep at night. I saw my dad infrequently, as we lived nearly 2,000 miles apart, but we would reunite for visits at my grandmother's house in Central Florida in a beautiful place called Mountain Lake. Golf was a staple of life there, and as my interest in golf surged, my dad's perked as well. He followed me into the game, and I felt from the outset that his nascent interest might just be a well-meaning effort to connect with me on my terms.

The other fifty-one weeks of the year, I batted the ball with square-grooved Ping Eye 2's around a Tillinghast track in Dallas, while Dad bought a few secondhand blade irons and started beating balls at a driving range in Connecticut. "God, I was just hitting the ball great the other day," he'd say to me over the phone. Sure you were, I'd think, but say something more like, "That's great, Dad, keep up the good work." Then he bought a cheap driver and became even more enthusiastic about his game. "I was hitting the ball about 250-260 today," he'd say, though experience told me that unless he had managed to straighten out his swing and had substituted a super-ball for a Spalding, he was probably hitting the same short duck hooks and power fades that made five-hour rounds a staple of our Floridian get-togethers.

But you couldn't help but admire the man's enthusiasm, nor fail to find the humor in his flouting of conventional golf etiquette, which ran to driving carts up to the fringes of greens, striking a pose after errant tee shots and asking, "Hey, did you see what happened on that one?" as he knelt down to place another ball on the tee, and trampling on more putting lines than I could count. I'd attempt to correct him occasionally but he'd simply wave me off and say, "It's not like we're playing the final round of the Masters, now is it?"

I knew from hitting some balls with his makeshift set that his clubs weren't helping him at all. Every now and then I'd persuade him to use one of my newer irons and he'd hit the ball longer and straighter than before. "I really ought to get myself some new clubs," he said more than once, but I knew that a man who slept on old, ratty sheets, and ate Stouffer's frozen dinners more often that not, would never splurge on something like that. I knew he didn't feel worthy of using better equipment. If the upgrade of his arsenal were ever to happen, I'd have to be the one to do it.

There were many times that I thought about doing just that, but it always seemed like something else needed my dollar more urgently. My dad and I grew more distant for various reasons and I never got around to getting him a decent set. That's a regret, and a wrong I'll only be able to right with someone else in some other circumstance. I hope that moment comes one day.

My dad never did find that elusive business triumph. Eventually he ended up driving for a car service that transported high-flying Wall Street hotshots (like my dad had once been and tried very hard to be more so) from their suburban homes to the New York airports. He worked sixty-hour weeks into his early sixties before relocating just a few miles from the PGA Tour's headquarters in Ponte Vedra Beach, given a grub stake by my grandmother to invest in the market. He spent the remainder of his days watching CNBC, making trades and scrawling out investment ideas on the same yellow legal pads that also served as address book and grocery list. My sister and I never did become corporate officers or own a share of the any of the dozens of prospective companies my dad talked of starting.

My dad may not have been the world's most realistic or self-aware man, and my golfing experience with him only confirmed that impression. We never really played a memorable round together and his golfing etiquette never really improved. But what I'll remember more is walking into my grandmother's sitting room one chilly December afternoon after breaking 80 for the first time and saying to my dad, "Hey, guess what I shot?" He let me provide the answer myself: "I shot a 77, Dad!"

I'd rarely seen him so pleased. "That's just terrific!" he said, his pride in my accomplishment nearly equal to my own. His happiness at my success made clear that my dad really did have some character, just not where I'd been looking for it all those years.

~Whit Sheppard

42

Pings Left in a Will

My grandfather didn't only provide a guide to living; he lived life fully and modeled for me how to do it — mostly with love and kindness.

~McAllister Dodds

Grandpa George used to come over to the house and try to get me to go play golf with him. He'd always say with his big grin, "Jason, I know you'd be good so let's get you out there." My high school years consisted of playing guitar in bands, skateboarding and generally goofing off. After his pleading, my inevitable response was, "Sorry Gramps. I'm not playing an old man's game." Still, every Sunday he came by offering up the possibility of playing some golf. From what I've been told, Grandpa George was a great high school athlete and picked up golf late in life and "never hit it that far but was always right down the middle." The sight of his consistent tee ball regretfully I will never get to see.

Golf never held any interest for me growing up, even though childhood memories of visits to my grandparents' house in Reno spark images of Jack Nicklaus and his yellow polo shirt on television, an aluminum golf cup on the carpet and red striped range balls all over the apartment.

My grandfather contracted throat cancer from years of smoking and was treated at the local Phoenix Veteran's Hospital. The doctors removed parts of his throat and tongue to battle the disease and I remember visiting him in the hospital. I remember everyone locked in a grim state as the cornerstone of our family lay helpless in bed. I never realized how important he was until that moment because as a kid, the world revolved only around me.

A few months later, he returned from the hospital and took my brother, sister and myself out for pizza. He had lost a tremendous amount of weight and looked very frail, but was pretty much upbeat. He spoke of his desire to get back out on the golf course and asked me to join him out there for once. I refused. I was upset with him for lighting up an unfiltered Camel as we ate our pizza, but also because I was then in full teenager rebellion. I felt I was a grown up. I loved him very much but didn't have time for anything so trivial as golf.

The following year, I moved to Seattle to pursue a dream of infiltrating the burgeoning music scene. I only lasted nine months, during which time I received news that Grandpa George had passed away. The cancer had resurfaced and this time it was just too late. In his will, he left various articles to members of the family. To my surprise, he left me with his prized golf clubs, a set of Pings, with a personal note that read:

Dear Jason,

I am leaving you with my golf clubs, as I know you'll have a knack for the game and will enjoy it for the rest of your life. This game will bring you tremendous pleasure and you'll learn more about yourself and the world than you thought possible through it. Please get out there and give it a go.

Love, Grandpa George

I was tremendously saddened by the loss and upset that I never got to say goodbye. I was also confused that even in death he continued to push me towards the game of golf. I returned to Phoenix and forgot about the note as my entry to adulthood was getting the better of me, consisting of jobs, girl problems and the everyday stresses of carving a niche in the world. After a few years of trying to make it on my own, financial pressures forced me to move back to my parents' house.

One hot afternoon, my good friend Scott drove by and I happened to be out front washing my car. He stopped, rolled down his window.

"Hey Jason, we need a fourth for golf," Scott shouted. "Do you know how to play?"

I looked up and was immediately flooded with memories of Grandpa George, requesting the same thing of me for years as a teenager. "I think I have some old clubs in the garage and haven't ever taken them out. Is it cool if I join you guys?" Little did I know this would be an unbelievably satisfying and awakening decision for me.

Like everyone else, my first round was filled with pain and frustration but sprinkled with moments of brilliance. I was overwhelmed by the whole atmosphere of the course; the smell of cut grass, the relaxed and open air, the beauty of the landscape, and the combination of power and finesse the game provided, along with the enjoyment of hanging out with friends. It reminded me of home more than my own home did. I felt like I belonged on the course and as comfortable as if I had been there hundreds of times previously.

After finishing up on 18, Scott added up the scores and to my surprise I had beaten everybody. My friends were shocked that I had never played before. "I think you might want to think about playing this game," Scott said. But I had already made that decision by the turn.

I haven't looked back since. I feel closer to my Grandpa George every time I walk onto the first tee than I ever did when he was alive. I know in my heart that he is there with me, guiding me down the fairways. For the past twelve years the game of golf has been the most influential and consistent thing in my life. It has taught me about life and myself more than any other experience or person, and I owe all it to my Grandpa George. I know I can't relive those early years, and painfully regret not taking him up on those early requests to accompany him on the fairways. Not too far but straight down the middle.

~Jason Kileen

Two Feet Short

Romance fails us and so do friendships,
but the relationship of a parent and child,
less noisy than all others, remains indelible
and indestructible, the strongest relationship on earth.
~Theodor Reik

I struck my drive on the 5th. Long and down the middle and before it came to rest my clubs were on my shoulder and I was walking after it. By the time I reached the fairway I was thinking back to my earliest memory with my father on the course. I hadn't thought of this memory in so long that I found myself smiling as it came to me. Playing alone is something I enjoy every once and a while.

Growing up, our home was along the 6th hole of our local course. Every so often in summer, my father would go out in the late hours when no one was on the course and walk just a few holes. One evening, just ahead of the setting sun, my father asked if I would like to tag along. My reaction was immediate, ecstatic. It would have been the same had my father asked if I wanted to watch him mow the lawn or haul some trash to the garbage dump. Because when you're little, you long to spend time with your dad. Before the angst of the teenage years sets in, when all a young man wants is to spread his wings and experience life on his own, a boy just wants his father, to feel part of his life.

So the two of us made our way out the back door. On the tee, I listened intently as my father explained where to stand when someone was hitting and how vital it was to keep the left arm straight. I took it all in, then watched him stripe a beautiful draw down the middle. "That'll do," my father said.

It was funny to think back on this, because I now utter that very phrase often after a good shot. Little things like that never cease to amaze me. Now in my later years, I find myself mimicking things my father did: a phrase, a facial expression, or (as my wife would note) his horrific taste in neckties. No matter how we try to do things differently and be our own person, inevitably we find ourselves turning into our parents.

My father's drive that evening put him 185 yards away from the green, which was guarded by a small water hazard in front. I remembered thinking how incredibly far away the flag seemed, and I remember the determined look on my father's face as he selected his club. He hit a high towering shot that flew over the hazard and landed on the front of the green. The ball took the break of the green and began to head for the cup, rolling and rolling until it finally stopped two feet short.

Excited, my father turned to see my reaction. But instead of the awe he was expecting, he saw me looking at my shoelaces. After a moment I walked over, placed my hand on his back and said, "That's OK Dad, you got it real close. It was still a pretty good shot."

No doubt my father was surprised by this reaction. It was a shot that Jack Nicklaus would have been proud of. So why the disappointment from his son?

But then my father realized why I'd felt the need to console him—I'd expected it to go in. After all, that was the goal of the game as understood by my naïve young self, to put the ball in the hole. He smiled, placed his hand on my shoulder, said, "Yep, I'll get 'em next time." And off we strode to finish the hole.

That's how it is with sons and fathers. When you are young, you see them as superhuman, capable of doing anything. So what if it was a 185-yard shot over water, my dad can do it, he can do anything. Seeing one's father for the first time as a human being, warts and all, is something a child never forgets. In my later years, I found a strange sense of comfort in seeing my father fail. It lead me to the realization that we all struggle in life, no matter who we are, and that it is not the times we fall short, but rather how we deal with adversity that defines our character.

That day I learned that my father couldn't simply hole out a 5-iron from 185 yards. Later in life, I would see a man who worked to control his temperament, provide for his family, and offer words of encouragement to a son who at times desperately needed it. Often times he came up short in his endeavors, but he always approached them with the same steely determination he displayed late that summer evening on the golf course.

This memory faded by the time I arrived to my ball. I lined up and struck my approach shot. It landed right in the heart of the green.

"That'll do," I said in a whisper as I gathered my clubs and walked towards the green.

~Gregg Mills

The Twenty-Seven Year Challenge

A parent never dies. He or she lives in your heart.
~Robert Trent Jones, Jr.

t was two days after the funeral, and I was helping my mother sort through some of Dad's personal belongings. Placed where I would be sure to find it was a scorecard from the Hawley Country Club dated July 18, 1981. On that day, my dad, Vint McDonald, had played eighteen holes with one of his golfing buddies and shot a 73, 3-over par. This was a remarkable score, especially in view of the fact that he died of cancer fifty-three days later.

On the bottom of the card, he signed his name and made the notation that he was sixty-six years old. I recognized this as a challenge for me to try to match his score when I reached that age. At the time I was thirty-nine, and sixty-six seemed like a century away. It was then I made a promise to my father that someday I would answer his final golf challenge.

Last winter I celebrated my sixty-sixth birthday. It was a sobering reminder that I had just turned the age my father was when he passed away. I located the twenty-seven-year-old scorecard, which I had carefully stored in my top desk drawer, and prepared to answer my father's unspoken challenge.

So on the morning of July 18th 2008, exactly twenty-seven years to the day that Dad played his round, I left my home in Luverne,

Minnesota, and drove two hundred miles north to the Hawley Country Club. During the five-hour trip, I thought about my father and reflected on the wonderful relationship we enjoyed both on and off the course. He was my father, golf coach and best friend.

Upon arriving at the country club, I was greeted in the parking lot by Leroy Dauner, a close, personal friend of both my Dad and myself. Everybody called him "Sam" because his favorite golfer was the legendary Sam Snead. Sam was the retired grounds superintendent at Hawley Country Club, and despite being on the sunny side of eighty, he was still in great shape. In a telephone conversation earlier that month, I had explained the uniqueness of the match and asked if he would serve as scorekeeper and rules official for this contest. He eagerly accepted and had been anxiously waiting for the arrival of this day.

Sam put my clubs in his golf cart, and we rode directly to the first tee. Without wasting any time, we teed off, and after twenty-seven years, the match was on.

I got off to a shaky start with three bogeys in the first four holes. If I didn't get my game together soon, the match would be over by the ninth hole. Then, I remembered what Dad would always say, "Relax, enjoy the game, and give it your best." He never measured success by wins or losses; he only asked me to give my best effort. This advice, given to me over fifty years ago, helped me in golf as well as my personal life.

With my refreshed attitude, I relaxed and finished the last five holes of the front side with three pars and a couple of birdies for a respectable 1-over par score of 36.

On the back nine, I continued to play well. As we played, Sam and I recalled stories about Dad. It seemed like every hole on the course brought to mind a fond memory. I could feel the presence of Dad's spirit with us.

I lost a stroke to par on the tough 11th hole, but I got it back when I made a long, downhill putt for a birdie on 15. I was fortunate, the putt was hit too aggressively and would have run off the green had the ball not hit the center of the cup, popped up, and come down in the hole. Sam and I agreed that sometimes it is better to be lucky than good. This unexpected birdie left me only 1-over with three holes to play. Life was good.

The 16th hole is considered an easy par 4 because it measures only 345 yards. Carelessly, I hit my drive into the rough and my second shot landed in a greenside bunker. It took two attempts to get out of the sand and two putts to complete the hole. "A six," Sam lamented, as he recorded the double-bogey on the scorecard. "You are back to three over."

The members consider the 17th hole the most difficult par 3 on the course. It plays 180 yards uphill to a small backstop green. From experience I knew not to leave myself putting from above the hole. I carefully played both my tee shot and chip shot short. The strategy was sound, except now I faced a ten-foot uphill putt for a par.

When I stroked the putt, I immediately felt that it was short. Then, almost as if the ball defied gravity, it kept rolling to the hole, paused at the edge of the cup, and dropped in. "A par!" Sam shouted. We exchanged high-fives, and moved to the final hole.

The 18th is the signature hole of the Hawley golf course. The scenic 505-yard par 5 plays from an elevated tee to a generous tree-lined fairway that meanders back to the clubhouse.

I hit my best drive of the day and followed with a solid fairway wood that ended up 10 yards short of the green. My approach shot almost hit the pin and came to rest six feet past the hole. The stage was set. The twenty-seven year challenge match would be decided by this six-footer.

I studied the putt from every angle. It appeared absolutely straight. Slowly, I took the putter back and then moved it forward in a fluid stroke. The putter blade kissed the ball and it rolled straight for the center of the hole. When the ball was three inches in front of the cup, for no apparent reason, it veered to the right, caught the edge of the cup, and rimmed out.

For a moment both Sam and I stood in silence, staring at the ball lying next to the hole. Gradually, I looked up at Sam and saw a big smile on his face. He extended his hand in friendship, and said, "That's the way your father would have wanted the match to end."

As I tapped in the final putt for a par, a score of 73, and a tie with my father, I realized the same force that propelled the ball into the hole at the 17th, had kept the ball from dropping in at the 18th. The challenge was complete.

~George McDonald

Generations Linked

I was born in Kitchner, Ontario, Canada, May 20, 1930. While going through my dad's things, I found several poems in a box along with a letter addressed to me.

These poems were written by my grandfather, John Russell Dauberger, in the German language in the late 1800s. He was a woodworker by trade, loved golf, and made his own wooden clubs. He started me in the game before he passed in his early nineties. For many years I used a persimmon putter he made especially for me.

My Dad translated the poems into English before he died. Here's one:

Golf the Game

Golf shall teach you patiently
Adversity to meet
It shall teach you philosophy
To keep your temper sweet
It shall teach you still to grin
With mirth no matter what
You are a victor if you win
A loving cup or not

~Harry L. Dauberger

Chicken Soup
for the Soul

Hallowed Ground

He didn't tell me how to live; he lived, and let me watch him do it.
~Clarence Budington Kelland

My closest friends say that if you substitute golf for trout fishing, our family story would read like "A River Runs Through It." A father passes the lessons of a sport onto his children, and that sport becomes an anchor in the family's history. For almost forty years, my father was my teacher, coach and playing partner. The golf course was our river, our golden pond, our field of dreams. The golf course was where I learned the most about Don Massé as a man, competitor and friend. The course was also where I, his second son, was tested, taught and inspired. It remains the most pleasing place for me on this earth.

In the fall of 2000, toward the end of a beautiful golfing season, we lost our beloved father to lymphoma. On his last day, I joked with him that we had a tee time. He smiled weakly, and I know he would have willed himself on the course if he could. His voice that day was soft, though his grip was surprisingly strong. Years later, I remember that grip. More important is the voice I still hear from long ago, that of a low-handicap golfer encouraging his five children to play this wonderful game. My father had me hooked the first time he let me clean his clubs, those magic irons and woods that sent golf balls flying high and far into a deep blue sky.

My lessons began when I was nine. We first went to the driving range where I learned the basics: the stance ("Shoulder width, feet slightly open."), the grip ("Interlocking: That's what Jack Nicklaus uses."), the takeaway ("Keep the left arm straight.") and the follow-through ("Head down. I'll watch where your ball goes."). We would start with the high-numbered irons and work our way down to the longer irons and woods. I groomed my young game on the rock-hard fairways of the Green Valley Par 3 Course in Purchase, New York.

I wasn't allowed to play a full-length course until I was ready in my father's eyes. That memorable day came in June 1964, when I was eleven, a fresh graduate from sixth grade at Harrison Avenue School. Dad and I played nine holes at Maple Moor Golf Club in White Plains. To be on a regulation course with him made me feel as if I were strolling through heaven. I don't recall my score, but I remember when Dad nodded, patted me on the shoulder, or gave me that "OK" sign with his short thick fingers. His OK would still guide my golf game well into middle age. And it's no coincidence that my two lowest scores ever, a 79 and a 36 for nine, were both played with my father.

Every time I step on a course, his words guide me. "Hold the club like you're holding a bird... Swing easy... Tempo, tempo, tempo... Let the club do the work... Don't try to finesse the shot, just swing down and through... When in doubt, go with the longer club... Never give up."

Dad didn't give lessons to just his children. He regularly tutored golfers of all ages. His gift was a friendly, nurturing style that made people trust him. He was an avid reader of golf magazines and instruction books, notably *Play Better Golf* by Jack Nicklaus, one of his idols.

Shortly after my father was diagnosed with lymphoma, he received a wonderful, generous call from Nicklaus, a fellow Ohio native. They chatted for fifteen minutes about family (Jack also had four boys and a girl), golf and the fighting spirit. Another of the golfing gods, Sam Snead, also acknowledged my father in those final months. On an 8x10 photo of my father teeing off at a tournament years earlier, Snead attached a note:

"Hi, Don. Your swing is great. All the best. A friend, Sam Snead."

Dad proudly displayed that framed photo atop the console TV. On those days when he was too weak to do much else but sit in his recliner, he could look up and see that picture of his younger athletic self finishing his fluid swing in Snead-like fashion. We were grateful that two of the game's legends had taken the time to recognize another in our father.

I remember being a wide-eyed boy when Dad brought home trophies and gifts won in local civic tournaments. I remember how he regularly scored in the 70s when he played the championship West course at Westchester Country Club, not as a member but as a popular guest. I remember how he broke 80 out in Las Vegas, just months shy of his 70th birthday.

The last awe-inspiring swing I ever saw my father make was with a 3-wood, a classic uphill shot that flew about 180 yards and came to rest some ten feet from the cup. Not bad, you say? Consider that just days earlier, Don Massé had been in a nearby hospital receiving chemotherapy at eighty years old. My brother Drew had the video camera running during our final round with Dad. His address, set up and swing were remarkably unchanged by time or illness. I studied his waggle and the slight forward press before his smooth takeaway. After he made contact, and his shot landed softly on the distant green, Dad raised his club in triumph and turned toward the camera. His smile was full and timeless as he stood on that hallowed ground.

~Mark H. Massé

Emergency Nine

When I was eighteen I spent the summer in the home of my favorite aunt and uncle with the understanding that I would help out around the house. Then, when the time came for the delivery of their expected baby, I would assume responsibility for the care of the household as well as my two younger cousins, who I adored.

Since nobody in my own family played golf, I was somewhat surprised to learn, early on during my stay, just how much the game meant to my uncle. Every morning he would meet friends for a round, and often he would return to the course again in the evenings. Even though my aunt's expression sometimes indicated she was not pleased with his departure, she was still getting lots of rest as I was enjoying the opportunity to practice my meager cooking and housekeeping skills, as well as mother my cousins.

One beautiful Saturday morning, my uncle had arisen earlier than usual. His plan, he confided in me, was to beat the weekend rush at the golf course. As he hastily loaded his clubs into the trunk of his car, my aunt called down to him from her bedroom window. Somewhat reluctantly, he returned inside and went upstairs. The hushed conversation behind closed doors that followed gave me the sense that all was not completely well. I worried, and waited.

There was a slight coolness between them when they emerged from the bedroom. My uncle was carrying the travel bag that had long since been packed with hospital necessities and baby clothes.

It had sat, undisturbed, for several weeks, in readiness for this very special moment. The baby was on its way and it was time for my aunt to go to the hospital, some thirty miles away.

I was so excited. She sat at the kitchen table drinking orange juice calmly, while I flittered about trying to concentrate on her last-minute instructions. Outside, her bag was being put in the trunk while the golf clubs were being taken out.

My uncle returned to the kitchen and asked hopefully, "Do you think I have time for nine holes before we go?"

~Lyn Larsen

In Michigan

Macho doesn't prove mucho.
~Zsa Zsa Gabor

There was not a weekend in the summer that I do not remember my father either playing golf or watching some event on TV intermittently while doing something around the house. It did not matter what event it was or who was playing. PGA or LPGA, Champions or European, if it was on TV, he was watching it. He could look at any player and tell you their name and how good they were.

He taught me the game when I was ten years old, giving me an old set of clubs with rusted heads and wood shafts. He told me that once he knew I was truly into it, he would buy me a better set. After a couple of years of playing on a weekly basis he kept his promise. I remember those clubs and wish I still had them. Probably a collector's item these days.

He bought me some no-name discount clubs, which were still a serious upgrade.

As Chicagoans, we could only play five months out of the year. We had a summer cottage in southern Michigan where we played most of our golf together. I miss those days.

My father died eighteen years ago while my wife was pregnant with my only son. There are two reasons why I really wish he were still around. First, to be in my son's life as those two would have gotten along fabulously. And second, to have a few more of those weekend golf games in Michigan.

I never beat my dad at golf, not even once. I was always too impatient to be very good. I'm the type of golfer who is happy when he breaks 100 and ecstatic when he breaks 90. I always wanted to do it my way, which eventually made my dad just give up on giving me pointers. At first, I think I used to aggravate him because I did not listen. And to be honest, it used to aggravate me that he was always trying to correct my game. Looking back, I know that he was just trying to help me to get better. I just laugh about it now and wish he were still here to play a round of golf with me every once in a while.

Once, at the cottage in Michigan, my older sister, who had never played golf before, informed my father that she wanted to start. So my father took her out during the week when he knew the course would not be crowded. When they got back from playing, my sister was all smiles and bragging about how she had shot a 45.

This got me very upset right away. My pride was out the window. "The first time she ever played the game she shoots a 45?" I asked my dad angrily. He pulled me over to the side so that my sister would not hear and whispered into my ear, "Calm down, she only played three holes."

The other story about my father I remember vividly occurred on a busy holiday weekend at Glenn Shores Golf Course, the nine-hole in Michigan where we played more than any other. We were on deck, and on the tee were three young men in their early twenties. A woman walked up to them and announced that she was a single and that the manager in the pro shop had said to join them.

Disappointment washed over their faces. These macho guys made it clear they thought she would slow down their group and didn't want to have to put up with her.

The 1st hole at Glenn Shores is a short par 4, only 285 yards. The first guy hit his drive down the middle of the fairway around 200 yards. The second guy sliced his drive down into the valley on the right. The third guy pulled his shot to the left, probably around 225 yards. The three then started to walk ahead towards the ladies tees, but the woman told them to stop, that she would hit from the men's tee.

At that point, my father turned to me and with a huge smile, and whispered, "Watch this; this will be very interesting."

I did not know what he knew, but he definitely knew something that nobody else did.

The woman teed up her ball from the same back tee which the young bucks had hit from. She made a beautiful backswing, followed by an explosive sound at impact, and the ball flew high into the air, never seeming to come down. When it gradually began to fall, it landed softly on the green, and rolled to within five feet of the cup. The mouths of the three young bucks, as well as everyone else waiting around the tee, dropped.

"I recognized her as soon as I saw her," my father said. "She's on the LPGA tour."

~Thomas Munson

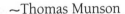

We Played Golf Today

When you look at your life, the greatest happinesses are family happinesses.
~Joyce Brothers

I t was a day I had long awaited. Having gained membership to Rock Ridge Country Club, a private club in Newtown, Connecticut, I invited my father, brother and nephew for a round of golf. The reason for my anticipation was two-fold. It was the first time the four of us would play in the same group and the idea of having three generations of our family on the course together was a photograph waiting to happen. The other reason was not so heartwarming. I wanted to show off the fact I had made it—that I was a member of a private club. And to rub in the fact my brother—eight years my senior—still played at well-worn munis. Sibling rivalry doesn't stop when you hit your forties.

I arrived early to make sure the guys in the bag room and locker room knew I had guests coming. I couldn't wait to buy lunch and drinks after the round so I could sign a chit instead of having to whip out cash or a credit card. Big spender that I am, I bought each a sleeve of Pro V1's. And when the pro said, "Mr. Johnson, you have a minute?" I swelled with pride. In front of my family I was now "Mr. Johnson." How cool.

The pro calmly explained to me that my brother, who had shown up in cargo shorts, would have to change as that style was not permitted. The information left me partly embarrassed, but also armed with the type of story brothers can use on each other at a later date. That was, until the follow-up question came. "By the way, how old is the boy?" the pro asked.

"He's sixteen. Why?" I said.

"I'm afraid there's a problem. No one under eighteen can play until two in the afternoon," said the pro. "It's a club rule."

I was stunned. It had never dawned on me to ask. And I felt even dumber because I had worked in a golf shop years ago and had made fun of members who made similar faux pas.

After explaining the situation to my dad, brother and nephew, I whipped out my cell phone (which was allowed under club rules) and dialed every course within striking distance. A lack of tee times or similar rules provided a stymie with each call. Finally, I said to them, "You know, I bet we could get on Sunset."

Sunset was Sunset Hills. A nine-hole, privately owned course built in the 1920s, the locals refer to it as a hardhat course because of the close proximity of one fairway to another and, indeed, greens to tee-boxes. It's the type of place where yells of "Fore!" outnumber the fours on the scorecard. Not that making a four at Sunset is difficult. A par 70, the course measures a Lilliputian 4,720 yards. The score-card does not feature a photo of the course's "signature hole" because, well, there isn't one. Instead the card is made of a paper just a shade stronger than paper that you would print a letter on. The standard scorer's pencil was yellow—sans the name of the course. Sunset's the type of place without a pro, but rather a man in his sixties sitting behind the counter who takes your money, all of $76 for the four of us, cart included, (which I was surprised didn't go immediately into a cigar box) and hands you the key to your cart. "No. 17," he said in a gruff, yet somehow friendly voice. A starter? Not so much. Place your ball on the tee-box and wait your turn. Still, for a Sunday morning it wasn't a bad wait. About twenty-five minutes in which the four of us talked and my brother took every opportunity to needle me about my failure to know my own club's rules, leading us to this "dog track" of a course.

It was hard to argue against him. Sunset is not a place where closely cropped fairway grass softens your steps, but rather offers a patchwork of *poa annua*, crabgrass and hardpan—mostly the latter two—as fairways. A firm push of the thumb often was not enough to get a tee in the ground, either. The greens? The length of the grass would be fairway height at most private clubs. "I think those guys have better playing conditions than us," cracked my brother, gesturing to the adjacent graveyard.

Yet despite the change of venue, it was a normal round of golf in many ways. My brother continued his annoying habit of talking to himself while standing over the ball and my nephew kept waggling the club more than Sergio Garcia on a bad day. Another constant was that my dad was clearly enjoying the day, being with his sons and grandson.

Sunset bills itself as "The Area's Friendliest Course" and it would be hard to dispute. As play backed up at the 3rd—a blind, down-hill par 3—conversation flowed easily among the three groups on the tee-box. During the wait we learned that Gene Sarazen was the course's first professional, a claim I would normally have deemed ludicrous if not for the fact I knew Sarazen had lived in Brookfield, not far away. The course, they said, was open from early March to December. We also were told on the next hole, the 4th, that we had to keep it down the right side or else we'd have no shot into the green. Without hole diagrams on the card, this was useful local knowledge for Sunset first-timers.

The second time around on the 7th, Dad, then seventy-seven and having taken up the game less than ten years ago, hit an approach shot that thudded short of the green, but happily bounced, as if off cement, onto the putting surface. The shot elicited jabs of derision from my brother and me, but brought more than a hint of a smile to my old man's face. It mattered not how the ball got there. It was just a few feet from the hole and he made a rare birdie. He then stepped onto the 8th tee and announced, "I think I have the honor."

That's when I realized that despite all the shortcomings of the venue, the fact was golf—real golf—was being played. We were hitting shots, playing a match, having fun. Stories were being shared and interesting folks were met. We learned about Sarazen's involvement in the course. We enjoyed the warmth of the sun. My nephew was allowed to play. My brother could wear his cargo shorts. And Dad made a birdie.

As it turned out, it didn't matter where we played or that there was no one to clean our clubs or polish our shoes at the end of the round. We took our dirt-caked clubs and carried them to the car. We then went and had hot dogs and soda paid for in cash. Not a chit to be signed in sight. And like any other round, we replayed the good and bad shots and settled the wagers, Dad and I raking in $2.

We played golf today.

~E. Michael Johnson

The Mediator

My two sons usually got along pretty well. But when they were fourteen and seventeen, the older one arrived home from a camping trip one evening, and the younger jumped all over his case for borrowing his sleeping bag without permission. One word led to another, which led to nasty remarks, which then led to even nastier remarks. They were downstairs by the front door and I was upstairs listening to it escalate. It wasn't long before I heard bodies slamming and furniture breaking. I hurried down, grabbing a club from my husband's golf bag, which was often kept at the bottom of the stairs.

My intention was to insert the club between the boys, separating them while I could remind them of the "brothers don't hit brothers in my house" rule. Somehow the club got mixed up in the fray, hit the older son on the chin, and he started to bleed.

"He's bleeding, Mom," the younger cried. "You've hurt him!"

"What were you trying to do?" I retorted. "Kiss him?"

With that, they both left the house, headed in different directions. I leaned dejectedly against the wall, bloody golf club in hand, as my husband came down the stairs to see what all the ruckus had been about. He put his arm around my shoulders and took the club out of my hand.

"You shouldn't have hit the kid with a 9-iron," he said.

"I know, I know," I replied tearfully. "I feel terrible."

As he put the club back into the bag at the base of the stairs, he said, "You should have used a wedge."

~Jackie Fleming

51

My Little Girl Golfer

A daughter is a day brightener and a heart warmer.
~Author Unknown

My wife and I went to China to gain a daughter; getting a golf partner for the rest of my life turned out to be a bonus.

Like all adoptive parents, especially those in the close-knit community of families with Chinese children, we traveled halfway around the world with all sorts of anxieties and expectations, but no real idea what to expect. Our daughter, Liza, had been abandoned when she was a month old, dropped off by her birth parents in front of a government building in the small mining town of Jinning near the Laotian border. Turned out she was lucky. One of the infants adopted by another couple in our travel group had been left under a train trestle before being rescued. Yet another had been dumped on a concrete piling under an expressway overpass. All the children looked shell-shocked. A couple of them looked like they might die before the flight home.

But everything worked out. All the children we met in China thrived in America, and our daughter has melded into the family as if she had been here all along. As all parents want to do, we bought her dresses and dolls, pink frilly curtains, and lots of bows for her hair. Being a good dad, I did my part by getting her a beginner's golf set, four tiny clubs and a knee-high bag. Expectations were low; my sons played football, basketball, baseball, soccer, rugby, and tennis, but all shrugged at golf, only playing a little here and there when nothing else was going on, never treating it as a legitimate sport. I expected nothing different from Liza. Exposing her to the game was my job as a golf-loving father. Anything beyond that was up to her.

Then came one of the greatest and most undeserved blessings of my life: my baby girl, somewhere around age six, began crawling up in my lap and saying, "Daddy, can we *pleeeease* go hit golf balls?"

You can imagine how many times I said, "No."

Not only does Liza love golf, she shows an extraordinary aptitude. For her seventh birthday party, she asked if she could have a few of her friends out to our club for a golf clinic, and it wasn't long before she was challenging dear old Dad to closest-to-the-pin and putting contests.

All of the local teaching pros I know have said something to the effect of, "Just don't screw this up, Steve." No pressure there. Since I had nothing to do with her genetic predilection to the sport, all I'm expected to do is raise, encourage, motivate, teach, coach, finance, manage, and play with my little prodigy.

Caddying was not something I put on the list. That, too, changed when Liza asked if she could play in a few tournaments at the ripe old age of seven.

I had carried a few bags in my time. As a kid, I had caddied for my father and a few of the better players at our home course during tournament weekends—nothing noteworthy other than the fact that I had never been fired. Then in my early adulthood, I took looping to the next level, caddying for my friend Laura Baugh on the LPGA Tour for a few months. That was when I realized that I could never make a legitimate living as a glorified porter. Not only did I fail to suffer gladly the petty foolishness of Laura's fellow competitors (one witless tour veteran actually complained about me standing 30 yards behind her because she thought I might be staring at her ample rump), I found the lives of LPGA Tour caddies borderline pathetic. One of my fellow bag-toters regaled us one morning with his boundless knowledge of illegal horticultural practices, only to admit, five minutes later, that he thought Al Gore was that guy who shot 59 in Memphis a few years back. Laura understood when I retired early.

Who would have guessed that my next stint carrying a golf bag would be in a junior tournament for seven- and eight-year-olds? The bag was a little small, and pulling the right club is more of a struggle when the player is wholly dependent on you making the right call. But other than that, the job of caddying remained unchanged. I was there to do whatever I could to help my player perform, a task I wasted no time screwing up.

In only our second event of the season (note the royal use of "our," typical of caddies and college football fans, none of whom actually participate in the contests they are describing), I realized that with one hole to play, "we" were tied with another little girl in our group. The final hole was a 100-yard par 3 with water on the right. As I pulled the headcover off my daughter's 3-wood, I casually said, "You need to make par here to win."

As the last syllable traveled from my lips to her ears, I reached out and tried to snatch the whole thing back. Such nincompoopery would have gotten me fired from all previous caddying jobs, even those where I was the only looper in the pen without a possession-of-a-controlled-substance arrest. How I could have thrown my darling baby under the bus like that was beyond me.

I tried to keep my expression calm and my voice upbeat as I said, "OK, honey, just relax and make a good swing," but I wanted to drown myself in the water hazard on the right.

Thankfully, Liza hit the ball in the center of the green and two-putted for par. "Did I win?" she asked after holing out.

"Yes, honey," I said. "In spite of your father's stupidity, you won."

The rest of the summer was a joy unlike anything I could have imagined. We won a few, lost a few, laughed and cried. I got to relive all the emotions I had gone through as a young golfer, only this time I did so with the tender smile of a man who was seeing the game with new eyes. Liza might become a fine player, or she might never win another event; at eight years old it's impossible to tell. But the most important thing is that she loves golf.

For years my wife has teased me that even though I have five biological sons (in another age, I would be king), I had to travel halfway around the world to get a child just like me. I don't know if that's true, but I do know that I have a daughter who loves me. And I have a golf partner for the rest of my life.

What man could want for anything more?

~Steve Eubanks

The Golf Book

Recovery Shots

Resolve never to quit, never to give up, no matter what the situation.

~Jack Nicklaus

52

Chicken Soup for the Soul

Quitting

Golf is full of reward but seemingly incapable of forgiveness, which makes it an ideal endeavor for those whose lives need a bit of reshaping. When I quit drinking in 1990, I had no idea golf would become my personal salvation. A chopper who had taken up the game six months earlier probably has no business leaning on it so heavily. Maybe the calling was subliminal. Eighteen years later, I still haven't devoted much mental energy to wondering why.

As a sportswriter with too much idle time, no wife or kids and not a lot of money, I found my roots in the rubber mats at the driving range. There came evenings when I was striping 2-irons like a real player, those cruddy balls soaring wonderfully into the night, but without a mentor—someone to show me how to play and play with me—I might not have stuck with the game.

So if I never see Michael Keating again, I am indebted to him beyond my last breath. A former sports editor at the *Washington Times*, Keating was shot in the head execution-style during a robbery in 1986. He hired me two months later, an occasion made memorable by his showing up for my interview in a jacket and tie instead of a wheelchair.

The guy was bulletproof. Keating returned to the golf course within six weeks after the incident, and if that bullet hadn't crashed into his skull in December, the end of the golf season in the mid-Atlantic, he might have come back sooner. Acknowledging Keating's toughness made my nine-beer nights easier to avoid. His intelligence and patience had me breaking 90 less than a year into my sobriety.

On what seemed like hundreds of mornings, we had the 7:03 A.M. tee time at Lake Arbor Golf Club, a semi-private mousetrap that runs through a nice neighborhood of a Maryland suburb. A 3-handicap who couldn't make a four-footer unless his life depended on it, Keating taught me the swing, the rules, strategy and etiquette. When I overslept one morning and missed our scheduled appointment, he made it very clear that if I stood him up again, the previous round we'd played together would be our last.

I'm sure he has gone through a few dozen belly putters by now, but the guy could sure hit a golf ball. Keating's old school, one-piece takeaway served as my swing template, and by the time I left town in 1995, I could consistently shape an iron shot and score in the mid 70s. For all the ten-second parcels of advice he gave me, there was never a formal lesson. You can talk and demonstrate all you want, but five minutes of instruction won't get you anywhere. Five hours of practice will.

When Keating thought I was ready for it, he took me to southern Virginia to play in my first tournament. I remember holing a few putts and realizing that competitive golf is a different game than the one we'd been playing at Lake Arbor. There have been a lot of good days since, certainly plenty of lousy ones, but not drinking hasn't been a problem for me. My wife keeps beer in the refrigerator. My friends have a glass of wine or three at dinner. The demons of temptation haven't come knocking.

I look at my drinking days as a phase of my life that has come and gone. The only Alcoholics Anonymous meetings I've ever attended were by a court order twenty years ago. But I know the AA route has worked for a lot of people, so I don't knock any method. When a struggling drinker asks for advice, I keep it short and simple. You won't quit until your heart tells you to, and if you do, quitting isn't going to solve the rest of your problems.

Quitting will, however, make them easier to deal with, although a snap hook or a chunked bunker shot are sure to test your resolve.

In September of 1995, I took a job with *Golf World* magazine, which meant moving out of the Baltimore-Washington area for the first time. Five years of clean living made the transition to Connecticut easier, but after covering mainstream sports my entire career, the game that had saved my life was quickly becoming my life, which isn't to say a man can't suffer worse fates.

I eagled marriage, joined a club, got a little better each year. By then Keating had launched his own magazine, *Washington Golf Monthly*, and we hooked up six or seven times between New York and D.C. for a series of best-ball matches with our editors. The north duo lost just once. My editor-in-chief, Geoff Russell, and I collected several hundred dollars in wagers. This is funny, because I do remember Keating telling me years earlier that he'd give me $100 if I ever beat him straight up.

Maybe the check's in the mail, or maybe I'll see him again someday, although it's fair to say Michael Keating is the reason this game has given me more than I ever could have imagined. The guy was bulletproof. I have a strong sense of gratitude. We'll call it even.

~John Hawkins

53

Get Legs

Last Friday morning I pulled into my home track, Skyland Golf Course in Hinckley, Ohio, and my heart sank. The parking lot was jammed. After passing several identical window decals and a quick word with the cart boy, I ascertained the Cuyahoga County Firefighters Association Golf League was playing.

I went into the clubhouse to talk to Tim Rhodes (who is the second generation owner along with his brother Rich) about my chances, however slim, of getting out to play.

From the pro shop to the 10th tee is only about 50 yards. We could see a threesome on the tee and Tim suggested I join them. "You'll love these guys," Tim said. So I grabbed my sticks, walked over and introduced myself.

Their names were easy to remember: Steve, Steve and Steve. One was a fireman and his dad was a retired fireman. The third Steve was a retired fireman with no legs. He'd lost them at mid-thigh in a terrible accident. He had stopped to help a woman change a tire, and had parked his car on the side of the road behind hers. He was between the cars when another car slammed into his.

Instead of prosthetic legs, Steve did without. He simply walked on what was left—two stumps. To ride in the cart, he would back up to the cart floor and then jump backwards. He would ride on the floor of the cart. When they got to his ball one of the other Steves would hand him a club.

Steve played pretty well, despite what was likely the flattest swing plane in golf. The shot I remember best was a 5-wood from the fairway. As the ball landed and started bouncing down the fairway towards the green, he yelled, "Get legs!"

I have no doubt he said that to make me feel comfortable. It did.

Later I was talking with Phyllis, the barmaid, and told her the story. She said, "Oh sure, Steve. The guy is wonderful. Sometimes I'll see him in the parking lot and I'll yell, 'How's it going, Steve?' and he'll yell back, 'Can't kick.'"

~John Tidyman

54

A Walk in the Woods

A passion, an obsession, a romance,
a nice acquaintanceship with trees, sand, and water.
~Bob Ryan

I was in Florida, on vacation, playing golf with my eighty-something-year-old mother and two of her peers. On the 12th tee-box of a lousy round, having just swung as hard as I could, I found myself listening to the oohs and aahs of these octogenarians as they watched how far my ball traveled, and how high. Then I heard these oohs and aahs change to silence as the ball sliced and veered deep into the woods.

The shot went so deep into the woods that I could actually feel my blood pressure rising, rising as least as much as my self-esteem was plummeting. I seriously considered storming off the golf course right then, giving up the game forever. I was just about to slam my driver into the ground to blow off a little steam when my mother said, "Say hello to your father for me."

I turned for an explanation, clearly curious, a rash of frustration spread over my face like hives.

"Your father," she began, "told me just before he passed away, that if I ever needed to talk to him, or spend some time with him, or just be in his presence, I could always find him right here on this golf course traipsing through the woods. He'd be searching for his lost golf ball, he said. And he said it with a smile that made me understand he knew something that I didn't."

My father worked hard all his life, picked up his first golf club when he was about sixty. By that time, his muscle memory had full-fledged amnesia, so even though once in a while he'd manage to hit a good shot, he could never do it twice in a row. He was a hack.

"Your father never got frustrated," my mother continued. "Never made excuses for his bad shots, and he never stopped smiling. Even if he took a swing and missed the ball completely he still had a smile on his face. When you go into the woods and see all the dings in the tree bark that have been made over the years by errant golf balls, you can be sure that at least some of them were made by your father.

"And your father truly looked forward to each walk in the woods." She looked straight at me. "So go find your ball, and say hello to him for me."

With a lighter feeling in my head and my chest, I set off to find my ball. Entering the woods, I did sense my father's presence. At first I was aware of how quiet the woods were, but soon I became aware of how the woods had sounds all its own.

As my mind wandered I was paying little attention to the task of trying to find my ball. Yet, after walking far into the woods, I looked down to the ground and there was my ball within inches of my feet, resting in the center of a small clear patch of grass.

"Thanks, Dad," I said quietly.

Not only was the ball perfectly placed for a clear swing, there was also a window between the trees up ahead that gave an open shot to the green.

I sized the yardage and picked a club, stood behind the ball and pointed the shaft at my target. I went through my pre-swing check-list: yes, I was lined up properly; yes, my hands were lightly gripping the club; yes, I was taking deep, relaxing breaths.

I swung, somehow knowing that nothing further was going to go wrong on this day. Not on this golf course under my father's presence. The shot was going to be perfect.

The ball came off hot to the right and smacked a tree in the middle of its trunk. It ricocheted off a number of other trees and ended up fifty years deeper into the woods than where I was standing.

This time, as I started off to find the ball, I had a smile on my face. After all, it gave me more time to spend with my dad.

~Neil Rosen

"The easiest way to hook a ball is to try to slice it!"

Reprinted by permission of Bob Zahn ©2005

55

Chicken Soup for the *Soul*

Arnold Palmer's Greatest Rescue

Cancer is a word, not a sentence.
~John Diamond

With notebook in hand and media badge on my jacket, I walked toward the podium to interview the King. The reporter who I was shadowing was determined to get me right up front. My stomach fluttered; this was the closest a junior in high school could get to being a real journalist. As I reached out my hand to introduce myself I heard a loud voice from behind me say, "This is Caroline Stetler. She had cancer too."

Shock and fear delivered a sucker punch robbing me of air. My big moment to interview Arnold Palmer and I could not utter a word for fear my voice would crack and tears would well. The reporter who was mentoring me meant well, but in an instant she told the world—my world of Southwest Florida—my biggest secret, my biggest hurt.

Mr. Palmer sensed my absolute helplessness. He took my hand in both of his. We were standing about two feet apart and he looked me right in the eyes and said, "We've got to get better about talking about cancer and not being afraid to say the 'C' word." He went on to talk about how important early detection is and how people could live a long life even after getting a cancer diagnosis. As he spoke, I could feel strength emanate from his big, grip-calloused hands and I began to regain mine. He was eloquent. He was the King.

At that time, Palmer was returning to the Senior PGA Tour after undergoing surgery for prostate cancer in 1997. A few months before he was diagnosed, I had been diagnosed with thyroid cancer. At the time I didn't even know what my thyroid was or how it functioned, but I quickly learned that papillary thyroid cancer is highly treatable. After doctors remove the thyroid, patients undergo a radioactive iodine treatment and then simply take a daily supplement for life to replace the hormones that the thyroid would have produced. My survival rate was ninety-nine percent, so I was more concerned about my next golf tournament than the cancer.

When I met Mr. Palmer, I was playing the best golf of my life and was even entertaining aspirations to become a professional golfer (it was fun to dream). But my other passion was reporting for my high school newspaper. The golf columnist for a local magazine knew of my interest in journalism and had asked if I wanted to shadow her at the LG Championship, a Senior PGA Tour event held in my hometown of Naples, Florida. I was ecstatic because the opportunity to have media access to the pros was as good as it could get, the best of both worlds.

I interviewed a lot of players that week and tried to absorb their greatness. Dave Stockton talked to me about where I was thinking of going to college and told me one of his daughters had attended Wake Forest. I had of course heard of the university before—after all it was where the King went. When Stockton asked about my grades, I told him they were pretty good. "Your grades have to be better than pretty good to go to Wake," he said. I smiled, knowing I had a better shot of earning an academic, rather than a golf, scholarship there.

At the end of the week, I worked with my mentor to write my first published story. I wrote about my experience interviewing the pros, learning about print and broadcast media, and sitting in on a live ESPN golf broadcast. I quickly became acquainted with the term "hard edit," but I loved the learning experience. When the *N Magazine* issue (N as in Naples) with my story came out, I was happy with the final product.

As luck would have it, I would meet Mr. Palmer three years later at an event honoring former Wake Forest golfers. This time I was introduced to him not as a journalist but as a member of the Wake Forest women's golf team. I didn't mention meeting him before in Florida, and I prayed he didn't remember. I was just thrilled we now had something besides cancer in common.

After graduating from college, I joined the professional ranks—as a journalist. I still get the same rush of excitement from interviews as I did in high school and love laboring over my keyboard even more. Yet twelve years since my diagnosis, I still struggle to say the "C" word. I went back and forth several times just trying to bring myself to write this. So this one's for the King: Go get checked. Regularly. Cancer is not a death sentence. Smile. Keep those you love close. You can still live the life you dreamed.

~Caroline Stetler

56

Chicken Soup
for the *Soul*

The Six Stages of Golf Grief

Golf is essentially an exercise in masochism conducted out-of-doors.
~Paul O'Neil

All of us would be most fortunate if we could go through life without ever having to experience the five stages of grief. But grief touches us all eventually. And most of us will find a way to get through it and move on.

Golf grief is a different matter entirely. I once played with a scratch golfer who, after missing a makeable birdie putt, slammed his putter against his shoe in disgust, his face contorted in anger. He went on to shoot even par for the round, but was still steamed about that missed birdie that would have broken par for the day.

I, on the other hand, would have needed that birdie putt for a smooth 94, instead of the 97 I wound up shooting, finishing the day steamed that my putt for double-bogey on that same hole had lipped the cup. Golf anger is fungible; it can be expressed the same way by a golfer who fails to break par as for one who fails to break 100. But anger is only one of the six stages of golf grief. Yes, in golf, grief is extended by one additional stage, the one that eventually gives golf grief its eternal quality.

The denial stage begins on the first tee, and generally follows what you just confided to your playing partners is the best warm-up on the range you've ever experienced. Then you step up and send one dead right and short over the OB stakes. "That can't be me!" you scream in protest.

But the anger stage soon follows as hole after hole fails to generate anything near the effortless and flowing swings from the range. In your tempestuous, club-slamming wake you leave fairways mottled with divots that resemble a strip mining operation.

The start of the back nine is where the bargaining stage of golf grief commences. You tell yourself it's a whole new nine, and that you can still salvage a sub-90 round (overlooking the naked fact that you'll have to break 40 in order to do so). Your buddies may confuse your bargaining stage simply as denial all over again, since there has been nothing in your game so far to suggest that the back nine won't actually be worse than the front.

And so the depression stage inevitably appears around the 15th hole, when your mental calculations indicate you'll need to go birdie-birdie-eagle just to finish on the number at 90. "Guys, I hate to say this, but this is the last round of golf I'm ever going to play. I just can't take this anymore." Of course, your buddies, who have kept a running diary of such pronouncements, take this statement in stride, believing it to be just another form of denial on your part.

Suddenly, however, you step up to the 18th tee, and for the first time that day, stripe a drive that splits the center in a gentle draw, reminiscent of what you had produced back on the range. Your approach shot flies high and on target, landing on the green ten feet from the cup. You firmly drain for a birdie, resulting in that smooth 94 you would have settled for just a couple of rounds ago. Acceptance, this fifth stage of golf grief, now flows like honey through your veins, as your buddies tell each other, "Well, that'll bring the moron back again," and you realize at last that improvement will be episodic rather than progressive. "Maybe I will play tomorrow after all," you announce, confirming what your buddies had already (and reluctantly) deduced.

And it is that that brings you to the doorstep of golf grief's sixth and final stage: repetition. It is the stage that proves that golf grief is something we continually aspire to, rather than try to avoid. From the guy who can't stand life itself because he failed to break par, to the guy who can't stand life itself because he failed to break 100, golf freely provides the grief that keeps on giving for those who just can't ever seem to get enough of it.

This is why the question "How much golf is too much?" really has no answer, until we can first answer "How much golf grief is too much?" And so we continue to return in Buddhist-like repetition to torture ourselves through the stages of golf grief all over again. But it is those who ultimately learn to embrace that eternal grief who attain golf's Nirvana, the stage at which we learn to play without a scorecard or a handicap, but just to enjoy a pleasant, unspoiled walk in God's great universe.

In other words, the cycle of denial is complete again.

~Reid Champagne

No Carts

Golf is not just a game; it can save someone's life. I know it did mine.

Fifteen years ago, I went through a divorce. I had married my high school sweetheart, but after nineteen years together, it was over. I was devastated.

I moved into a two-room apartment in the center of town. The place was a far cry from the four-bedroom, three-acre ranch in the country where we had been living previously.

All of my friends were married and after a while I realized I couldn't spend every day at their houses. So when I wasn't at work, I found myself sitting on a barstool.

I was in the worst mental and physical shape of my life. I didn't care if I lived or died. And believe me, there were times I wished it was the latter. I was drinking heavily just to fall asleep at night.

My best friend kept trying to get me to go golfing with him. I had played football, basketball, and baseball in school and couldn't see how anyone could call golf a sport. You didn't run or jump and the uniforms were really ugly, especially the ones the older players seemed to fancy.

I had a birthday coming up. My children secretly asked my friend what I wanted. Instead of telling them what I wanted, he told my children what he thought I needed. So on my fortieth birthday, when I opened my card from the kids, out dropped a gift certificate for eighteen holes of golf at our local municipal course, cart not included. My friend and I set up a tee time and met on the day.

I kept saying, "Let's get a cart," as we made our way from the parking lot to the clubhouse, but he kept insisting we walk. I offered to pay for both of us to ride but he wouldn't budge. "But this is my birthday," I said. "What kind of present makes you lug thirty pounds on your back for six miles?" But my friend won out. We walked.

I didn't realize it at the time, but it was the best birthday present gift I could have received given my circumstances.

I hit a couple of shots from 100 to 150 yards that landed within ten feet of where I was aiming. I was hooked. My friend said he hadn't seen such a look on my face in a long time. It was a mixture of surprise, excitement, and joy all rolled into one.

We finished the round and I actually had a couple of bogeys on my scorecard. Before we got back to the clubhouse, we were already making plans for our next outing.

By walking, I was getting all this fresh air in my lungs, and you know, the bag really isn't that heavy when you set it down every 100 yards or more. I found that swinging the club served two purposes. It stretched my back out so I was ready for the next haul. It also helped to beat away the stress and frustrations that life had handed me.

That night I found myself exhausted, but in a different way than the other nights when I had went to bed at closing time. I slept like a baby, dreamt of pars.

Thanks to my friend and my children, I was introduced to the greatest sport ever invented. Yeah, that's right, I said "sport."

I truly feel that the life I was living wouldn't have lasted very long at the rate I was living it. And today I still head to the course instead of the bar.

This weekend, I'm taking my eight-year-old grandson to the course and am looking forward to that look of surprise and excitement and joy on his face when he gets a hold of one. Also the thought of him going to sleep dreaming of pars.

If you know of someone who's going through a rough time, buy them a round of golf without a cart. You might just save their life.

~James Swigert

58

Coming to Grips

I'm not saying my golf game went bad,
but if I grew tomatoes, they'd come up sliced.
~Miller Barber

After fifty years playing this game, my skills have abandoned me. I actually shanked a three-foot putt yesterday. I see chips heading in directions unknown. I find my once trusty driver to be a foreign object in my hands. I can take comfort in no part of my game. I am a stranger masquerading as myself as I wander helplessly for eighteen holes.

I took up golf at six, and from that point on it was a natural fit. I took a few lessons when I was eight or nine, but I don't think it was this professional advice that molded my game. I was an athlete, and the flow of the swing came to me as easily then as walking.

Now, fifty-six, as I look in the mirror, I see little evidence of that young boy. I play with a friend, same age as me, who regularly hits 300-yard drives. I find myself struggling to bunt the ball 200 yards. The distance with my irons is equally pathetic. I often find myself lying to my fellow players when they ask what club I hit, so as not to be embarrassed by my lack of strength. My friends who took up the game late in life are now passing me on the golfing highway.

My sister insists I should be taking lessons. For someone who is inherently lazy, cheap, and has been forever convinced that corrections are ultimately within one's own power to make, I have rejected her advice. For so long, a tweak here and a tweak there have been enough to bring my game back. I was always able to pull out from my memory bank some forgotten secret that aligned me physically and mentally. I could handle whatever little missteps I made, and bring my game back to the level I was comfortable with and enjoy moments of pride in my accomplishments. Now, all I find when I look for these guides is an empty box. Someone has hidden the answers from me. The CliffsNotes have been lost. I am looking into the abyss and am having trouble maintaining my balance.

Is the answer to swallow my pride and admit that after half a century the golfing gods have been wooed away? Must I make that dreaded phone call to a pro asking for help? I still cling to the belief that the light will be turned back on with my next swing. That the high, short, ugly slices and complete mis-hits that now inhabit my game will be replaced with beautiful low draws that travel forever. That I will find birdies and pars to be regular staples of my golfing diet once again.

I think I will give myself one or two more bad rounds before I cry uncle. I will get the names of some teaching pros I can call upon, and carry their phone numbers with me at all times. If and when the weight of my disappointments becomes too much to bear, I will start dialing the phone. Until that moment comes I find myself like an addict who believes that salvation can be attained by the sheer belief that you have the inherent power to achieve it.

As I look in the mirror, I like to think I am still the six-year-old boy who could play. However, until the magic reappears, I would strongly suggest that you stand behind me whenever I swing because I have no idea where the ball is going.

~Robert Scott Nussbaum

59

A Widow by Choice

*I think the press made a grave mistake in calling Arnold, Jack,
and myself the "Big Three." I think the "Big Three" were
Winnie Palmer, Barbara Nicklaus, and Vivienne Player.*
~Gary Player

I never would have imagined that a game could save a man's life. But a bucket of practice balls, a cheap set of clubs and three lessons from a local pro did for my husband what no therapy ever could. Gave him a reason to get out of bed in the morning.

In the early fall of 2008, my husband's entire construction division was dissolved. For years he had worked long, hard hours for this major corporation, but soon enough it came his turn to pack his desk and join the growing line of unemployed people posting their resumés online.

My husband Curt is a workaholic. His job has always been his passion. Many evenings, he wouldn't come home until his dinner had turned cold and I'd already changed into my pajamas. He had no time for hobbies except for the occasional game of catch with our daughter as she grew up. But after he lost his job, his days spread before him like a vast wasteland.

"You need a hobby," I announced one morning at the breakfast table, as he was reading the closing pages of what was probably his tenth book that month. "Besides going to the library."

He raised his eyebrows. "What about getting my pilot's license? I always wanted to finish that."

I shuddered at the thought. "Too easy to crash. I'm not ready to be a widow yet."

He got up from the table and walked over to the living room and plopped in front of the television, flipping the channels. After a few cycles, a swath of green grass and lush waterfalls filled the screen. He put the remote down.

"I would like to learn how to play golf for real," he said. Curt had played a few times with the guys at work but the set we'd found him for $25 at a yard sale when we first moved to Florida left little to inspire.

Within the hour, we drove to the biggest sporting goods store in Orlando and Curt discussed every club option available with the zealous clerk. A week later, he took his first lesson.

My girlfriends had warned me about the addiction to the game of golf. I never believed them at first, but reality is starting to sink in. The other day I tripped over a ladder he'd placed opposite a chair in the garage for working on his swing plane. Every time I tune into the news I have to switch the channel from The Golf Channel. My daughter asked me what her dad wanted for his birthday, and I had to tell her the truth; a subscription to *Golf Digest*.

My husband found a job, but it isn't one that makes him leap out of bed every morning eager to start the day. But he manages to get through the week filled with one hope, the weekend and a round of golf. At least I haven't come home to find our house sold and our bags packed, him ready to move to the nearest golf community. At least not yet.

I'll take being a golf widow over a pilot widow any day.

~Terri Tiffany

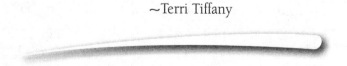

60

Chicken Soup for the *Soul*

The Strongest Memory

The ball, a scuffed Walter Hagen 2, is cemented to a tee, and is mounted to a small polished piece of oak. A brass plaque reads: POLAND SPRING, MAINE, HOLE- IN-ONE, AUGUST 26, 1986. The memento sits on my father's nightstand in his room at the nursing home just outside of Boston.

He really was not much of a golfer, but he enjoyed the game immensely. A sub-100 round at the local city-owned course was a triumph. Never one to spend a lot of money, his clubs were branded "Rivalists."

Then, a most remarkable day. While on vacation with my mother, he decided to play a round of golf on the resort's course. My mother chose to sit by the pool.

Paired up with a partner he had never met before and whom he would never see again, he somehow managed to hit his tee shot 148 yards, over a pond and into the cup at the 6th hole of Poland Spring Golf Course. Truth be told, neither of them saw it go in, and they looked around the green for several minutes before looking in the hole.

It would give him pleasure for years to come, and at family gatherings he would seldom fail to remind any of his six children about the accomplishment. Since I was the only son who took up the game, he would also occasionally ask whether I had ever shot a hole-in-one.

My father is ninety-two now and suffers from advanced dementia. Visits to him at his nursing home over the past year have been difficult as each week seems to bring further deterioration. While he remains physically able, his short-term memory has declined markedly over the past few months and the foggy days outnumber the clear ones. He struggles to communicate, often choosing the wrong word or manufacturing words altogether.

We are grateful, though, for the wonderful care that he receives, and comforted by the fact that he is seldom angry or unhappy. We are resigned to the fact that he will never fully regain his memory.

His caregivers suggest that when talking to him you mention people, places, and things from his past, as a way to jog his memory. I try to get him to recall my mother, who passed away ten years ago, or his ailing sister, or his grandchildren, often with little or no success. The family photo album on his dresser brings little response. And, yet, there is that golf ball and plaque. Even on the darkest of days, if I pick up that plaque, and show it to him, and ask whether it was he who shot the hole-in-one, he will light up once more. The twinkle in his eyes returns and he grins. And if I ask how he was able to do that, he may even swing an imaginary club, his smile broadening. With even more prompting, he can even recall that he had a witness, lest there be any doubt about the veracity of the event.

It was for him, I think, his life's greatest achievement. And nothing else comes even close to bringing him back to an earlier, happier, time. Nothing.

~Timothy J. Larkin

The Golf Book

Swing Thoughts

Serenity is knowing that your worst shot is still pretty good.

~Johnny Miller

Trusting Instincts

Instinct is the nose of the mind.
~Madame De Girardin

As methodical as golfers try to be; pacing yardages with their noses buried in course notebooks, calculating pin sheets and carry distances, throwing bits of grass in the air to gauge the wind, and as is the case with modern players, using launch monitors and computers to tune their equipment to meet their exact specifications, what really separates winners from losers is instinct. When you've got to decide whether to attempt a certain shot or not, all you can go on is your instinct. More often than not it's the feeling in your gut, not the sparks between your ears, that will tell you how a ball is going to come out of an odd lie. When's the right moment to go for the pin and when you should play to the heart of the green.

Trusting my instinctual nature was the one of the most important common sense lessons my father ever taught me, and he taught me many.

One day, when I was a young boy, I asked my father who the best friend he ever had was. Without hesitating, he answered, "A rat."

I was flabbergasted. "A rat?" I said. "What do you mean your best friend ever was a rat?"

My father worked in the gold mines of South Africa. He made very little money, a couple of hundred dollars a month. The tunnels were built as far in as 12,000 feet. Whenever a tunnel was about to cave in, which they did far too often, the rats, on pure instinct, would come scurrying out like mad. All the miners of course would then take the cue and get the heck out as well. Because they relied on the rats' instincts to save their lives, my father told of how he and his fellow mineworkers always gave pieces of their sandwiches to the rats at lunchtime.

Years later in my adult life, I took Arnold Palmer and Mark McCormack and their families down some mines for a tour. (For those who don't know, McCormack started IMG and was the promoter most responsible for bringing golf where it is today.) They all couldn't believe how far down it went.

"Trust instinct to the end even though it render no reason," my father used to say. I've heeded this advice my entire life, not only to know which kind of shot to hit in a golf tournament, but also when to walk away from certain people in business.

I'm not a jewelry person, but to this day whenever I look at my Rolex wristwatch I think of my father. I truly know what it took to get that gold.

~Gary Player
as seen in the DVD *Chicken Soup Conversations for the Golfer's Soul*

62

The Charms and Challenges of Links Golf

Playing links golf is a great pleasure to me, the most fun I have in the game. I enjoy the feel of the golf, the feel of the courses, the history of the game in Great Britain. The people there understand the history, even if they don't play.

The history has been a big part of my life since I was a youngster. My dad talked about it to me, and I read books about it. The crowds are usually more knowledgeable than our crowds in the United States. Golf is more the fabric of their lives. It's the national pastime.

Plus the public can play many of the finest courses, like the Old Course at St. Andrews. They've experienced the situations you sometimes face in a championship there, and identify with you. You feel very welcome. It's going back to the cradle of the game. People consider it hallowed ground.

If I hadn't been playing the British Open all these years, I would have been going over to Scotland and England anyway just to play the great links courses. I've made it a custom to leave a week early for the Open to play different courses with friends. I may continue to travel to the United Kingdom after my Open eligibility runs out at St. Andrews in 2010.

At first I didn't particularly like the type of golf you have to play over there. I preferred target golf to the luck of the bounce. On our tour you pick a club that will fly the ball a certain distance over hazards, and it stops. Over there the game is played more on the ground than through the air. I didn't like blind shots where you had to aim at a church steeple off in the distance.

And I didn't like the condition of the courses. The ground is very firm. The greens are large but very flat. You have to run the ball rather than just pick a club for the yardage as you would on a soft course.

But by 1980 I was learning to appreciate the subtleties (and lack of them) of British golf. Bob Jones went through the same sort of adjustment before he accepted that golf is not meant to be a fair game. Now I consider links golf the supreme golf experience.

At a bumpy Open course like Royal St. George's, you can get some severe bounces, and what you thought was a good shot down the fairway might kick into a deep bunker. You have to be able to handle that kind of disappointment—expect bad breaks and figure they will even out over time.

You anticipate and play the bounces, try to land the ball in flat areas as much as possible. It takes me back to my boyhood, when I wasn't big and strong enough to carry the ball onto the green. You had to think about how the ground affected your shot. In links golf you go back to that style of play. There are openings into the greens so you can roll the ball up. The greens are much slower but the ground is a lot harder. You have to bump and run the ball more, and that perplexes Americans used to the ball stopping much quicker.

Links golf requires more creativity, more imagination. It presents more options, which can be confusing. You have to choose the proper shot and then commit fully to it. For too long, I was trying to force the ball into the air and stop it near the hole, and finally I told myself it wasn't working. That's the learning curve you go through to understand links golf.

The weather can confuse newcomers. The joke is that you can sometimes get all four seasons during a round of links golf. The wind also can be a major factor.

Bump-and-run golf can be the better way to go in bad weather, especially for weekend golfers. Too many modern courses in the U.S. are not designed with wind in mind. When it blows, they become virtually unplayable. I try to keep this in mind with my course design work.

Growing up in Kansas City, I practiced in all kinds of weather year-round. Just like the Scots, Kansans are crazy about their golf. It was nothing to tee it up when it was 30 degrees and windy. I didn't mind. And I've never minded seeing the weather turn bad at tournaments, because I figure it eliminates much of the field that won't like it.

It's the ultimate test, and I love it.

~Tom Watson as told to Nick Seitz

63

The Space in Front

Golf is not a good walk spoiled. It is becoming a good walk prohibited.
~Lorne Rubenstein, on compulsory carts

The pleasures of golf are muscular. Laying into your driver, throwing a shot as high as possible in an attempt to both clear a brook and stick the green beyond it, plucking a long iron clean on the second shot of a par 5. You feel these things in your bones.

And the more you feel them, the deeper you sense the physicality of the game. It's hard to convince a non-golfer of this deep physical thread. They scoff; to them golf is played at an amble. It looks lazy, self-indulgent, slow. They don't understand that it is a game of distance, of space negotiated. I suppose it's a cliché to say that a round of golf is a journey in itself, but there is little question in my mind that the physical nature of the game, its aspect as a test of the body, is reflected in that journey, in the very distance one undertakes by setting out on a round. That distance must be experienced, not ignored. The only way to do that, to truly understand the test of golf, the challenge of it, the surprises it offers, is to face up and feel things in your bones. You must walk.

I stand in the middle of the 16th fairway, 147 yards from the pin. To get to this spot I have walked the better part of three miles, crossed three different creeks (one of them four times), traversed a cranberry bog, climbed a small escarpment and trailed along two manmade berms, each a quarter mile long. I've trod gravel, asphalt and turf and walked ruts cut into the mud by a pickup truck. I've climbed steps, railroad ties, followed a twisting path into the mid-day darkness of the woods, emerging on the other side, surrounded by prairie grass. There was a fox following me down the 2nd hole, and two deer crossing on the 4th. I moved by them, and through them, each of us noting one another with a look. I have walked all this way, through all that, to stand here.

There is no sound. No crackle of tires on gravel. No rattle of clubs on the backside of a golf cart. My clubs are right here on my shoulder. I'm a spot-on 8-iron from the hole. Because I have scrambled along the mantle of the earth to get here, I have earned this very spot on the course, this moment within the round. Nothing took me here. I carried myself.

Now I take a deep breath and go still.

I'm meeting my girlfriend for dinner in an hour at a Mexican place about three miles from here. That isn't all that far. If I left now, I could walk it. But, that is not my way. Besides, there isn't even a sidewalk that would lead me there. Three miles, most of it on the shoulder of a state highway—the truth is, no one in their right mind would walk it.

Walking is not the American way. Except in a handful of major cities, no one walks anymore. Not really. Not to work, not to buy cigarettes, not to the supermarket. That's because even on the local scale, the world we have created is far flung. The best sandwich shop clings to one edge of town, while our eyeglass repair place, or the dry cleaner we favor, sits on the other edge. So, we drive. It's quicker, easier and allows us to do more. It appears to give us choice. It is our way. I accept that. I participate in it.

But three miles isn't that far. The landscape of our culture forces us to forget that. That's barely fifteen holes on a decent municipal course. In the world outside the game, we short circuit distance routinely. I drove eight miles yesterday to see a movie. And then six more to price out a table saw. None of this seemed very out of the ordinary. We compress the world. Is it any wonder then that the golf cart seems to be a natural part of the universe at the start of a round?

Golf is a game where the lesser habits of the culture sometimes creep in. These days, there is a lot of riding in golf. That's to be expected. At some level, I think, why not? The benefits to riding on the course are similar to riding off it; it's faster and easier to use a cart, to be sure. You can't argue with a quick round, and with so many new courses designed with huge gaps between green and tee, you can't get a quick round unless you ride.

But think about it. Golf was created by shepherds at a time when the only way to ride involved loud clattering wagons and horses. Golf was created as a means of feeling distance, not outwitting it.

Golf shoes, unlike any other sport, rather than making it easier to move quickly, make it easier to stand still.

It's a game where every ounce of technology is devoted to giving you more distance. The first time you really hit a golf ball, it is a remarkable thing, as if the laws of the universe bent a little in that moment. It's like hitting a super-ball with a tennis racquet. But you don't stand there and enjoy it. Unlike other sports in this way, you don't return to the bench, or wait for the judges' score, or head to the dugout. When the shot is over you follow. You set out after the ball. You take responsibility for the distance. You don't jump to the next action, you set out after it. Slowly, and with purpose.

Let's face it: walking is slow. You can play briskly, sure, but you still lose time to the game when you walk. And it hurts. At the end of eighteen holes walked, your body reports. Your feet hurt, or your knees, or your hips. Some feel it less, and set back out straight away. Others sit in the clubhouse nursing a beer, licking their wounds. You feel the game, even after it is over. But a day more felt is a day better lived.

There are golf courses that do not allow walking. They have been stretched over too much acreage, wound through too much residential development, or the management wants more greens fees and must pack the course hole by hole with golfers speeding along on carts. To my mind these courses are no less beautiful than ones that allow walking, or encourage it. But the difference is profound. A course that doesn't allow walking is like an animal in a zoo, exotic, well-cared for, held captive against its own nature. The walking course is the animal in its element, full, unpredictable, a bit more elusive and rare.

A golf course wanders the landscape, cutting back on itself, turning suddenly into the sun or up the hills. At the outset, the golfer is handed a map, and yes, there is a perceivable route. But each journey is different, defined by the course of a few small mistakes and, likely, fewer miracles. The game then is a sort of sea. The golfer, a navigator. His tools for measuring distance are ancient. The wind. A row of trees. Perhaps the distant shore of a reservoir. Forget technology. Forget GPS loaded golf carts. Leave the rangefinder out of this for the moment.

The elemental challenge of the game is you against the space in front. Your best tools against this space are your wits and your sensibility. The best way to understand the space in the next shot, the next hole, is to do what golfers have done from the beginning of the game: start walking.

Stand with me a moment over my 8-iron, 147 yards out. I can feel the wind, judge its effect in the movement of the branches. I can see the green baking in sunlight. And I know the distance in my very gut. Like all golfers, I can stand over this shot and see what is ahead. But I have walked all this way, and that is what gives me the momentum of the game, the day, the afternoon and the moment.

I feel all that in the soles of my feet.

~Tom Chiarella

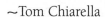

"LATELY, I HAVEN'T BEEN FEELING QUITE UP TO PAR."

64

Golf and Music

A few years ago I played in the Arnie's Army Battles Prostate Cancer tournament at Wilshire Country Club in Los Angeles. I had no idea Palmer liked or even knew of my music, but apparently he did, otherwise I wouldn't have been invited.

I was thrilled. Having been born and raised in Augusta, Georgia, where most babies are given cut-down 7-irons the moment they come out of the womb, I've always been a keen golfer and an even keener Arnold Palmer fan. As much as he's a legend across the world, he's even more so in our town. Like so many of my friends growing up, The King was my idol. And now I was getting to meet him.

How it worked was each group got to play one hole with Palmer. I wasn't exactly on top of my game like I'd once been (my freshman year at Ole Miss University I attended on a golf scholarship) but I was still swinging decently. Nevertheless, Palmer, who was in his mid-seventies, drove it past me off the tee.

I had a pretty thick beard going at the time, though I remember being dressed more appropriately than a few of the other musicians playing in the event (at least in my opinion). Still, my appearance made the wrong impression on a traditionalist like Palmer. As we approached my ball in the fairway, Palmer turned and said to me, "Young man, you'll hit it a lot farther if you shave that beard off." And there was no joking to his tone. He seriously wanted me to get rid of it. If you look at all the thousands of photos taken of Palmer over the years, I don't think you'll ever see a single facial hair on him.

So meeting my idol didn't go exactly as I hoped, but at least it happened. As a junior I was a pretty serious golfer, so it's somewhat ironic that it's been music, not playing ability, that's gained me entry into the circles I used to dream about. Just the other day I was flying on a private jet from Burbank to Las Vegas, and who should be sitting across from me but '92 Masters winner Freddie Couples. I told him what a huge fan I was, and that I had actually shagged balls for him at the '97 and '98 Masters. (The local aspiring juniors used to get awarded inside-the-ropes jobs at The Masters; I drove the ballpicker.) Freddie laughed at this, said he was a fan of my stuff, too.

Watching the world's greatest players come through our town every April never turned me into a professional golfer, but I still think it cultivated my career. Golf and music share a great affinity as both are fundamentally about timing and tempo. I used to study players on the range at Augusta National, trying to absorb their tempo, grace and discipline. I wanted these qualities to bleed not only into my golf swing, but also into my guitar and drum skills. The rest of the year, growing up with my brothers, we used to play golf until dinner and then music until bed, each skill feeding off the other.

But as much as the skills are similar, the styles can be worlds apart. Though I acquiesced to my hero. After the round with Palmer, I took the razor to my face as soon as I got back to the hotel room. And I haven't worn a beard since. At least never anything more than some stubble.

~Josh Kelley

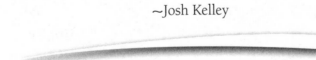

65

Confessions of a Snap Hooker

H i. My name is Mark, and I'm a snap hooker.

I don't really know how I got to this point: all that matters to me now is successfully completing my 12-step program, attending meetings every day and picking up the pieces of my broken golf game. Right now, I'm just taking life one hole at a time and hoping to one day find a foursome that will accept me as I am—a recovering snap hooker.

I was at the top of my game. Twice Long Drive Champion at the annual Labor Day golf tournament in Ruidoso, New Mexico, along with three other top-five finishes; I was the most sought after "D" player in scramble tournaments within a fifty-mile radius. My nickname in those glory years was "Long Drive Man." Shouts of "Sandbagger" could be heard whenever I walked up to retrieve prize money. I swept in Ruidoso in 2000 and walked away with the coveted championship silver buckle.

In retrospect, I didn't handle success well. Subconsciously I was flirting with the golf demons, living too close to the edge and trying too hard to hold on to that rush of adrenalin that comes from being on top with a 26-handicap.

In the beginning it was innocent enough—out with my friends for a quick round, just looking to release a little steam, forget my worries and continue the celebration. Like most stories such as mine,

I started out just hooking a few. You know, coming out of my shoes once or twice a round just for jollies. But soon that wasn't doing it for me. More and more often I found the need to tee it a little higher and swing a little harder.

Early on I thought I could control it, that I could go back any time to the way my swing was before. How stupid I was! You don't control a snap hook—it controls you! I know that now, but back then I was so sure I could be longer I just didn't see the warning signs. I was so seduced by that feeling of nirvana when I hit a really long drawing drive that I didn't see all the damage it was doing to me. I didn't realize that my divots were getting deeper and deeper. Looking back, I guess I just couldn't face the reality of all the bad snap hooks I hit, so I just blocked them from my mind.

A few tried to warn me. "It don't matter!" yelled my old caddie at Pinehurst when I asked which club I should hit. This caddie eventually dropped my bag and stalked off into the woods to underscore his point. "You use a pillow to smother that one?" became a common refrain.

But there was just nothing like it. Standing there at address, staring at my knuckles as they turned white from my fearsome grip, seeing every muscle in my forearms rippling with tension, feeling my body tighten up like a statue as I prepared to channel all this pure energy into my swing. And oh the swing! Like a lighting bolt, the flash of speed both back and forward can only be described as sexual. In those seconds of address I thought I was Tiger.

Never mind the ultimate fate of the ball—whether just off the box, in the woods, the water, the rough, it made no difference—it was the rush I was after. I was totally blind to the damage I was doing; there was no turning back, I was addicted.

My buddies wanted to help, but what could they say? I don't blame them for my situation. Some people asked them, "Why did you wait until he completely lost it?" No, looking back, I don't blame them. They would turn away on the tee-box, clean their golf balls, do anything but watch. No man can stand to see another throw his swing away as cavalierly as I was doing.

Soon, just snap hooking off the tee wasn't enough. I lost all control, and all self-respect. I needed more and more bad shots to satisfy myself. I began to feed my habit other places on the course—fairways, rough, around the green, the traps. I changed grips, stances, weight shifts and takeaways in order to feed my habit.

Snap hook addicts ruin their games as well as the games of those around them. It takes a lot of time to snap hook as much as I was. Four hour rounds became four and a half hours, then five. I had to have more and more hits to satisfy my habit. Never mind my score; it didn't matter any more. It was the rush I was after—not par.

Then there came a turning point. I hit bottom. My friends finally stopped helping me search down the left side. They allowed me to play my game, but at their pace. That was fine with me. A fast snap hook, and another and another, faster and faster until my body just couldn't keep up after the years of abuse. I was so out of control I began cutting my fingers with broken tees. I broke down. I didn't have the strength to snap or smother another shot. Emotionally spent, wasted and bleeding, I was done.

The next night in Fort Worth I found myself in the backyard in nothing but my boxers, golf shoes and my championship belt, ferociously hacking at the grass and snapping golf balls left of my practice net and into the pool. I heard a noise and turned to find my three-year-old son watching me. "Let me hit balls in the pool!" he said. And finally reality hit home like a 1-iron—is this the legacy I want to leave my son? It had to stop now.

I have sought help. Professional help. It's going to take time. Years of urges and habits can't simply be changed overnight. The demons are still lurking whenever I see a driver or long iron.

In the mean time, golf goes on. I have to try to put my shattered game back on the course, one round at a time. I have to try and rebuild the relationships that I have allowed my habit to destroy.

I will have to learn to simply "pick up."

My name is Mark, and I am a recovering snap hooker.

~Mark Fowlkes

Me and My No Problem Putter

Selecting a putter is like selecting a wife. To each his own.
~Ben Hogan

Several years ago I was at a driving range and met the owner who had given lessons there for many years. The older man idled over and watched me as I laced a few iron shots. After I'd worked down through a few irons, he said, "You about a 2- or 3-handicap?"

"No," I replied, "more like an 8."

"That's strange. I can usually tell pretty well what a guy shoots from watching him hit balls."

"You've never seen me putt," I replied.

I've never considered myself a bad putter, nor a particularly good one either. To me the real joy of golf lies in hitting the ball solidly, making the right tactical decisions, and trying to suffer gracefully the slings and arrows the game throws at you. Putting never appealed to me as much as the full swing, or even the other fine points like chipping and sand shots. Putting was always a side issue, and something that players of lesser skill needed to get in the barn in a somewhat respectable number of strokes.

I like the quote attributed to Ben Hogan in which he expressed that putting is totally unrelated to the rest of the game of golf. He proposed that matches be played where whoever is closer to the flag in the regulation number of strokes wins the hole. I suspect Mr. Hogan spoke those words after a particularly frustrating round in which he struck the ball solidly—as he always did—but couldn't get a putt to fall. Most of us can relate to that, at least the putting part.

Last year a friend gave me a putter to fill out an extra set of clubs I keep around the garage for visiting friends. He said absolutely not to return it, as it was one of many he had inherited from his father-in-law who had recently passed away. The deceased gentleman must have had his putting difficulties too, judging by the number and variety of putters with which my friend was now burdened.

The putter he gave me was called the "No Problem" putter and it had the letters "NP" stamped on the sole. Eventually, one day I took a serious look at it.

I took my stance over the concrete of the garage floor. It had two conspicuous parallel lines on the flange that set up squarely right behind the ball. Unhappy as always with my putting, I decided to trot the NP out to the practice green at my course. Something about those two aiming lines behind the ball seemed to make the putter align itself. I felt like I couldn't hit a putt off line.

I put an extension on the shaft and re-gripped it and took it out to the course. Oh my God, did I start making putts. Lots of them. I didn't pull or push the short ones and was canning 20-footers more often than not.

Since I was a boy I could always hit the ball on or around the greens in regulation and usually made a couple of birdies each round and hoped for an eagle or two each year. During the two-month stretch after I started playing with the NP I made eight eagles, countless birdies. On the closing hole at my regular course, a par 5 that measures only 480 yards, I made eagle on three consecutive days. That hole is more like a par four- and-a-half as it isn't difficult for me to reach in two, but still, miraculously I made the putts! The NP was Nearly Perfect.

Visiting another course in that period I shot a 71, my best round ever. For the next few weeks my scores dropped and my handicap fell into the 3 range that the driving range owner had tried to bestow on me.

Then, as quickly as she had arrived, the Putting Muse moved on. I wasn't putting horribly, just more like normal. I worked with my alignment and continued to play well but I wasn't making much of anything. Standing over a 20-footer the NP was Non Productive, and eventually Not a Prayer. I decided to stick with it though because, well, because I was putting no worse than I always had, and once in a while I still made a long one.

Anyways, this blip of greatness forced me to rethink my closed-minded view of putting. Maybe there had been some sour grapes there. I now realize that making putts is good, as is shooting low scores. On the other hand I would still rather hit a bunch of greens in regulation and have an average day putting than hit poor shots and sink a lot of long putts for par. At least I think so.

The NP is still in my bag. And who knows, maybe someday the magic will return. The NP could again make me the Number-one Putter and bring me Newfound Pleasure on the golf course.

~Don Patton

67

If It Weren't for Golf

*Golf is played by twenty million mature American men whose wives
think they are out having fun.*
~Jim Bishop

I do not like to play golf. I reluctantly have had to admit that to myself. The game is just too frustrating because my performance falls so far short of my lofty aspirations.

My late father, on the other hand, was a real player: club champion, course record holder, two holes-in-one, 2-handicap in his prime, shot his age a couple of times in his seventies. He was solid, a natural. From him I received my devotion to the game. Too bad I can't enjoy it. Though I still, of course, play almost every chance I get.

Oh, I've managed to scrape it around to a 6- or 7-handicap for most of my career (lifetime low Index 5.0). I know that to a lot of people a single-digit handicap would be an achievement, but one must consider that I've been playing for fifty-four years, since the age of five. I actually have pretty good knowledge of swing mechanics, so I know how I should do it, but my lack of athleticism impedes. It is even less fun now with my current 11-handicap. My distance is adequate, probably long enough to be scratch, and my swing is considered conventional and aesthetic enough. But it is erratic despite copious practice.

The highlights of my golf life have mostly been comical. Like the time my friend drove one so far off line that he was stymied by an equipment shed, until he realized that if he opened both end doors, and kept it low, he would have a shot, as he did.

In the early days of those electronic, self-propelled individual bag carriers, my friend Barry's cart was dutifully following him over a bridge—until his transmitter fell off his belt and into the pond, closely followed in by his bag and clubs.

Once, on a hole with a big lake on the right, my buddy Lefty pull-hooked one so badly that we actually had to yell, "Fore in the boat!"

I once hit one *out of* a boat. Really. My drive trickled off the fairway into a lateral lake (same one), but came to rest, as I found, on the seat of a small rowboat tethered there. If I stood on the edge of dry ground and really reached with a long iron, I could, and did, hit it back onto land. Probably illegal because the ball was surely in motion, imperceptibly.

Which reminds me, do you know what the worst shot in golf is? No, not when your putt ends up going into a greenside bunker. That is only the third worst. The second worst is putting into a water hazard. The worst, therefore, is when you putt one out of bounds.

At least I thought that was the worst until a friend posited that the worst shot of all is when you play the wrong ball, and whiff.

I've seen people get negative yardage on shots even without the ball hitting an object, such as a tree, and ricocheting backward. For instance, a very fat hit into a very strong wind will accomplish this.

As for my own career highlight, I'd have to offer my easy win last year in our local "Bad Pants Open," which as the name suggests, was won by my pants, not my golf. In fact, my vintage golf pants are so bad that I was invited to model the whole collection. All my extreme pants have individual nicknames. My winning pair is named "The Jimi Hendrix Experience" for their mind-bending appearance, obvious era of origin, and mythic construction of industrial-strength, triple-knit, polyester. Just try to visualize. But dare not look at them for too long or you'll have an LSD flashback, whether you've ever done LSD or not.

And I've had some great 19th holes, notably one in 1973 at appropriately named Turkey Creek outside beautiful Gary, Indiana, when I tried to pick a fight with the legendary Chicago Bear bruiser, Dick Butkus. My friends still talk about that one. Fortunately, Mr. Butkus discerned that I was only kidding.

But why do I keep playing, practicing, and punishing myself if

I don't enjoy golf? Economists might aver that I *must* enjoy it, that I derive some utility from the activity, or else I wouldn't do it. To the contrary, it is a matter of abstractly recognizing that there is some slight positive probability that I will straighten my game out. In other words, I keep trying and hoping for an epiphany, the right swing key that will be the ultimate fix, which would deliver future "utils" in excess of the present negative state. But I do not expect that ever to happen, so the game of golf only makes me miserable in my futility.

I trust you can see why, relative to how long I've been playing and the effort I've put into it, I think I must be one of the worst golfers who ever lived. If so, at least I've achieved that one golf distinction.

I guess I'm addicted.

Of course I revere the game as an institution for its culture, traditions, challenge, and beauty. How can one not? My personal relationship with golf, though, is strained and conflictive, to say the least, but that reality leads us to a poignant lesson. It is easy for golfers to be captivated by the game if they enjoy it. For the sport to have such a grip on people such as me who dislike playing it, however, is a profound commentary on golf's attractive power and gravity. Perhaps my sad story is an even higher tribute to golf than the more favorable testimony you will encounter elsewhere.

It must be conceded the game of golf does mean something special to me, as I have arranged to be buried next to a favorite course and the inscription on my gravestone, already in place, reads, "Ironically, I rest where my drive on old #16 often did"—as in, out of bounds. The alternative epitaph I scrapped was, "See, I *told* them I was sick."

Or maybe golf is my way of maintaining a link, so to speak, with my departed father.

Regardless, you won't get any effusive, over-the-top sentimentality from me about how "golf means everything to me" or "how I owe it all to golf." But, on that score, there is one other detail I should mention about the game. My parents met on the golf course.

So, if it weren't for golf...

~John Gaski

68

Golf in Duluth

*One of the most fascinating things about golf is how it reflects the
cycle of life. No matter what you shoot, the next day you have to
go back to the first tee and begin all over again and
make yourself into something.*

~Peter Jacobson

t's been said, probably too many times and in too grandiose a fashion, that golf is a spiritual endeavor. Nevertheless, I've found there's more than a modicum of truth to that notion and here's why.

As I approached mid-life in the late 1980s it was apparent that I'd never be married or have children. Most of my friends and companions had "grown up" and pursued this more natural path into adulthood. This left me with a gigantic void in my life that had to be filled.

Out of the blue, a fellow my age suggested we both get season golf passes at the local public courses as spring (or what passes for spring under the cold standards held by Duluth locals) approached in 1989.

I'd originally quit the game in the early 1970s due to a combination of a lack of talent and a volcanic temper—these two qualities often go hand-in-hand I've discovered. However, this time around I relented to this fellow's suggestion and began the game again in earnest.

It just so happened I got laid off from work that summer. So I played daily, absorbing the more existential aspects of the game as my future lay rather precariously in the balance.

Golf season in Duluth lasts six months if we're lucky, and is replete with winds like massive sheets of air ripping across the sky, temperatures in the 40s. Golf in these conditions lends itself to an aura of survivalist mode. Since I played most of my rounds solo, a certain golfing introspection born of extreme concentration came to me as I walked the fairways for hundreds, and then thousands, of hours.

Now, twenty years later, I can say that golf has been the single most enriching thing in my life. Nothing else comes close. Sure, I've spent a lot of time cursing (literally and often quite inventively if I do say so myself) my decision to play on an obsessive daily basis. But I've always kept coming back for more. The inner competitiveness and exercise proved vital to a largely autonomous man.

What I've found is that life, for some people, isn't about the love and warmth of other people. Rather, it's about the equally intense and fulfilling love of a thing, an entity, and in my case this thing is golf. The game has been my life partner.

And I doubt it just happened to play itself out this way. I'm firm in the belief that God brought golf back into my life at that exact right juncture so as to give my existence a richness that for me, couldn't have been gained elsewhere.

~Bob Landfield

69

Chicken Soup for the Soul

Foreplay

Friends are people who help you be more yourself,
more the person you are intended to be.
~Merle Shain

I dreamt last night with a vividness that can only be brought on by the familiar.

My feet shuffled across the gravel parking lot, the echoes scratched off the unfinished stucco facade of her building. Only the walls protected her from me. My gait was slow and deliberate and my bare legs shook from the early morning chill. Arriving at the door, I threw it open as if I owned the place. I waltzed in and bobbed my head to the Latin beat playing in the background of the room. I went immediately to the large window and took in the view. The azure sky, peppered with high white clouds, the warm sun drawing me closer to the glass. I was excited. There she was, spread out before me. Naked. Pierced with just a few bits of jewelry. A long leg, bent slightly to the left, spread out to accommodate me. Moisture, like dewdrops, glistened and steam rose from her like an offering to the gods. Her slender hips dipped and undulated. I hung my head in a short prayer, hoping that my performance would be worthy of her grace and beauty. I turned again and was met by a casually dressed man.

"You all set?" he asked.

I shook my head yes.

"Hundred and fifty bucks." he said, without a trace of guilt. I gladly paid him. It would be worth it. I already wanted a smoke. My smile stretched from the New York cold to the Miami heat.

"Good luck buddy." he chuckled slyly. "Keep it long and straight." And, he exclaimed, "Welcome to Miami Beach Golf Club."

The thing about golf is that, like sex, when it's good, it's really good and when it's bad, it's just plain embarrassing. And worse, there are witnesses. The anticipation is new each time and the results vary day to day. Technique that worked well yesterday is forgotten quicker than a waiter's name, replaced with mis-hits, poor swings and bad reads.

The sport lends itself to camaraderie. Good-natured ball-busting is a staple. Conversations that would never take place at the office are commonplace on the course. There's a certain sensation that takes over once you reach the 1st tee. Trust and confidentiality are the unwritten rules. Things get talked about on a golf course that will be left there well after the round is finished. Stories covered in sand, left to be raked out by the Great Greenskeeper. It's a place to sort things out, bounce things off your friends — confessions of marital problems, financial woes, problem children, bad jobs, cancer. The only things out of bounds are marked by white stakes. We rely on that maleness, a sort of athletic and spiritual multi-tasking, to allow a vulnerability that cannot be expressed in any other place. Walking therapy.

I've strolled many fairways with friends, new and old, and I am often amazed at the candid conversation. Ambling up a fairway with a buddy is a solemn act of confidence. You talk about strategy, both on the course and in life. I've shared my history, and my present, on the course. My close friend Kenny talked about living with prostate cancer and his fears for his family.

"Paulie," he says, "I just want my family to be OK." Confiding, "That's all that matters."

I nod silently, looking him in the eye. There's no need for words. This moment of undisguised honesty takes place during club selection. He's 135 yards out and, without my advice, chooses a 9-iron. Kenny, who needed an 8-iron, lofts an admirable shot that falls far short of the green. Then I put my arm around him and we start walking towards the green. The gravity of the moment not lost, I look at him and say, "Nice shot, Alice. Your husband play?" He smiles, balls-busted, knowing he's been heard. You hear everything on a golf course. It's only a moment like that, on a fairway, where you can forget about the day-to-day and live in the moment. I respect that intimacy.

On a Friday morning, sometime near the end of March, I'll be in Miami with my friends. We'll get in at 11:00 A.M. and be on the course by one o'clock. The ball-busting will have started weeks prior. Who's going to kick whose ass? Who the partners will be? Who gives who strokes? I'll play right into it. And I'll cherish those singular moments that define men. It's as much a part of me as my dreams.

~Paul Ehmann

70

What It's All About

The biggest liar in the world is the golfer who claims that
he plays the game merely for exercise.
~Tommy Bolt

There is so much about this game that I love. And I don't mean those syrupy things like the azaleas at Augusta, a family round with Dad and my two brothers, the morning dew on the greens, or those motivational office posters that show a picture of a golf hole with some cheesy metaphor for life inscribed underneath. I mean the "other stuff" that really stokes the fire within. I'm talking about things like...

Hitting a brand new ball over a lake... Finding a brand new Pro V1 in the woods... Wondering why a guy who shoots 115 believes he should be giving golf advice... Watching Woody Austin fall into the water... *Tin Cup*... Never going a complete round without someone in the foursome making a reference to *Caddyshack*... Dropping an approach in tight to the 18th green in front of a packed 19th hole patio... The cart girl... Getting the golf cart onto two wheels and living to tell about it... Wondering why your partner who just topped his tee shot ten feet past the ladies tees is asking for a yardage... When the gods of the pro circuits are proven human, thank you Jean van de Velde... Hogan's 1-iron... Tiger's chip-in at Augusta at the 16th... All trick shots... Three-hour rounds... Ibuprofen... Always keeping the first putter your dad gave you... The Old Course... Caddies that can read greens... Charles Barkley's swing, I laugh every time... Striped shirts with plaid pants... Realizing that Rocco Mediate can hang with Tiger... Out-driving your friends without bouncing your ball on the cart path six times... Sansabelts... The simple fact that every shot makes somebody happy... Amen Corner... Nailing a long triple breaker for par... Hitting a half-submerged ball from the water and not ruining a pair of pants... Always believing that somehow profanity will change the flight of a golf ball... Bushwood... Playing in the worst weather imaginable and loving it.

This is what it's all about.

~Steven Floyd

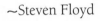

71

Chicken Soup for the Soul

Saturday Singles

Alook in the bags tells you right away that these golfers are different. Blades—old Mizunos and Titleists, even knife-like Wilson Staffs from the 1970s. Right there, before you walk into the pro shop, you know these men aren't the type to give a hoot about commercials or professional endorsement contracts. Their clubs aren't the most expensive or the flashiest, just the ones that work, and maybe used to work a little better back when they practiced. These golfers know their games, and they know how they want to play.

On weekend mornings throughout the year, we gather at first light in the pro shop at Poppy Ridge Golf Course in Livermore, forty-five miles southeast of San Francisco. This is the only time in our crowded lives that we can play, what with work, marriages and kids. So when we do get the chance we want purity. We have no time for an ugly hybrid with a thick topline, even if it meant an extra mis-hit or two would finish flag-high. There's no fun in that. Nothing's like a blade 3-iron struck in the heart, and that's the feeling we're chasing.

The country club life doesn't work for us. Where we live in Northern California, entry fees at good private courses go for a whopping $50,000 and more. In an era when many of us started our families later in life, and because we live in an area known for account-draining mortgages, we simply can't afford it. We're in the full bloom of adult responsibilities, like coaching kids in youth sports and taking care of backyards. There's college tuition to think about and 401K accounts to manage. And, finally, quality time with the family outranks the desire for a regular Wednesday afternoon foursome. So, daily fee life it is.

So while most of our free time is scheduled around these duties, there is one sliver of a blank slot—very early on either a Saturday or a Sunday. We set the alarm for five A.M. and rise in the dark, check the weather (windshirt, rainsuit or sunscreen?) and off we go.

We walk and carry. Any eighteen-hole configuration works out to be about a five-mile hike with steep elevation changes and long transitions from green to tee. It's also our two-for-one deal (another concession to lack of free time): recreation and exercise.

Though we may not know each other's names, we play enough to recognize each other. But upon reintroduction on the first tee you'll hear, "Oh, yeah, we played last year." A few of us might call ahead for tee times, but most of us don't know if we can escape until the night before, so we show up as a single and fit in wherever the starter deems. That's why we don't see each other for months at a time. But we recognize the kindred spirit, on the first tee right away, as evidenced by the blades, of trying for perfection in a very, very difficult game.

The equipment is personal. It's not so much about score but about hitting shots the way they should be played—a high fade to a back-right pin or a wedge past the hole that spins back for an easy putt. It's about control and artistry, and it all happens when iron meets ball and turf precisely. Approach shots that calculate triple factor issues of swing, conditions and lie; to us that's what the game's all about.

"What'd you hit?"

"I jumped a 5."

Hogan, the greatest ball striker of all time, said maybe one shot a round came off as he envisioned. For us, maybe it's one shot a month. But that's our goal. There are plenty of pulled drives and topped approaches and skulled escapes from bunkers. But every once in a while one of us will strike a pattern of fairway-green-one-putt that lasts a few holes, and we'll rise out of our solitary quests to recognize it in each other.

"Great shot. Tough pin placement."

"Yeah, the only way to get it there was to hit it low and run it up. That's why I dropped to a 7."

In our lives, with the demands of career and family and financial pressure, much of which is out of our hands, it's nice to occasionally feel the power of precision and know that it can make a difference.

Hogan's proficiency was so much greater than ours, and we know that. But we take the same approach anyway, even though the limits of modern family life cut back on the time we can devote to developing the mastery of the game we love.

With blades, when that attempt at the perfect shot comes off, it lingers in the hands for days. It puts a smile on our face and brings us back. That, for us Saturday morning singles hoping to squeeze into the tee sheet, is the majesty of the game.

~Ted Johnson

72

The Genealogically Isolated Golfer

Until you have a son of your own... you will never know the joy,
the love beyond feeling that resonates in the heart of
a father as he looks upon his son.
~Kent Nerburn

Lightning fried our automatic garage door opener last summer. With more than a little dread I took a screwdriver, removed the cover panel, replaced a small-but-expensive circuit board, hooked up new safety sensors and tightened the chain drive. Then I plugged it back in and stood in the driveway with the remote. When I pressed the button the door went obediently up.

"Atta boy." The two words came involuntarily from my lips.

It was my own utterance, but I heard it in my father's warm, distinct timbre. The ears of any son are super-tuned to the song of his father's praise, especially praise for something the dad might consider a manly art. It's a sensory memory that keeps its imprint long after boyhood ends. My own congratulatory whoops for a drive down the middle have been savored by my son, Nathaniel, and ought to be stored in the boy's consciousness somewhere.

I saw to it Nathaniel was introduced to golf in the parentally correct manner. I built him a few kiddie-length irons when he was four, taught him chip shots in the backyard, got him the half set of whippy-shafted clubs ideal for an eight-year-old, took him to the cool little nine-holer in the next town, told him we could quit after six holes if he was sick of it. All that enlightened stuff.

And the two of us had a fine time out there. He managed to hit a few greens, made at least two pars I can remember, canned a downhill 40-footer. But the golf bug never bit him. Nathaniel is seventeen now, and his bag of Junior Tour woods and irons leans against a cracked toboggan in our basement. And the conclusion of my experiment has long been plain: I am not the dad of a golfing son and — since I didn't start out as the son of a golfing dad — I belong to that odd subspecies called Genealogically Isolated Golfer.

There was no other way for it. The males in our lineage are contrarian types. We may not be pioneering visionaries, but we chafe at conformity. My father's golf career unfolded in a single afternoon on an Army base at Fort Dix, New Jersey — a nine-hole round with borrowed clubs in which he shot a 47 he insists was legit. And though fully aware of the many blue-collar, municipal golf courses in his midst, he always chose to associate the game with starchy yes-men who vote Republican.

Imbued with the old man's mutinous nature, I saw golf as open territory and took right to it, starting out as a "B" caddie at a small club two miles down the train tracks from our house. Golf's slate was clean. I could have it to myself. I've often read about boys who grew up caddying for their own fathers and learned to love the game through Dad's patient tutelage. According to these narratives, whatever fatherly wisdom a man can muster for his son's guidance, it will always sound truer and wiser if uttered while the two are striding the fairway toward father's well-struck drive. No reason anyone would lie about such a thing, but the thought of caddying for anyone and neither getting paid for the effort nor feeling free to mock the guy's crummy swing sends a shiver through me.

My father ran his own business — still does — and was rarely free of its demands. His lack of availability for sports coaching and other forms of suburban heroism eventually became spun. My parents made a virtue of necessity, saying it was better for boys to be among their peers as they discovered sports, not doted on and hovered over.

Dad had been a devout tennis player in high school and college and tried several times to encourage me to play. The only thrill I ever got from tennis came from wild, bombed shots that soared over the fence surrounding the court and bounded along the softball field. Distance was what counted.

Jean-Paul Sartre wrote in his autobiography that father-son relationships are by nature stifling and oppressive to the son. The noted Existentialist was openly thankful for the free path he had in life because his father had the foresight to die just months after Sartre was born. I would never go that far, but it shouldn't have surprised me that my son would do what he did, which was leave the golf to me and spend his high school Saturdays playing electric guitar in a garage band.

The weekend after I fixed the automatic door opener, he and the boys were in there with the amps cranked way up. I reached in the side door to grab a rake and hung around long enough to hear my son nail a long, throbbing solo on "Cinnamon Girl." When the last note faded I gave him a dignified little fist pump. "Atta boy," I whispered.

~David Gould

The Golf Book

The Lifelong Game

*Once a golfing champion allows himself to suspect that
playing a superb round is not the be-all and end-all of life,
he is lost.*

~Author Unknown

73

Remembering Mr. Meticulous

A good teacher is a master of simplification and an enemy of simplism.
~Louis A. Berman

As golfers, Davis Love III and I have little in common beyond wearing a glove on our left hands (except when we're putting).

He is a twenty-five-year veteran of the PGA Tour, where he is known as DL3. In 2008 he won his 20th career tournament to earn a lifetime playing exemption. He drives the ball 300 yards or longer when the situation demands it.

I, on the other hand, am a forty-year veteran of *Golf Digest* magazine, where the boon of my existence has been sampling—yes, without charge—the applied wisdom of the top teachers of our time. This windfall also has been the bane of my existence.

The pluses are stimulating to say the least, and have led to improvement, especially when contact with the gurus was maintained and a modicum of discipline occasionally exercised. But the minuses—warring brain waves from different approaches and vocabularies—have often proved considerable.

In spite of all the world-class instruction, I can count the times I have broken 80 at good courses on my gloved left hand. With a stiff back I now drive the ball so short I can hear it land. It doesn't help either that so many dear readers think golf writers play all the time rather than brood over their typing machines.

However, DL3 and I *do* share the bittersweet bond of his father's classic teaching. Davis Jr. was a former tour player who became a leading teacher before he died at age fifty-three in a small-plane accident. He was on his way to a meeting of the Golf Digest schools staff in bad weather at night.

I remembered him once saying it was safer to fly at night. Besides, he added with his usual sly wit, you can't play golf at night.

Golf was his consuming passion, beaming out of small, observant eyes. He favored casual bucket hats that protected a hairline receding toward baldness, and he conveyed an air of competent calm that put even the most nervous student at ease. He was prepared to work harder than you were if you wanted to improve at the game.

Once you knew him better, you realized that he was wound tightly, which should have resulted in the odd explosion of frustration. Yet I never saw (or heard about) a letdown in his professional demeanor.

In manner and appearance, Davis Jr. could have passed for a small-town Midwestern druggist. If he'd been a doctor, it would have been said he had a terrific bedside manner. He accorded you his full, undistracted attention no matter how crowded his schedule. And inevitably it was overbooked.

He was my favorite teacher, the rare guru with the ability to give a student, whether beginner or prize pupil like son DL3, only as much information as the student could handle at a given stage of development, and making that message as simple as possible. I have always been prone to taking the club back too far and pausing too long at the top of the swing, costing myself control and timing. His advice was terse but effective: "Try to keep the club moving at the top."

He converted my small hands to an all-finger grip. "It gives you support both ways," he said. "You have more feel of the club." When I parroted something I'd heard about pressure points in the grip, his advice was to forget all that. Those pressure points would change on their own as I swung.

Playing golf with him and watching his buttery-smooth swing was a wonderful influence on anyone's tempo. His driver action was upright and relaxed looking, and consistently put the ball in the fairway. "If you want to hit it far, hit it straight," he would say.

At meetings of our old *Golf Digest* Professional Panel he was quiet-spoken but keenly attentive. Sitting in the same room with prestigious peers like Bob Toski, Paul Runyan, Peter Kostis, Jim Flick, et al., Davis Jr. was the best listener. He picked his spots to interject fresh, well-considered comments.

The topic one day was the everlasting problem of average golfers not hitting enough club for approach shots. After a while Davis said, "We have been talking about this subject forever. I'd like to see one-day tournaments where every time you hit a shot to the green with a club and it doesn't get there, you can't use that club anymore. Whoever has the most clubs left at the end wins."

Talking about the typical weekend golfer kidding himself about making a long carry over water, he said, "The thing that trips you up there is that the body is smarter than the mind. If the mind makes a stupid decision to go for it, the body is going to lock up at some point during the swing and say 'I can't do this.' It knows."

He filled legal pads with extensive notes during these meetings. Once I asked him about it. "If I write it down," he said, "I'll remember it." He was Mr. Meticulous. A few days after the meetings, he, alone among the esteemed group, would send us, unsolicited, a detailed list of article ideas he envisioned growing out of the sessions, outlined with textbook precision.

Always he would stress that we needed to find ways to make the game enjoyable. More fun. DL3, so close to him for so long if not long enough, says his dad emphasized having fun as much as mastering mechanics when he was growing up. I feel fortunate to share that legacy with DL3, even in a limited way. Setting aside that he can hit it a football field past me these days, end zones included.

~Nick Seitz

74

Just Call Me Jack

Focus not on the commotion around you, but on the opportunity ahead of you.
~Arnold Palmer

I played on the PGA Tour for two years. If I proved one thing, it was that I was a pretty good player on Monday and pretty bad one come Thursday and Friday. In 1978, I entered thirty Monday qualifiers, made it through twenty times, but only made two tournament cuts. 1979 was pretty much a repeat performance. I entered thirty-one events, qualified for nineteen, and made the cut in only four. Let's just say I was more accustomed to traveling on Saturday and Sunday than I was to playing.

One of the rare events where I made the cut was the 1979 Doral Open. On Thursday and Friday I was paired with Mark McCumber (the eventual winner of the event) and in these first two rounds I somehow got caught up in McCumber's draft and played pretty well. After Saturday's round I checked the leaderboard, just to make sure my name was actually on it after three rounds. Not only was my name on it, there was a chance I was going to play with Jack Nicklaus on Sunday as we were at the same score.

So after dinner I called to get my tee time and casually asked who I was paired with for the 10:10 starting time. I was told Bob Murphy and Jack Nicklaus. So, I did what any twenty-three-year-old green pro would do. I immediately laid out my clothes for the next day and started ironing my underwear while breathlessly repeating, "It's no big deal, it's no big deal, it's no big deal...."

The next morning I arrived at Doral my usual hour and a half early to warm up. I didn't notice a sizeable difference in crowds around the putting green or near the practice area. I was relieved. It really was going to be no big deal.

With about thirty minutes remaining before my tee time, I left my gallery on the range, estimated by my caddie to be three, which was including the range picker-upper guy. As I walked over to the putting green I noticed perhaps a hundred people gathering at the far end of the practice tee. Mr. Nicklaus was over there. A hundred people I could deal with. As my caddie and I arrived at the putting green we noticed a few more people milling over, but still, "no big deal."

The practice green was only about thirty feet from the 1st tee. We finished our warm-up with three straight ten-footers made, decided on the Titleist 4's since we all know the 3's are unlucky (and it was the fourth round after all) and turned to go to the 1st tee.

"Uh oh," I said to my caddie. "Where'd the 1st tee go?" The tee had been right there in plain sight a few minutes ago. In the span of time necessary to roll a few putts the gallery had exploded.

I swear there must have been more than a thousand people around that 1st tee. It took my caddie and me five minutes to negotiate the thirty feet from the practice green to the tee. By the time we wiggled through the starter was already announcing "and now for the 10:10 starting time, first on the tee is Bob Murphy playing out of Delray Beach, winner of four PGA Tour events... top sixty money winner each of the last eleven seasons... U.S. Amateur Champion." Yada yada yada.

Bob gets up and with his usual chicken winged high-handed backswing, just smoothes a little cut right down the centerline. The crowd applauds and I'm thinking, that's pretty loud for a 260-yard drive.

"Next on the tee in the 10:10 group and playing out of North Palm Beach is the winner of sixty-eight PGA Tour Events... Top Money Winner eight times... Scoring Leader eight times... Member of five Ryder Cup teams... Winner of five Masters, three U.S. Opens, three British Opens, and four PGA Championships... PGA Player of the Year five times... ABC's Wide World of Sports Athlete of the Year... Winner of two Trans Mississippi Amateurs... Winner of two US Amateurs... Walker Cup Member twice... 1961 NCAA Champion... Ohio Open Champion at age sixteen... won five straight Ohio State Junior titles beginning at age twelve... overcame polio as a child... and has been named by most every golfing authority in the world to be the Golfer of the Century... and on and on and on... Jack Nicklaus!"

The crowd goes crazy. Mr. Nicklaus waggles over the ball, and hits a perfect shot down the middle of the fairway. This makes the crowd go even crazier and I'm thinking I better get used to this noise ASAP.

"Next on the tee in the 10:10 group and playing out of Missouri City, Texas... Bobby Baker... good luck" That was all the starter said.

I was standing there listening to the starter, and it took me a moment to realize he said I could play, too. I walked to the teeing area, teed the ball up somewhere between the markers and noticed for the first time that my hand was shaking and was absolutely amazed when the ball actually stayed on the tee.

I hit that drive with so much adrenaline that it went 50 yards past Mr. Nicklaus. I had a 6-iron left to the first hole at Doral, normally a fairly long par 5. We walked off the tee and the gallery started walking along with us, then running, and it sounded like a herd of cattle. The only thing missing was actual mooing.

So now I am walking next to the Greatest Ever To Play Golf and realize we haven't met yet as I had had trouble getting to the tee in time due to the crowds. I looked at him and said, "I've grown up watching you play and I don't know whether to call you Jack or Mr. Nicklaus or Mr. Bear or what?"

He chuckled, put his hand on my shoulder and replied "I'm not that much older than you so just call me Jack."

Maybe I was a little nervous, and still don't know why I said what I did, but I put my hand on Jack's shoulder and said, "You're probably not used to the noise so let me know if my gallery bothers you today."

~Bob Baker

"I JUST FOUND OUT MY WIFE RAN AWAY WITH MY BEST FRIEND—<u>NOW</u> WHO AM I SUPPOSED TO PLAY GOLF WITH?"

The First Lesson

Golf was easy for me as a kid. I had to play a while to find out how hard it is.
~Raymond Floyd

It was a midweek day in February when I paid a visit to John Dobson's golf shop on Clark Street, a commercial avenue about four miles north of Wrigley Field. Dobson was the pro at Bunker Hill, a public course I played during my first summer in the game. In the winter, Dobson did club repairs and gave lessons in his storefront, which had one stall with a sheet of heavy canvas marked with a bulls-eye.

I walked in as though my intent was to look for a putter in the big barrel of used clubs he had near his workbench, and to price re-gripping my driver, which I had with me. In truth, I couldn't afford a putter at any price, or to have my driver re-gripped. I just wanted to hit some balls into his canvas, and thought Dobson would let me, no charge. He seemed the kind of person who would help kids just starting out in the game. I was right. When I asked him what he thought of Hogan's swing and if he knew the secret, and mumbled some other inanities, a smile crossed his lips. He knew why I was there, and asked if I would like to hit a few. I was at the mat before he completed his offer.

After I hit one or two, Dobson's wife pulled up a chair and sat next to the stall to watch me. I was smacking the canvas pretty good, which I suppose got her attention. After a couple more hits she said there was one thing I needed to learn if I was going to be a really good golfer. She spoke in a soft voice, and I was immediately drawn to her, as I came from a family with a few loud and nervous women. Mrs. Dobson was none of that. And what's more, she took an interest in me without my asking. I was all ears.

She said I needed to pivot. I wasn't sure what that meant, certainly not in a golf context. She said I was swinging the club the way most caddies do when they begin to play. On the backswing, my right side slid laterally to the right and formed a kind of bow, or one side of a parenthesis. On the downswing my body slid laterally in the opposite direction and closed the parenthesis. Though she didn't use the parenthesis image (I did only after I became a writer). Mrs. Dobson said I needed to turn my body as if it were in a barrel. She showed me what she meant, putting her hands on my waist from behind and spinning my hips around as if there were a swivel.

"Now try it," she said. Somehow, I got it right the very first time. The feeling was like nothing I had ever known before in my very short history as a golfer. When I threw my wide-swinging curveball as a baseball pitcher my arm ached. My hands almost always stung when hitting a baseball. I won a 100-yard dash once and although it felt good to be a winner, afterwards I thought my chest would burst. During my first rounds of golf in the summer just past, I hit behind the ball a lot, and topped more than a few. I of course hit a few decent ones by accident, but none that felt like that first ball I hit into Dobson's canvas sheet. Not only was there no pain, it was almost as though it didn't happen. I hardly felt the impact. I hit another, and another, and another. Same thing. I looked up and Mrs. Dobson was nodding and smiling. I noticed Dobson himself, from behind the counter at his grinding wheel, give me a glance and a nod.

I hit a few more. I could have hit a million more, but Dobson finally said he was ready to close up for the day. I had to leave. He said I could come back anytime I wanted. I said thanks. No more, no less, just thanks. For the golf lesson that metamorphosed my being. Well hell, I was only fourteen and in an enchanted state. I had just had an out-of-world experience, an epiphany.

In Chicago, February is the cruelest month. When I left Dobson's shop the wind was slashing like a razor across my face. The sky was an unbroken sheet of deep and ominous gray. The ice-sheathed pavement crackled under foot like splintering bones. I was aware of the conditions, but felt nothing of them. It was for me a balmy day in Elysium. All I felt was those swings, the clean whirl of my body as I hit the ball. I could hardly wait for the weather to break.

Then, on a day in early March when the temperature rose into the low 40s, my golf season began. I schlepped my Johnny Roberts irons and Wilson Strata-Bloc woods on the Montrose Avenue streetcar to Milwaukee Avenue, transferred to another streetcar that went north on Milwaukee to the end of the line, walked four blocks from there and arrived at Bunker Hill to put the pivot in play.

The very first shot, with a driver, was as pure as the snow that had been driving so fiercely only ten days ago. The ball had just the right height, and a slight draw. The short iron through the gap between overhanging trees had the same flight pattern, landed on the green and stopped after a single low bounce. This second shot was most satisfying because taking the ball off the ground had given me the most trouble the prior season. But now I had hit the ball first, the divot was square and aimed at my target, and the mark of impact on the clubface was dead center. Oh, man! For the rest of the round, almost every shot I hit was the same. One after another. At the end I shot 75. It was my first round under 80.

I had played the round by myself, but didn't need anyone to help me celebrate my ascension to the golfing heights. Golf is a loner's game, and I was a loner under any circumstances. Later, in the salad days of my golfing life I would sometimes remark (as others have and often do) that hitting a perfect golf shot was sometimes better than sex. On that chilly afternoon in March, 1946, a fourteen-year old naïf was unable to make such a comparison. Eventually I could and would agree that it was... well, close.

As I walked back to the streetcar after shooting my erotic 75 I felt flushed, inflated. I was six inches taller, twenty-five pounds heavier, and I began to think I wasn't such a bad looking kid after all.

I said to myself, with the fervor of a novitiate priest taking his vows, that I would never again, never ever, shoot in the 80s. Riiiight!

~Al Barkow

Nine Holes in Eighteen Years

The greatest good you can do for another is not just to share your riches but to reveal to him his own.

~Benjamin Disraeli

"I hit those Pings Eye 2's *great*," said my brother-in-law Chris as I walked through the door of my house. He was sitting at the kitchen table, beaming. I'd just finished giving a few lessons at the course. Chris had mentioned the possibility of ducking out for a few holes in my absence. I bit my tongue. I contemplated whether to tell him the history behind those eighteen-year-old Pings he was so excited about. A set that had never, ever been hit. Until now.

Chris had just flown in from Chicago for the Thanksgiving holidays. Like a lot of northerners would be, he was happy to be in sunny New Mexico with a golf course across the street. Smiling for his good fortune and industriousness, he told me how he'd discovered the Pings in the corner of my garage, strapped them onto my golf cart and squeezed in a quick nine, all in the little space of time I'd been gone.

I smiled, asked him to give me a play by play of each hole. Secretly cringing behind a curious expression, I listened as the shots were recounted, which included one notably successful approach from a scrappy lie in the dirt.

As Chris progressed through his round, my thoughts floated to the special journey the Ping Eye 2's with Serial #34066A had taken in finally making it to the golf course.

Back in 1988, the favorite hobby of a man named Joe H. was the game of golf. That year, he suffered a heart attack on a commuter plane and was left in terrible condition. It was hard for him to walk, and even talk. At the beginning of his rehabilitation, Mrs. H. bought a set of brand new Pings; a full set of irons 3-SW and the wooden pear-shaped 1-, 3-, 5-woods with the famous black lacquer finish. She set them purposefully in clear sight, in the corner of perhaps the cleanest garage I have ever seen, to serve as an inspiration for Joe to make it back to the golf course. For eighteen years, the clubs were only touched when the garage was swept on a weekly basis. Believe me when I say there was zero clutter in this garage. Only a lawn-mower and car were ever in the company of Joe's Pings.

Then in 2006, Mrs. H. and their son decided to walk across the street to where I lived. Since I teach golf for a living, they wanted to know if I could find a home for the Pings. Joe's condition had only become worse through the years and he was now wheelchair bound.

As soon as I saw the Pings I realized how special they were, as would any golf pro with modest historical knowledge of equipment. Their condition was perfect. The stickers were even still on the face of the woods. But more amazing than the condition were the years of hope invested in these Pings. To think they had been sitting for nearly two decades calling out the name of a man in a wheelchair so that recovery might come sooner.

Chris sat on my sofa, beaming as he recounted his nine holes, as most golfers tend to do when their love of the game has been rekindled through good play. He must have been somewhat curious as to why I was inquiring so specifically about each and every club he hit, wondering why I was so suddenly showing such keen interest in his game that I had never really shown before. But oblivious, he kept on. In the end, I ascertained that the 3- and 4- irons and 1-wood had not been hit.

I didn't tell Chris the real story that afternoon, and nor have I since. Figured there was no point in making him feel badly for devaluing the set. But I think Joe and his family will be happy to know that my brother-in-law became excited again about the game after his nine holes of magic that sunny day in November.

In January 2010, I plan to post the Pings on eBay. The last I heard from a collector, the near-mint set should still fetch a remarkable bid, perhaps as much as $4,000. Half will go to Joe to add comfort to his last years. The other half I will use to buy clubs for aspiring juniors. So in the end, even though the Pings didn't successfully get Joe back to golf, their redirected value might introduce dozens of others to the game. And I will make sure the seeds of growth occur in Joe's namesake.

~Todd Kersting

77

Everybody Should Play

Television is what made all sports boom. When we formed the LPGA back in 1950, a typical purse for one of our tournaments was $1,000, or maybe $1,500 if we were lucky. Because we were just trying to get the whole thing jumpstarted, at times it could be kind of a shoestring operation. Us girls would pack our clubs and show up at a town, never exactly sure what to expect.

One year about twenty of us went up to Syracuse, New York, to play a 54-hole event booked by a man up there. That's how it happened. Anyone could call up the LPGA president and put up a purse, and then that's where we would go play. At this Syracuse event, they said, there would also be thirty amateurs playing, but the last place professional was guaranteed to make fifty dollars.

At first it seemed great. Each one of us got to stay in a nice house for free, and the people helping run the tournament took us out to dinner and entertained us a couple of nights. The only thing we had to pay for was our caddies. We always took local caddies.

Our galleries were never too large in those days, but I remember the gallery at this tournament being smaller than usual.

As to who won, I can't exactly remember. I think it was either Babe Zaharias or Patty Berg. Whoever it was though, in the end was only playing for pride. Because when it came time to hand out the money, no one could find the man who organized the tournament.

We hunted all over for him — in the clubhouse, in the parking lot, but to no avail. We asked some members of the hosting course about him, but they didn't really know anything. It turned out the man wasn't even a member of the course, like we'd naturally assumed.

As the sun started to set and the sky grew dark it was pretty clear what had happened. The man hadn't made enough money selling admissions and had simply ditched town. There wasn't even a trophy. It was terrible, but there was nothing we could do. We just packed our bags and drove to the next event.

Of course, when it comes to unsure expectations, there can be good surprises, too. Another time I was invited to play in a pro-am tournament in Washington, D.C. My partner turned out to be none other than Stuart Symington, the Secretary of the Air Force. Mr. Symington gave me his limousine and his driver for my personal use during the entire tournament. The first time I got in that limo I saw there was a phone. I couldn't believe it. A phone in a car! I had the driver take me around so I could call every single person I knew. To each one of them I said the same thing. "Can you believe I'm riding in a car right now, with a phone?"

Golf has taken me around the world. Sometimes there have been good surprises and sometimes they haven't been so good. Even if you're not a professional, the game takes you so many places and lets you meet people you'd never meet. That's why I say everybody should play.

~Peggy Kirk Bell

Shrivel Disobedience

J ust as a plant takes up water from its lateral roots, I took up golf from its lateral hazards.

When the course was closed on the weekends—rather, open only to adults—my cousins, twin sister and I pedaled the short trip from our grandmother's house to Fenwick's 4th hole and parked our bikes next to the abutting cove's row of red stakes. If no one was hitting, we scurried through the Rosa Rugosa bushes to scavenge for stray balls.

If it wasn't a Titleist Professional or a Top-Flite Strata (our gamers of choice) or bore a neat logo, we sold it on the 4th tee-box, and shared the profits. On a busy day we could each rake in as much as $20, which was (and still is) a heck of a lot of money to an eight-year-old. Then come evening, when children were permitted to play, we had plenty of ammo.

Ammo. *Amo, amare, amavi, amatum.*

One time a guy joked, "If you ever find one of my balls, it's got this black elk logo on it, I'll buy it back from you for $15."

"Really?" I said, doing my best to hold back a grin.

"Yeah, really."

As soon as his foursome left the tee-box, I pedaled back to my grandmother's two-door garage. I was sure I had seen that logo before. The only question was, had I played with it and scuffed it up?

I found it. Within minutes, I reconvened with my new business acquaintance on the 4th green, carrying the object he had assessed. Cue the sound of a cash register; I made my daily salary in the time it took the guy to play one hole.

What we played with, we cherished. As self-described experts at looking for golf balls, we took pride in not losing what we had found. In the rare case that we did slice or hook one into the bushes, we made up for it by reemerging with at least five replacements.

One hot August day, business was slow. I was having daydreams of becoming a golf pro, and following the beliefs of yet-to-be-read Henry David Thoreau, I was ready to go show the tyrannical administrators of those invidious rules what I, a kid, could do.

No one was coming up the 3rd hole. Also, in the shade of the Rosa Rugosa bushes, I had just found a brand new Titleist Professional that I couldn't wait to try out. I raced home, threw my dad's stand bag on my shoulder and raced back to the vacant 4th tee-box.

Someone behind me, I'm guessing it was my sister, told me I probably shouldn't, that I'd get in trouble. I didn't listen or even look back. In my back pocket, I had my golf glove and a fresh scorecard as my alibi. If someone asked what I was doing, I'd simply tell him that I was playing golf. If someone told me children were not allowed on the golf course on the weekends before 4:00 P.M., I'd challenge him to a match.

I parred the 4th and was ready to hit my pitch shot up to the 5th green, when an E-Z-GO came up over the horizon. Janet Keeney, the 1969 ladies club champion, was at the wheel and she was gunning straight for me. When she pulled up close, her cart casting a shadow over my father's stand bag, she informed me I had cut directly in front of her and her guest, without checking in with the starter.

"Young man, I'm sure you're aware that children aren't allowed on the course on Saturday morning," she said. "I'm going to have to ask you to stop playing."

A small part of me wanted to challenge her to a match, but I feared she'd probably beat me. I stood there, mute. Mrs. Keeney and her guest played on.

To this day, the 342-yard 5th still gives me trouble.

~Jeff Patterson

79

Band of Golfers

We few, we happy few, we band of brothers.
~William Shakespeare, Henry V

As the USS *John F. Kennedy* pulled out of her homeport we stood on the flight deck knowing that it would be at least another six months until we'd see home again. To the north we could see a sliver of green, which was the course at St. Augustine. And somewhere to the south, I knew, because I had flown over it so many times in the past weeks, was TPC Sawgrass.

As if our families were not enough of an incentive to return home safely, the great golf around Jacksonville was one more thing that some of us wanted to get back to, in one piece.

Gearing up for deployment is a lot like what I assume a professional golfer does getting ready for a major. In both cases, you're doing everything possible to make sure you have your "A Game" when it counts. This was our major. This was the culmination of a year and a half of honing our skills as pilots. We were going away for six months, to do a job that required a reliance and trust in our squadron mates that is unfathomable to those who have not experienced it.

A few days prior to the deployment, we loaded our bags and boxes into our staterooms. We were going away for six months, and I was not surprised to see other guys in my squadron lugging their clubs down, just as I was doing. Yes, we were deploying to the Mediterranean and then probably on to the Persian Gulf, but what if? Better to have them and not need them than need them and not have them. Chances were decent that on a day off we could blast a few out into the ocean from the deck of the carrier. Better yet, there might be a port call near a golf course. You know, join the Navy and see the world.

After a few weeks stuck on a boat, every person from the captain down to the guy who cleans the toilets has one thing on their mind, "Get me off this damn ship!" There are some rather strict rules about being on a United States Naval vessel, one of them being the equivalent of prohibition. Yes, despite what you may think you know about being on a ship, the mere possession of an adult beverage can earn you time in the brig, or even get you kicked out of the Navy. There were usually about 5,000 people running for the nearest bar whenever we pulled into port.

Rather than drinking into the wee hours at every port visit, which, sad to say, is often done, a few of us would instead drag our clubs off the boat and seek out the local fairways. Of the twenty or so officers in our squadron, there were about eight or nine that were always chomping at the bit to hit the links.

One round that sticks in my mind from this deployment was a trip to a beautiful course in Tarragona, Spain. To get there we had to pack six guys and six sets of clubs into a Citroen hatchback. Of the six, I know for a fact that I was the smallest at 5' 11" and 180 pounds. Our squadron had a reputation for the way we would eat on the ship. The term "fat party" was often said with pride around mealtime.

It was not a memorable round in the sense that any of us played very well, but it was very memorable in the sense that it was a day of normalcy, the likes of which we had not experienced for a while. No flight suit, no forty pounds of survival gear, no smell of diesel or jet fuel, and best of all, no night traps. It was one of the most picturesque golf courses I have ever seen. There were beautiful mountains in the background, an actual stone aqueduct running through the course and we were virtually the only people on it.

I smile thinking back to that day. There was JJ, who we always gave a lot of crap about how short he was off the tee. JJ was always right down the center and wore a wide grin after every shot. There was Gerbs, who likely had the shortest backswing known to man, but could clobber the ball. Then there was Torch, our version of Ernie Els, who had effortless distance, *smooooooth*. Though Torch's hold on the Spanish language proved smoother than his golf that day as he was able to negotiate our way out of a minor fender-bender with the Citroen after the round.

Not long after that round of golf in Spain, we were off through the Suez Canal heading for the Persian Gulf after a short stop near Bosnia. This whole time our clubs gathered dust in the corners of our rooms.

As with all the golf I managed to sneak during my time in the military, that day in Tarragona wasn't about the course, the few birdies, the many bogeys, the location or the scenery. It was about the playing with people I knew and trusted like brothers. Without them, it would have been just another round of golf.

~Lieutenant Ross Troike

80

A Miracle

The first miracle was that they'd actually pay you $3 or $4 to carry somebody's bag around a beautiful golf course. I mean, compare that to shoveling snow or cutting lawns.

The second miracle was that on Mondays, if you behaved yourself, they'd let you *play* the golf course. Just like the members! I had to pinch myself. The only stipulation was we had to tee off in front of the tee-boxes. One Monday, teeing off so early we could barely see our drivers in front of our faces, we played seventy-two holes. Total score: about 400 shots apiece. It was the most wonderful exhaustion I'd ever felt. One of the members sold me his old set of MacGregor Tourneys and from then on, golf was all I thought about. I was hooked.

The third miracle, the most amazing of all, was that they'd send you to college. Everything paid. The members told us about it, the Evans Scholarship, founded by golfer Charles "Chick" Evans, who won both the Open and the Amateur in 1916 but elected to remain an amateur and suggested the prize money be directed to start a caddie scholarship fund. The members helped us with the applications and coached us on what to say. My parents, Mary and Bill Carney, faced with the thought of putting six kids through college, couldn't believe the gift they got: two sons, two scholarships, and a million lessons in growing up.

It was not an instant miracle, of course. There was the application to fill out and, ugh, the interview. Can a person be more nervous than I was that day? Dressed in an un-caddie-like jacket and tie, finger nails scrubbed, I sat sweating in a small room at the Dearborn Country Club I'd never been in before—I think it was a Sunday—and faced a horseshoe of eight men, all in either green or blue blazers. These were the officers of the Golf Association of Michigan and the Western Golf Association, who would decide whether I was worthy or not. As a caddie, I'd grown used to sizing up members, had learned to sort the good guys from the not so good. I saw immediately that these were good guys, smart guys, confident and powerful. Despite their efforts to put me at ease, they were intimidating. For forty-five minutes I fielded their questions, explained why I thought I "deserved" the scholarship. Though, of course, I believed no such thing. In the end my grades (B+), my attitude (appropriately deferential), out-of-class activities, and the fact they knew my parents would never let me flunk out won them over. A few weeks later the letter arrived.

To me, Dearborn Country Club will always be a place of wonder and opportunity, a window into a world I used to think only "other" people inhabited. Did Henry Ford, when he established the club for his executives, have any idea that it would result in college education for dozens of his employees' children? That it would help to imbue thousands of kids—members and caddies—with the lasting values of a game he himself didn't even play? That he had, in fact, set up a crash course in the American Dream?

Maybe he did. Maybe he knew what he was setting in motion. He was a master of motion, after all.

The miracle Ford created continues for me today. I work for a golf magazine and have for almost twenty-five years. Being able to write about the game I came to love in a caddie yard thirty-five years ago has been a gift and a privilege. Sharing golf with my brother Tom, who caddied with me, makes it all the sweeter. Today Tom and I both belong to family-oriented clubs much like Dearborn and play in one another's annual member-guest tournaments. We take caddies, of course, never carts.

I still like to drive by Dearborn when I'm "home" to catch a glimpse of the kids in the caddie yard, knowing that there are members who'll keep the miracles coming for them. I look at the faces of the caddies at my own club and wonder if they feel the amazement I did. I hope so.

~Bob Carney

81

Mea Culpa, Riviera

What other people may find in poetry or art museums,
I find in the flight of a good drive.
~Arnold Palmer

f any veteran member of the Riviera Country Club in Pacific Palisades, California, is reading this, *mea culpa. Mea maxima culpa.* I'm the reason all those golf balls mysteriously appeared on your fairways lo those many years ago.

Please understand. There was no better place to practice than my parents' lawn. Bordering your club from the top of a hundred-foot cliff, Mom and Dad's backyard offered a sweeping view of Hogan's Alley and the Santa Monica Mountains beyond. With a perch like that for teeing ground, how could a youngster resist? It was one of the most gorgeous spots in Los Angeles's corner of the golfing world.

It also was one of the most challenging. Between my roost and your course lay a slope full of chaparral and, beyond that, five eucalyptus trees that rose well beyond a hundred feet—four to my right and one to the left. Just to get through to the rough of your fine course, I had to thread the ball through that 30-yard gap. Once I perfected my aim, I could choose between your par-5 1st hole and the par-4 12th. Those were the two holes that started not far beyond the fence that divided us.

I'd place my bucket at our yard's edge, just before the earth precipitously dropped, then sight between the trees and swing. More often than not the first ball would flop into the bush. Then the next few might ricochet against the aforementioned eucalyptus goalposts. But usually after a while I'd find my driving groove. Most days I would be hitting directly into the sea breeze, as that was the prevailing wind. On other days warm Santa Ana winds caressed my back, and that's when I could swear I had struck the balls so hard that they soared over Riviera and landed somewhere near the beach. Of course, they probably dropped onto your course, bounced a few times and then nestled to a stop on the kikuyu grass of your fairways. Or at least that's how I imagined it.

When my friends came over, we launched golf balls in salvo. My buddies played much better than I. It would have been cruel not to let them use my yard as a driving range. I'm sure you understand. And you have to admit we were considerate. After all, we held our fire during the L.A. Open and the PGA Championship tournaments that you hosted during our salad days. We waited for you to play through before taking our shots. We never hopped the fence to attempt a game at sunrise. (All right, that's because I'm not a morning person.) And you got to keep all my golf balls.

After thirty-five years, I must confess: you got your revenge. Spending all those days with my driver left precious little time to practice anything else. Now I can't chip, can't pitch, and I'm so clumsy with irons that I'm embarrassed to play. I content myself with driving ranges and miniature golf courses—my comeuppance for years of whacking golf balls from the commanding heights.

~Tony Mohr

82

Round of My Life

There, on the shelf, sits the white dimpled ball.
Cuts and stains show its age.
The birdie putt on sixteen paused at the edge,
then, like a mouse, disappeared into the hole.
On the next tee, the pond guarding the front of the green
which had swallowed many who had dared pass before,
Stared directly into my eyes.
Legs shaking, heart pounding, I took a swing.
As if guided by an unseen hand,
the ball flirted with water's edge,
then pranced onto the green.
The tension-packed walk up eighteen
filling my palms with sweat,
created images of Hogan, Jones, Palmer,
all who had taken similar steps.
As the tiny sphere jumped off course
and headed towards the newly planted trees,
my heart sunk like a lead weight into my toes.
As I approached, I saw that I had a clear view of the target,
and knew the guiding force had returned one last time.
The delicate chip suspended in the air
like a hot air balloon out for a Sunday flight,
softly nestled close.
As I lined up the eight-foot birdie putt,

I felt my heart pounding out of my ribs
assuring me it had returned to my chest.
There, on the shelf, sits the white dimpled ball.
It had successfully completed its eight-foot journey.

~Mark Rylak

83

On Moe Norman

The privilege of a lifetime is being who you are.
~Joseph Campbell

The first time I met Moe Norman I was conducting a free clinic and he was in the audience. After I finished what I thought was a perfect display of shot shaping, Moe came up to me and asked if I knew who he was.

I said, "Yes, you're Moe Norman."

Moe said, "How'd you like me to come next week and show everybody how a ball should really be hit?"

I agreed, and we did clinics together for eighteen years after that. He became a true friend.

A lot of everyday people don't know who Moe Norman was, but a lot of pros will tell you he was the greatest ball-striker ever. Tiger Woods once said that only two people in the history of golf have ever truly owned their swing, Ben Hogan and Moe Norman.

To watch Moe hit balls was riveting. Time after time you could not believe how good it was. But what was so amazing about Moe was he broke all the rules of conventional mechanics. He held the club in the palms of his huge hands (there was no wrist action in his swing — I always said it was like he just had arms with hands) and he took an abnormally wide stance. In the address position, his club rested about a foot behind the ball. He extended his arms out as far as possible and swung the shaft with his arms in one single axis.

I remember Lorne Rubenstein, a well known golf writer, once came to the Ocean Palm Golf Club in Florida to interview Moe. We went out on the course and Moe started hitting balls with a 4-wood. But because Moe was hitting in the direction of the sun, Lorne asked him to hit the other way so that they might get better photos. So Moe turned around to face the 9th fairway. There were two women playing the hole, walking down the middle of the fairway 10 yards apart, about 200 yards away.

I said to Moe, "Hey, you better wait until they get out of the way."

Moe shrugged his shoulders. "They'll never know," he said, and addressed the ball in his idiosyncratic way and swung.

The ball went like an arrow right between the two women. They just kept walking, oblivious.

Another time Moe was playing a practice round with George Knudson in the Canadian Open. Moe never gave much credence to putting, often played without even reading the greens, and so offered to George they simply play pins-in-regulation for five dollars each. As in, each time your ball hits the flagstick on the regulation approach shot, you get five dollars. George laughed, said OK, sure, whatever. Moe hit the pin in regulation on each of the first three holes. George walked in before they got to the 4th tee.

I love people who come along with unusual styles and beat your brains in. As a teacher, I've always told people not to change their inherent style but rather to nurture it as an asset. People who rebuild their swing to fit the mold risk losing their natural ability.

This truth hit home for me when I once asked Moe if beginning golfers should consider copying his unusual swing.

"How can anyone copy my swing?" he laughed. "No one can be me. Everyone is copying everyone else. Don't try to be me, no one can be me."

In golf, the only swing you can ever hope to own is already yours.

~Craig Shankland

Chapter
9

Grinders

I open the driving range and I close it.

~Vijay Singh

84

Large Bucket

Regard it as just as desirable to build a chicken house as to build a cathedral.
~Frank Lloyd Wright

The man looked like a slightly less groovy Jerry Garcia. His face was as weather-beaten as a retired fishing boat captain who had eaten too much, probably drank even more and hadn't caught enough of what he was fishing for.

"A large one'll cost ya four dollars American," the man said with a smile that revealed what happens when oral hygiene dips below other priorities. All around him lay the detritus of a secondhand shop that hadn't done much business in years. The rusted parts of a vintage tractor engine stood next to the cash box. Just by the door, there was an old lamp advertising a brand of beer I had never heard of. And the clock on the wall, with golf balls in place of the 3, 6, 9 and 12, seemed frozen at twenty past nine, 1973.

But it was a driving range. Housed in a cinderblock shack that seemed the sort of place Solzhenitsyn's gulag-prisoner Ivan Denisovich might have called home for a time, the All-Star Driving Range (as the hand painted sign out front read in semi-psychedelic lettering) in North Carolina was open for business.

It was the other side of golf. In fact, it was so far from the other side of the David Leadbetter Golf Academy, the PGA Tour and Tiger Jam, some would claim it wasn't even part of the same family. No laser range finders here, no artificially arranged greens with flags in them, no high-tech ball retrieval system. Fact is, I didn't see a picker of any kind and I wasn't so sure that the old captain didn't walk the empty field on his own with a twenty-gallon bucket picking up balls by hand, dreaming of the sea. The mats on concrete slabs had not been updated since ever. They were so thin and threadbare that attempting to hit a ball off one surely would have resulted in the fracturing of most of the bones in both hands.

Just as I began to reconsider my site selection for the day's practice session, the captain appeared from the cinder gulag, urging me to find a flat plot of grass away from the mats and hit from there, not that the grounds had been mowed to fairway length, or even backyard length, for that matter.

"Move way over," the captain said. "There's rocks right under the ground there."

I felt a little embarrassed, like I was doing something wrong, as I moved past a line of people lashing balls between the weeds and rocks. But I found a spot and I hit my large bucket, and it was good. Sure, the balls barely had dimples. And sure, many hadn't merely yellowed with age but instead featured burnt discolorations like they had rusted in spots over time. And sure, the turf was only slightly more yielding than the concrete beneath the worn mats. And sure, judging distances was marred by the fact that half the yardage markers had fallen over and the other half were illegible.

Still, the experience was as worthwhile as hitting balls can be, as much a spiritual lift that a day of hard work usually rewards, like riding fences or fixing the garbage disposal or shoveling out a truckload of sand. You feel satisfied at the end because meaningful work has been done. And so I took a moment to take stock of the landscape. The balls had been scattered about, many of them hidden in clumps of grass, and while it was clear that not every shot had held its line, I congratulated myself that after the first few Tin Woodsman chops my swing slowly returned to something that almost felt like rhythm.

I don't know what to make of the hour I spent at that real-life and metaphorical rock pile, or whether I'd even want to stop there again, but I know a picture of the captain and his driving range, tucked between a Gold's Gym shopping plaza and a foreign car repair shop, won't ever leave me. I've played Augusta National, Pebble Beach and Pine Valley, and while I'm not equating those dreamy locales with hitting dimple-less, out-of-round golf balls off gravel and hardpan, because of that day I am certain that good shots at golf's cathedrals feel no different than when they're struck at one of the game's storefront chapels. At least that's what I was thinking when I got back home and noticed a nick in the sole of my favorite wedge.

I didn't replace it until I couldn't see the grooves anymore.

~Mike Stachura

85

Strangers on the Range

One fall morning when I was fourteen I was playing with my dad. I was down the fairway off to the side on a par 5, and just then, I heard his second shot veer overhead and crash into the woods. I glanced back in time to see him throw his club down the fairway as hard as he could. This was a man who raised five energetic sons, and it was the only time in our entire lives together that I ever saw him express anger. We never spoke about that incident. And I completely forgot about it, until many years later.

On a September morning not long ago I headed out to the driving range seeking, as always, a straight 3-iron shot. There were only two other guys at the range that morning, and as I walked out to the line I noticed that only one of them was hitting balls.

I set up about twenty yards down the line, did my stretches, and hit a few shots. As often happens, my first few shots were relaxed and straight. Then, as I was getting ready to hit again, the guy who hadn't been hitting balls, who was fairly young, approached. I was surprised. To me, the driving range is a solemn and sacred place, especially on a chilly morning. It's a place to go to keep the dream alive, the dream of hitting a long-iron so far and so straight that life will bring forth new bounties.

So I must have seemed a little cranky to the man who came walking up to me that morning. When he got close he said, "Excuse me, my friend down there has a terrible slice. Do you know how to get rid of a slice?"

I've been playing golf more than fifty years. When I was a teenager my father started getting me up at dawn every Sunday to get in nine holes before the crowd arrived at our public course. I never took a lesson, but during those early years I developed a swing that looks good, feels good, and is almost guaranteed to deliver a very acceptable short iron shot. But my quest for a decent long iron shot has taken me to driving ranges up and down the eastern United States. I have stood at the line almost in tears after slicing yet another 3-iron, without any idea what I was doing wrong. And the golf course is the only place I ever saw my father angry.

That's what I wanted to say to the young stranger who was breaking my driving range code. Or, "I know how your friend feels, but, hey, I got my own troubles. He really oughta see a pro." But I couldn't think of a congenial way to say that either.

So I leaned on my 3-iron, looked down at the ground and said, "Geez, could be a thousand things. It's really hard to say."

The young man responded softly, "I know, I know," like a parent to a disappointed child. A very sympathetic guy, obviously, out on a cold morning trying to help his friend with a problem. And now I suddenly felt like he was feeling sorry for me and his friend. He must have realized, now, those first few shots of mine were a fluke.

But I felt like I had to give this nice guy something, even though I knew it would be like giving a pack of chewing gum to someone who is trying to quit smoking. So, as he started to back away and head back down the line, looking a little perplexed, I said, "Tell him to slow everything down." I hadn't even watched the guy take a complete swing, but felt I had to offer something. I took a glance over my shoulder to make sure no one could have overheard me. Sure enough, we were still the only three people out there.

"Sounds good to me," the sympathetic friend said, and turned and kept walking. His response indicated he probably understood the value of the advice he had just been given. Like at the office, when somebody says, "This is a bunch of crap. Let's all go to Hawaii for a month." And you say, "Sounds good to me." I went back to my 3-iron shots, afraid to look down the line at the two people after that. I just wanted to finish my bucket and get out of there as fast as I could.

Later, I thought about my wife in the same circumstances. I'm sure she would have told that young man, "I'll be happy to come over and try to help if you like." She wouldn't be able to help much, given her 40-handicap. But, for her, the desire to be kind would transcend anything related to hitting a golf ball. Some men would have gone over and shared their 20-handicap wisdom, for a whole different set of reasons. But there is some indefinable point in the psyche where golf becomes, for some of us, more than a game. It becomes a shadow of our entire existence.

I help stranded motorists on the highway. I carry jumper cables in my car, and enjoy the opportunity to assist people with dead batteries. Although I know the world is an often hostile place, I still believe in the kindness of strangers. But I can't help feeling that if I had gone over to help that young golfer that morning I would have had to share too much of my soul with a stranger.

~Neil Haldeman

86

It Was Colder Than I Thought

Sunshine is delicious, rain is refreshing, wind braces us up,
snow is exhilarating; there is really no such thing as bad weather,
only different kinds of good weather.
~John Ruskin

A sane man doesn't expect to play golf in Wisconsin in the middle of the winter. But the particular winter in question had seen little snow, though it had been plenty cold. Without snow, outside activities are limited in Wisconsin. Cabin fever had set in, and bad. So one Sunday, when the mercury in my porch thermometer inched just above freezing, I decided it was golf weather. I put on several layers of clothing, got my clubs out of the basement, told my wife and three children I'd be back in a few hours.

I decided to play the back nine first since it was more sheltered from the whipping winds. The greens were staked to keep off cross-country skiers, but the tees were open. The ground was frozen but I did manage to force the tip of a tee into the ground.

Number 10 is a par 4. The tee is elevated above a creek that feeds into a small lake hidden from view by fir trees.

After a few warm-up swings I whacked the ball pretty well, considering both my lack of recent practice and blood circulation. The low liner easily cleared the creek but was heading for a sand trap on the right side of the fairway. The ball didn't even slow down when it hit the trap. It bounced hard and high off the nearly petrified sand and down the fairway, finally skating to a halt just short of the green.

After getting that much roll, I remember thinking, this was going to be fun. As I crossed over the creek bridge, I glanced over at the lake to my right. It was frozen solid. Out in the middle were three guys in orange overalls, ice fishing. One of them saw me at the same time I saw him. For that moment, we just stared at each other. Simultaneously we smiled, doffed our woolen caps at one another. I stepped off the bridge onto the fairway and headed towards the green. He returned his attention to his hole in the ice, and I mine. I imagine he was as hopeful as I was.

It was colder than I thought.

~Y. John Lee

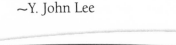

Chip and Putt

On a crisp day in January 2003, a bright and energetic sixteen-year-old boy named Kevin played a cold round of golf in Oregon. He arrived home shivering and starving, yet proud of his score. While his mother cooked him dinner, Kevin warmed up in the Jacuzzi. There, he suffered a grand mal seizure and died. He had no prior seizure history or signs leading up to his shocking death. My son, Dusty, was fifteen at the time and Kevin was his best friend. They'd been two peas in a pod since age five, counting the days until they could be on the high school golf team together. They never realized their dream. We are still in disbelief and heartache over the loss of Kevin, as he was an amazing young man who loved the game.

In preparing for Kevin's funeral, we discovered a short essay he wrote at age fourteen entitled "Chip and Putt." His insightful (and true) essay makes us chuckle every time we read it.

•••

Chip and putt, chip and putt, that's all I ever stinkin' do, chip and putt. I wish just one time I could go out like my friends and actually play on the golf course. Sure, I get to go on the course every once in a while when I save enough money or the pro lets me play for free. But it's nothing compared to how many times my friends play in a week. I usually never set foot off the dumb putting green.

My dad says, "Kevin, if you can chip and putt, then you will be better than all your friends."

I don't understand that because I only chip and putt, while my friends get to do everything. The one reason I sort of believe my dad is because he played four years of varsity golf in high school. But still, I don't think what he says is all true.

Well, after about a century of practice, Larry, the pro at the McNary Course, finally let me play. He probably thought I was getting sick of the practice green. He was right about that!

It was once in a blue moon for me, but sure enough, my friends happened to be playing that day too. So we all golfed together. And guess what, I smoked them all! After the round was done, I ran home and told my dad that I did great because of my chipping and putting. He just smiled.

So now I listen to him about everything in life... everything except girls.

~Kevin Butler and Tamara Bowers

88

Why Do We Dream?

The future belongs to those who believe in the beauty of their dream.
~Eleanor Roosevelt

Some say our nightly escapes are extensions of reality. Others say our dreams are predictors of the future, as the Biblical Joseph was adept at interpreting.

Both views have merit, but one must take into account whether the dream in question is unconscious or conscious, nocturnal or day. When a rookie makes his debut at The Masters, for instance, he's usually quoted at some point as saying, "It's always been a dream of mine to play The Masters." This falls under the latter, daydream category, a goal we hope to achieve through some extraordinary effort often yet to be shown. It's the same as when we "dream of Jeannie with the light brown hair." We desire a relationship with the girl of our dreams, although we feel inadequate in our crooning.

I, however, am for the moment more interested in the dreams we have when we shut our eyes, the ones fantastical and outrageous in scope. Particularly, what am I to make of this recurring golf dream I've had a few times over the years? It goes like this:

I'm playing The Masters, but there's nothing specific about the people around me. I don't know who my fellow competitor is. There is the usual big crowd around the first tee, the course is in Masters magnificent shape, and I'm called to tee off. "Fore, please, Cliff Schrock now driving." I bend over to tee the ball, step back and address it, but before I can take the club back, the ball falls off the tee.

I calmly bend over, re-tee, and set-up once more, but the ball falls off again. The dream continues with this comedy routine (although I never get razzed by the gallery). I never do tee off, never get to hit a shot, and the dream fades away to no conclusion.

I've developed a few theories about what the dream means, approaching it from the angle that this is an interpretive dream about my life.

Theory No. 1: I'm a success at golf. Even though I don't strike a shot at the Masters, the fact that I'm on that grand stage indicates I've shown some golfing prowess and have a legacy to be proud of.

Theory No. 2: I'm a failure at golf. The Masters background is just a tease. It symbolizes what I've hoped to achieve as a golfer, but because I don't step off the first tee, it indicates I'm just a pretender, a 12-handicap wannabe who can't play with the big boys. I'm not even allowed on the course with them.

Theory No. 3: It's a windy day at Augusta and it's just my bad luck that I got such a lousy day to play one of the world's most magnificent courses. But because everyone else is playing in the same conditions, I'm on equal footing with the field. The dream shows how the breaks usually level out in golf.

Theory No. 4: An amalgam of the above. The dream illustrates that I love to play the game, that I would have liked to have played at the highest level. As some consolation, it shows I have a natural competitiveness because I keep on re-teeing the darn ball. I'm determined to make a go of it despite all the circumstances against me. The fact that no one else stands out in the dream reflects the solitary nature of golf and how we only get out of it what we put into it. As a golfer who has played for more than thirty-five years, I find my passion hasn't abated, but my patience has worn thin. I feel time is running out to achieve a repeatable, dependable swing.

Some may find this peculiar, though other die-hards may wish they had had such maniacal foresight. I have kept track of every under-par hole I've ever made. I have had a double eagle, two eagles and 493 birdies at eighty-two courses. When No. 500 comes I expect it to be quite memorable. I have logged all my rounds played since 1984, from my old home muni of Highland Park in Bloomington, Illinois, to Winged Foot, Pine Valley and the Old Course. I've tracked fairways and greens hit, as well as number of putts. I look back at these rounds and read all the pithy comments I made about them. "Worst performance since moving to Connecticut," I wrote of a 97 in 1987. "Give it up," I noted after a round in 1990.

But I've been more complimentary lately, and have learned to be kinder to myself—being my "own best friend" as Bob Rotella would say—praising either my "eight one-putts" or my "parring of the last six holes."

I like Theory No. 4 because I think it speaks to all golfers who have a passion to play the game, yet lack the talent and wherewithal to be anything better than a regular Joe. Once the game has sunk its teeth in us, we have no choice but to stay strong mentally, keep striving to improve, and take the highs and lows with equal amounts of dignity.

And in the end, there's nothing wrong—or better—than dreaming of great things to come.

~Cliff Schrock

Reprinted by permission of Off the Mark
and Mark Parisi ©2006

89

Chicken Soup for the Soul

A Costly Free Lesson

Being left-handed is a big advantage.
No one knows enough about your swing to mess you up with advice.
~Bob Charles

Traveling through the Midwest one night, I came across a lighted driving range. In need of some recreation before I retired, I decided to stop and hit a large bucket of balls.

After purchasing the balls I grabbed my clubs and went to the nearest open tee. Halfway through the bucket an elderly gentleman approached, said he had been watching me struggle with my swing. He introduced himself and said he was the former owner of the driving range and a retired golf pro, and asked if I were interested in a free lesson. I accepted. He told me to grab what was left of the bucket and follow him down to the end of the range where we could have more privacy.

He brought with him a large pile of old clubs. He told me my problem was that I held the club too tightly, and the cure was to take the club and release it down the line. He picked up one of the old clubs he had brought, made a golf swing and threw the club 40 yards down the range. He said if I could learn to do this too, it would cure a lot of the flaws in my swing.

Alive with new hope, I grabbed an old club and tried to throw it as he had demonstrated. On my very first attempt, I held on too long and released too late. I watched in horror as it sailed over my left shoulder like an Olympic javelin. Situated behind me was a big picture window that was part of a grillroom attached to the driving range pro shop.

The club went through the window and hit the soda dispenser.

Patrons in the restaurant dove for cover under tables as glass fell and soda sprayed everywhere.

The proprietor of the restaurant came out yelling and screaming. I managed to calm him down after I told him I would cover all of the damages.

I then looked to the golf pro for some help in explaining how this all transpired. All he said was, "I told you that you were holding on too tight." Then he turned and walked away.

~Thomas Ashcraft

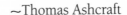

Walking On

Eighty percent of success is showing up.
~Woody Allen

As I sat at the breakfast table, my friend's mother served me a soft-boiled egg and the harsh reality, as she saw it, of my hair-brained plan.

"Ye think ye're goin' to walk on at the Old Course?" she said. "Ye might as well think ye're goin' to climb Everest without a sherpa and then surf down nude."

"Well, I might just do that," I replied. "But *after* today's round. At the Old Course."

I was just ten miles from paradise, in Kilconquhar, a quaint agricultural village where time seemed to stand still and the pub was barely standing. But in the eyes of my Scottish friend's mother, I was three billion miles away. On Pluto.

Her negativity didn't faze me. She had no idea what I had been through. No idea that I had been driving for three days in a Geo Metro, which was nothing more than a lawnmower with a windshield, and worse yet, a cracked engine block that had forced it to stall in fast-moving European traffic and nearly gotten me mangled. All she knew was that I had arrived on her doorstep the night before, soaking wet after navigating eighteen holes at Gleneagles in a downpour with another equally desperate American.

I hadn't come this far to be shooed away by some bitter starter. I'd be playing the Old Course at St. Andrews tomorrow, even if I had to create my own opening by following somebody from the starter's shack to the putting green and delivering a forceful whack to their kneecap.

When I arrived at the Old Course, I headed straight for the starter's shack. As I walked closer, the aura just seemed to overcome me. I stopped dead in my tracks. Something was tugging at me to savor this moment. I didn't feel the ghost of Old Tom Morris, but I did hear the voice of Jack Nicklaus, who said, "I fell in love with it the first day I played it. There's just no other golf course that is even remotely close."

I approached the starter, put my clubs down gently, smiled and did my best to avoid emanating The Ugly American vibe.

"Do you have any openings today?" I asked.

"Aye, ye're on the first tee," he said.

"What?"

"Join that twosome. Ye'll be goin' off at 10:20."

I looked at my watch: 10:17. I didn't ask what monumental change in plans had opened up this spot, nor did I moan that I had no time to arrange for a caddie or test the practice green.

My Scottish friend's mother's ominous forecast hadn't materialized. Neither had the weatherman's. He had forecasted rain, with perhaps a stiff wind driving those drops into my face like razor blades. Instead, it was sixty degrees with only a light breeze, and even patches of blue sky.

I joined Al and Patricia, a congenial couple from Chicago who had no idea what had happened to the rest of the group. After they teed off, I launched a pop fly that settled into the middle of the fairway 210 yards away.

As I turned to grab my bag, I saw a man frantically running toward us. He didn't look like a golfer. He wore a dress shirt over a turtleneck, khakis and Docksiders. But I couldn't help but hear the clacking sticks that were getting a wild ride along his hip as he raced toward us. It appeared that I wasn't the only lucky chap.

"I'm Paul," he said, shaking hands with us.

I launched a 6-iron 160 yards over the Swilcan Burn, then three-putted from sixty feet. Not exactly the start I had envisioned, but I hadn't killed anybody or lost a ball. I could feel the nervous tension dissipating.

On the second hole, the caddies, Colin and Alister, made it clear that they weren't going to confine their advice to whispers in the ears of Al and Patricia. They graciously guided Paul and me through the minefield of fiendishly hidden pot bunkers and massive patches of spiky gorse bushes. I had no idea how badly I would need their advice.

After bogeying the second hole, I went on a run of 3 pars. At the 6th tee, Colin eyed me and exclaimed, "Jehsus, didya par again?"

It would be the last par I'd get until the 12th. But instead of being demoralized, by then I was ready to bow at the feet of Colin and Alister. They had found at least three wayward balls that I had no clue about, saving me strokes and anguish.

However, at the 17th, The Road Hole, Colin and Alister were not able to rescue me from lost-ball oblivion and I staggered in with an eight. I checked my scorecard. I needed to par the 18th for an 89.

I ripped a majestic drive that bounced over Granny Clarks Wynd, leaving me just 120 to the flagstick, which was tucked into the right side of the dramatically tilted green. My 9-iron left me with a frightful 50-foot left-to-right putt for birdie. As I surveyed the path, I noticed that the fence bordering the green was lined with about fifty people. Some of them were just milling around, but many actually seemed interested in our play.

My heart pounding, I followed through and watched the ball trace a long arc and skirt the edge of the cup. After I tapped in, a raucous cheer erupted. I looked up to see a half-a-dozen young punks, who looked like they got lost on their way to hooliganize a soccer match, thrusting their fists in the air.

After the last putt of our foursome dropped and the pictures had been taken, I stood behind the green, trying to process everything. I futilely tried to remember every shot. How had four hours and twenty minutes passed so quickly?

Then I looked at my watch. 2:40 P.M. Still plenty of daylight. I thought, and impulsively grabbed my bag and headed toward the starter's shack. But Colin intercepted me.

"Savor the moment," Colin said. The best advice he'd given all day.

~Richard Weber

Embracing Mediocrity

I have always had a drive that pushed me to try for perfection,
and golf is a game in which perfection stays just out of reach.
~Betsy Rawls

It was the fall of 1985 when I decided to retire and move to Vermont. I was only forty-four years old, but I had done well in business and decided that I would devote myself to the pursuit of my passions. Golf, however, was not one of them. I was an avid skier, I had competed at the highest level in clay target shooting and I was also a die-hard tennis player. Shortly into retirement I took some jobs. I became a teacher at a local ski academy and a coach at a nationally renowned shooting school. I played tennis every day at my local club.

Upon turning fifty, I must have become afflicted by that "male menopause" thing I had read about. Noticing I was a step or two slower getting to a tennis ball, I decided to embark on a change of sports. I decided to take up golf. Unlike sports I had done since childhood, however, I vowed to be smart about this undertaking. Having spent the last couple of years in two intensive teaching facilities for sports, skiing and shooting, I had a plan of attack. I would hire the best teaching pro I could find, spend an intensive week totally immersed in instruction with him, and at the end of the week I would have it down.

One slight concern bothered me: did I have any aptitude for the game? I had been told it was going to be a long, hard road, and I didn't want to be a dyslexic trying to win a spelling bee. The Austrians, who rule the sport of skiing, have a cruel, but efficient, system in their state-run ski academy. They put little Hans through a series of physical tests at the age of seven or eight, and see how he compares to Franz Klammer at that age (for you non ski-buffs, Klammer was the dominant Austrian downhill-racer who won the 1976 Olympic Gold). As you can imagine, there's a pretty high rejection rate at that school. I wondered if they had a series of tests to predict if I could ever be a decent golfer.

At the end of my week, I was clueless. Looking back, I had done all the right things. Grip, posture, setup, alignment, pre-shot routine, one-piece takeaway, I had been taught all the fundamentals one needs to know. The problem is the golf gods just didn't think much of my efforts. All week long, I couldn't help thinking about little Hans in Austria, jumping between blocks and barriers only to be told that he would be better off taking up sailing or bowling.

I made a decision: It was silly to start this new venture considering how pathetic I was after a full week of lessons. It was probably better to try to adjust to being awful at tennis, I reasoned. I went to see my pro and gave him the bad news. "Thanks for the week, I really enjoyed it, but I'm quitting golf and changing my name to Hans," I told him.

Instead of wishing me well and sending me up the road, he said, "What skills do you think you lack, and what skills do you think are necessary for this sport?" I replied with the obvious. "Superior eye-hand coordination, flexibility, strength."

"How much value do you place on desire, determination, patience, those kinds of qualities?"

"None," I answered, as I had never really considered them at all. I figured one puts the ball down, holds the club correctly, lines up to the target, and swings away. What does that have to do with any of those other things? Not a hand-holder by nature, the pro shrugged his shoulders and left me to my decision.

Here I was, at a crossroad, unhappy with my tennis, and golf probably not an option. A voice, however, intruded into my thoughts. Sailing and bowling didn't appeal to me, and I happened to belong to a club with a fabulous golf course. Could I learn to accept playing a game where breaking 100 would be a life's quest? I consulted an old friend, a superior athlete who had started golf at just about the same time. He was as bad as I was, which perplexed me, as I had always envied his athleticism. But he was not about to quit, and berated me for even thinking about it. Another old friend, not a very good athlete, but a pretty fair golfer, offered the same encouragements. A third close friend, with probably the best eye-hand coordination of anyone I knew, begged me to reconsider. I began to see a common thread.

I found new resolve. I started going to the range every day. I took more lessons. I snuck out in the evenings and played nine holes. I kept reminding myself that I was undertaking a daunting task, one that, given my age and skill level, might prove impossible. Where should I set the bar? Too high and I would never find happiness. Too low and I would dismiss every achievement with the disdain of having just done something ordinary. In the end, I set the goal of becoming an "average" golfer.

How do you define an "average" golfer? The USGA, through the GHIN system, identifies the average male handicap at something a tad under 15, so that seemed like a good number. I would get a handicap and work towards that goal. And so the process began. As it did, however, something totally unforeseen began to take place.

Once I committed myself to the game, I began to really enjoy it. It was like setting out on a trip, a specific destination in mind, but finding that you enjoyed the scenery so much that the destination lost its importance. I realized the process of learning something new, with failures followed by triumphs, was a part of the game. Harkening back to my teaching pro's words, I realize now what he meant to say: I was failing to understand the depths of the adventure that lay before me.

At some point I passed the goal I originally set many years ago. To tell the truth, I never really noticed when it happened. It had ceased to be anything but a hazy memory. So where do I set the bar now? I just nudge it a little higher than where it happens to be.

~Chris Hagen

The Golf Book

Raconteurs

It isn't the big pleasures that count the most;
it's making a great deal out of the little ones.

~Jean Webster

Tomcat the Caddy

I drew a big gallery today. I was paired with Arnold Palmer.
~Gene Littler

Ever since I bought Bay Hill we've played a lot of scrappy shoot-outs in the afternoons. In the beginning days of this tradition there was a caddie nicknamed Tomcat who always used to make sure he got on my bag. Tomcat was one of those guys who seemed to have a line for every situation.

One such afternoon we came to the 17th hole and there were still quite a few pennies on the line with all the side bets. The 17th hole at Bay Hill is a 219-yard par 3 over water. As we walked up to the tee, I looked at Tomcat and said, "What do you think?"

"3-iron Mr. Palmer," Tomcat said.

"Whoa," I said. "I don't think I can get a 3-iron down there."

"Oh yes you can," Tomcat said. "You just hit that 3-iron."

So I hit the 3-iron. The ball grew small in the air as it sailed, and then I saw a big splash in the lake just short of the green.

"Dang it," I said, pretty agitated. "Give me that 2-iron." I then advised my playing partners I would play my third shot right there from the tee rather than going up ahead to drop. They all said sure, fine.

So I hit the 2-iron. It lands five feet short of the flag, hops once and rolls forward and goes in the cup. Par.

I turned to Tomcat and said, "I told you that 3-iron wasn't enough. 2-iron was the club."

Tomcat shook his head. He looked right back at me and said, "No sir, Mr. Palmer. You hit that fat."

~Arnold Palmer
as seen in the DVD *Chicken Soup Conversations for the Golfer's Soul*

93

Best Show in Sports

*Life is not dated merely by years.
Events are sometimes the best calendar.*
~Benjamin Disraeli

I had been playing golf for nearly three years, playing it decently for a city kid on scruffy city courses, but not that well and not that often. To me, pro tournament golf was something else entirely. In those years before network television, pro tournament golf was something I only read about in newspapers or saw in newsreels in the Loews Bay Ridge Theater in Brooklyn, not far from where the Verrazano-Narrows Bridge would be built a decade later. Sam Snead, Ben Hogan and Jimmy Demaret usually were the pros in those newsreels—a quick tee shot, a quick putt and a voice-over saluting the winner of the Masters or the U.S. Open. Those newsreels made it feel as if the big names of golf were on another planet.

But a day or two after Ben Hogan won the 1950 U.S. Open, having limped around Merion on legs battered in his Cadillac's 1949 head-on collision with a Greyhound bus on a foggy Texas highway, I read that he was about to play in the Palm Beach Round Robin at the Wykagyl Country Club in New Rochelle, a suburb of New York City.

I remember thinking, "I've got to see this."

The tournament was named for the Palm Beach clothing company, not for the posh Florida playground of the rich and famous. But in its time, the Palm Beach Round Robin was a big tournament, the only stop on the PGA Tour in the New York area except for the rare arrival of the Open or the PGA Championship. And now Ben Hogan, who had just won the Open, would be playing in a first-round foursome with Sam Snead, Jimmy Demaret and Jack Burke, Jr.

I had just finished my junior year at Holy Cross College. For nearly a decade I had been sitting in the centerfield bleachers at Ebbets Field to see Dodger baseball games, and in the balcony at Madison Square Garden to see Knicks and college basketball, Rangers hockey and AAU track meets. Going to sports events was something I would do (with a typewriter or a laptop) for the rest of my life. Now with Hogan in town, it was time for me to attend my first pro golf tournament.

Not that it was around the corner. I lived in Brooklyn. I had to get up at 5:30 A.M., walk four blocks to the subway, take the Fourth Avenue local to 59th Street, ride the Sea Beach Express all the way to Times Square, take the shuttle to Grand Central Terminal, board a commuter train to New Rochelle in Westchester County, then hop on a bus up North Avenue to Wykagyl. The trip took more than two hours, but it was worth it.

As I remember, it was cloudy that morning as Hogan, Snead, Demaret and Burke hit balls on the practice tee, then stroked a few putts on the practice green outside the pro shop. As famous as those four golfers were then, over their careers they would become even more revered, winning a total of twenty-two majors (Hogan ten, Snead seven, Demaret three, Burke two). And here they were in the same foursome, up close and personal. There were no fairway ropes then, only half-moon ropes around the backs of the tees and the backs of the greens. You could walk along the fairways with the four golfers and their caddies if you wished. And that morning there weren't more than one hundred spectators following that foursome. On the par-5 6th hole I clearly remember standing only a few yards from Hogan as he drilled a 3-wood toward the elevated green. On the par-5 10th hole I remember Snead, after a big drive, smoothly smashing a 3-wood up the hill toward another elevated green. I remember

Demaret's lime slacks and his wristy pitch shots. I remember Burke's boyish good looks and his velvety putting stroke.

I don't remember exactly what they shot (after all, fifty-eight years have transpired) but I know Hogan was over par, 73 or 74. But he was excused. Mentally, he was not grinding the way he had at Merion. Just seeing him was enough, seeing that tanned serious face and that tight controlled swing. And after the round, he autographed my $5 admission ticket.

On my way home, I realized that being a spectator at a pro golf tournament was better than at any other sports event. You were next to the golfers along the fairway and around the tees and greens. You could see them smile or frown, sometimes hear them talk. At other Palm Beach Round Robins and other tournaments, I remember Lloyd Mangrum addressing other golfers as "pro." And for more than half a century, I went to pro golf tournaments, usually as a sportswriter but occasionally as just a spectator. You seldom can get as close to the golfers now, but for a spectator, a pro golf tournament will always be the best show in sports.

~Dave Anderson

94

Kilspindie

I've had a wonderful evening—but this wasn't it.
~Groucho Marx

Keeping your opinion of a golf course staunchly separate from how well you happened to be swinging the day you played it is a tall order for even the most self-honest individual. In microcosm, the holes you birdie you tend to remember fondly, while the holes you quadruple-bogey tend to roil in your gut as ill-conceived scars of turf. This isn't always the case, but to not trend this way in your perceptions is almost cold-blooded. Golfers are emotional people.

It is safe to say that Kilspindie, a 5,500 yard par-69 in Aberlady, Scotland, will never make The Open rotation. However, it has fine views of Gosford Bay, a charming membership and a history that dates back to 1867. And if you've read this far you can probably guess why it's being discussed: when I played it I shot the lowest round of my life, at the time.

The eight of us were not even halfway through our biennial two-week golf trip to Scotland. It was unusually warm for September, and we were all feeling slightly out of place wearing short pants. On what was to be my big day, we played and were punished by North Berwick in the morning. We were then refortified with a pint and a quick lunch at a local pub before heading to Kilspindie for the afternoon.

With the group's average handicap hovering around ten, we were looking forward to a respite. As with all good links courses, most of Kilspindie's holes are very exposed, so weather plays a significant role. But on this day there were only occasional puffs of wind, followed by periods of complete calm. Without sunscreen, we would have burnt to a crisp.

The opening hole is a par 3, quite rare, and equal in this rareness was the groove that magically appeared in my game. All of a sudden there was time at the top of my backswing, and I experienced strong premonitions of where the ball was going before I would even swing down. If a putt needed to drop, it did. If a troubled tee shot required a miracle recovery, the golf gods came through for me. The entire three-hour experience was delight, followed by joy, with happiness always right around the corner. An up and down par on the last hole completed my pinnacle round. I won the afternoon prize pool from my fellow travelers by ten strokes.

I was a 12-handicap then. I shot 69.

My winnings were quickly depleted at the club bar afterward. I am not sure if it was the whiskey, the lager, or the accomplishment, but it seemed like I was hovering six feet off the ground. I would float in and out of other people's conversations as I smugly reflected on the accomplishment. If I had the time and money, I would have sent telegrams to every person I had ever played the game with. I literally could not stop smiling.

We headed out for dinner in Gullane that evening, and the partying continued. To cap off the evening, we found a suitable pub to go soak up some more Scottish congeniality.

A bearded, craggy old gent, sporting a tweed jacket and "smoking" a well-worn, unlit pipe, stood at the bar nursing a single malt. My friend Dale struck up a conversation with him, and the topic quickly turned to golf, and then to my exploit.

"See that guy over there?" said Dale. "He carded a 69 today."

"Did he now," the gent responded. He looked at me and said, "I am a wee bit of a golfer myself and I know what a fine round that is. I've never even been close to a 69. Where did you play?"

Truth be told, I really tried hard to keep my chest from puffing out too far as I replied. This was the first time this record-breaking news was leaving our group and I wanted to maintain certain decorum. The last thing I wanted was to come across as a bigheaded, arrogant "ugly American."

"A fine local links course, sir. Kilspindie, just over in Aberlady," I said.

I steadied myself, awaiting the gushing response, prepared to do my best to put on an air of bogus modesty over the event. But then I watched the old gent's face begin to distort. He looked me over crossly. Then he said words that are still with me fifteen years later.

"Kilspindie! Why that is a mere pitch 'n putt."

The first stranger given the chance to pay homage to me didn't buy me a drink. No slap on the back. He didn't even offer me his hand to shake. He turned my magnificent milestone into an ignominious incident in seconds. I was shattered.

I walked back to the hotel alone that night, contemplating the meaning of it all, wondering if I shouldn't take up a new hobby. I was convinced that golf could never again hold the same allure for me. It was over. If I were less of a man, I would have cried myself to sleep in a hotel bed, far from home and forever disillusioned.

Though prone to emotional swings, we golfers are a hardy lot. In the morning, a hangover successfully deterred my mind from the night's sour thoughts. There was lots of golf ahead, and if the sport guarantees one thing, it's healthy doses of positive (deluded) anticipation. We were headed to Carnoustie. From there we would play Cruden Bay, Royal Aberdeen, Nairn and then on to Royal Dornoch to finish. When we arrived in Dornoch, we were six hours away from Kilspindie and what seemed like light years from that horrible evening.

The bar at our hotel in Dornoch was very small. On that last night, Dale and I closed it. Near the end, as the bartender was drying the last few glasses, he asked if we were on a golf expedition. When we told him we were, he perked up a bit and inquired which links had provided our best golf experience so far.

"Muirfield was my favorite," Dale replied. "The course is terrific and the entire experience of playing a four-ball in the morning, having lunch, and then playing alternate shot in the afternoon is unique for us Americans. Muirfield it is."

I hesitated, looking like I was musing on my answer. In truth I was simply summoning the courage to repeat my story of Kilspindie.

We were hundreds of miles from the place, I thought to myself. And the course isn't exactly a household name. I did shoot a 69 there. This guy is only trying to keep the conversation going to be friendly. What the heck, I would be bold.

"I was fortunate to shoot 69 this week so that has to be my best experience," I said. "I was hitting it great. Everything went well. Putts dropped. All in all, a perfect golf occasion."

"Congratulations," he said as he poured us each our final single malt. "On the house," he added.

"And as we lift our glass in tribute, may I ask the venue of this great achievement?"

"Kilspindie," I replied. "In Aberlady."

Just as the glass was about to touch the bartender's lips, his eyes grew large and his brow wrinkled. He set down his glass, looked me straight in the eye and said, "Ach... Kilspindie! That's a dog track!"

I have never recovered.

● ● ●

(With apologies to the lovely members of Kilspindie.)

~Brian Clark

Reprinted by permission of Off the Mark
and Mark Parisi ©2001

Chicken Soup for the Soul

The Guy Who'd Play With Anyone

Blessed is he who has learned how to laugh at himself,
for he shall never cease to be entertained.
~John Bowell

Greg really loves golf. Any time. Anywhere. And as I recently learned, with anyone.

I met Greg about a year ago through my affiliation with the members' Men's Group at True Blue Golf Plantation in Pawleys Island, South Carolina. I felt like I had come to know him at least superficially well, and that we were on good, friendly terms. Affable and a competent player, I thought Greg might be a good addition to our regular Saturday foursome when one of us couldn't make it.

That occasion recently arose when one of my usual group begged off for the next day. Not wanting to play as a threesome behind a flock of foursomes on the seasonally crowded course, I called Greg.

"Hi, Greg. This is George Palmer."

"Uh, yeah. Hi."

I had always considered Greg to be on the gregarious side (no pun intended) and his laconic response to my greeting threw me off my rhythm.

Following an uncomfortable pause I tried again. "Well, uh, Greg. Um, I have a tee time tomorrow at Caledonia and wanted to know if you wanted to join me."

"Going to be kind of wet," Greg mused. It had rained the day before.

"Well, yeah, but it'll be playable."

"Yeah, yeah. I guess it will," Greg replied. I was growing uncomfortably confused. What was wrong with the guy?

There was another awkward silence until finally Greg said with a little more enthusiasm, "Yeah, OK. I think I will. What time?"

Despite the strangeness of our conversation, I was relieved to have found a fourth, and told him 8:15 A.M.

"OK, see you there," said Greg. He hesitated for just a second, and then, before I could hang up or say anything more, he went on. "Listen, I'm sorry. My hearing isn't what it used to be. Would you mind telling me who this is?"

I laughed long and hard at this, then identified myself again. "Damn, man, I was wondering what was wrong with you. I could have been a serial killer. What were you going to do?"

"Well," Greg said, "I was just going to show up. I figured whoever started talking to me was who I was playing with. Then I realized that might not work."

I laughed some more. Suddenly an embarrassing thought struck me. I hesitated, and then asked. "Um, well, you still want to play?"

We all enjoyed a fun round the next day, and now I know just how much Greg loves golf. He'll play with anyone. Even me.

~George Palmer

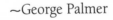

96

Golf and Love

*A pretty girl will always have the toughest time learning to play golf,
because every man wants to give her lessons.*

~Harvey Penick

Golf came into my life in pieces. My earliest direct experience was as the beverage cart girl for the chamber of commerce outing when I was in high school. Watching the small-town bigwigs play and drink and goof around, I marveled at the way golf seemed more of a club than a sport.

In college, I played for the first time with my then boyfriend, a generally impatient and anger prone person. As a lifelong non-athlete (despite several childhood stints in soccer, softball and basketball, all urged by my parents and all ending in disaster) it didn't come as a surprise to me that I was unable to translate what I watched him do into the actual moves my own body should perform. This boyfriend was unable to recognize my lack of natural coordination, and kept telling me to simply "do what I do!"

I would dutifully respond with my best impression of his swing, but only to either completely miss the ball or send it a disappointing few yards. This went on for seventeen holes, each successively more nightmarish for us both.

As I teed up on the last hole, he looked at me and said, "Why aren't you bending your knees?" I retorted that he'd never told me I needed to do that. So I tried it. And who knew, on that attempt I made marvelous contact with the ball, the kind that sparks an instant thrill as well as the intense desire to do it again. Instead of a fifteen, I scored an eight on that hole. While I wished I'd known about the knee thing all along, for a long time thereafter I associated golf with this miserable day and the guy who eventually became a constant source of misery. I wrote off the game completely.

After college, my only contact with the greatest game would come as appearances as drink-fetcher at work golf outings. Working in the financial services industry, I was surrounded by golfers all the time and it continued to strike me that playing made you part of a special clan. But a decade passed without my trying to play again.

Then, a later boyfriend turned out to be a golfer, though (as was his fashion) a bit of an outlaw about it. I lived on a lake, and he taught me to play on the seldom-used Frisbee golf course in the sandy state park that butted up against my backyard. We used the Frisbee goal posts as our flagsticks, and about 80% of the shots had to be hit from scrubby sand. I'm still amazed I stuck it out and was able to learn from this short-tempered, ill-mannered guy, but I did, eventually working up to nine holes at the local courses where he'd use his father's respected status in the local golf hierarchy to secure discounts.

For two seasons I played the game his way (on the make), improving slowly. Then, when I broke up with him, he took back the clubs he'd been letting me use. I decided that I'd only liked golf because it gave me something in common with him (there was little else) and not enough to purchase my own equipment.

The next season passed without my playing at all.

But the next winter I met my current boyfriend. About February, he started talking of the coming season and I mentioned I knew how to play a little. Aware of my general lack of athleticism, he was skeptical. When he went to play that spring, I asked to go along. Though apprehensive, he graciously invited me to join him and his friend. They were as surprised as I that with rented clubs and two years since my last round, I held my own and wasn't totally ridiculous.

For a while, I used his old clubs and we played together often. I really enjoyed learning from and playing with him. At last I'd found a great golf partner, someone who made me want to grow my game. Someone whose company on the course made me look forward to getting out there.

I bought my own clubs. My experiences had shown me that I liked golf, that it wasn't merely a fondness tied to any romantic interest but something I genuinely loved doing. For the future, I didn't want my ability to play the game to be subject to the ebb and flow of my love life.

I also realized that the best thing about golf, for me, is that when someone asks, "What sport do you play?" I can give an enthusiastic response for the first time in my life. Those who've always been athletic may not have noticed this, but sports are really a social expectation. The question is almost never phrased as "do you play any sports?" but rather, "which one(s)?" When you can't even name one, it creates unease in the person asking as well as the one responding. Now I can say, "I'm a golfer!" I'm finally a part of that distinct, elusive group I've recognized from outside all these years. When people are talking about the game, I know their pain and their joy and their dedication to improvement. I know the itchy feeling we members of the worldwide club of golfers get on a lovely day when the course calls.

Oh, and my golf companion? He's still inspiring me to grow in my game (as well as in my life). And his company, both on the course and off, makes me look forward to each day.

~Emily H. Allyn

97

The 670-Yard Ace

"Impossible" only describes the degree of difficulty.
~David Phillips

The 10th tee-box is where we stand. A cool spring morning in Forth Worth, and getting distance out of my high compression golf ball seems about as useless as trying to get sympathy from my ex-wife. The hole is a 340-yard par 4, with a 200-yard mandated carry over a large pond. Most players try to play a draw off the left edge of the large tree on the right side of the fairway, a shot which when properly executed, leaves a short approach into a green protected by a couple of large, ball-eating bunkers.

Since I have learned to play a draw with some kind of consistency (OK, it's more like a controlled hook than a soft draw, but I digress), I take out my driver to challenge this 340-yard par 4 with the determination of a battle-scarred warrior.

Strangely, as I draw back my club, well past parallel like always, I have a premonition. And on the swing down, everything feels oddly in sync. The planets are aligned, the sky has never seemed bluer, and my body actually completes this course of action without its usual flash episode of back pain.

As my club passes through the ball, I know this is a drive for the ages. The ball leaves the tee-box like a rocket ship headed for orbit. What's more, it never takes the draw (controlled hook) to which I've grown so accustomed. Instead, it traces high over the aforementioned large tree on the right. Yes, clearly over it and not next to it, which lets me know I have hit this ball like none ever before.

With my shoulders back and my head held high, I look to my fellow golf buddies and smile like a proud papa on his child's graduation day. In a way it was a graduation day for me, too, as I feel I have now joined the likes of long knockers John Daly and Bubba Watson. I will forever be remembered as the guy who cleared the 10th hole trees.

My buddies dribble their balls down the fairway in average manners, and we head down to encounter the glory that is all mine. They all hit their second shots, and because we can't see my ball, we assume it is probably in one of the green side bunkers. None of us have ever reached these bunkers from the tee, but we have heard tales of long knockers doing such a thing.

There is not a ball in any of the bunkers. We search the right side of the fairway, still there is nothing. Maybe it hit and bounced off the fairway into the right side of the trees? Or maybe it's buried in some of the remaining thick grass around the edge of the fairway? We look and we look. One of my fellow players even checks to see if it is in the hole, which even I think is a tad optimistic, but it is not there either.

After five minutes, time is called, and I have the unfortunate duty of trudging back to that tee-box to hit another ball. It is a sad trip.

I take my lump, hit another drive, failing to rekindle the greatness of earlier. I reach the green with a 9-iron and somehow, in some altered universe sort of way, make my putt for a bogey five. As we leave the green heading for the next tee, I can't help but glance back again hoping to see my first.

I feel there is an unsung glory in the way I handle the incident, and so I will sing it now. Please let history remember how I played the hole without cursing, whining or questioning the golf gods.

So we continue to the 11th, another relatively short par 4 at 330 yards from the middle tees. I hit another decent drive, and follow with a crisp wedge into a seemingly receptive, flat area of the blind green.

As I step onto the green, one of my playing partners congratulates me on a well-struck shot with an incredulous look on his face. He removes the flagstick from the hole. He allows me the honor of coming over to pick the ball out of the hole myself.

I take it out. It's the one I originally hit off the number 10 tee-box, the very one which sailed over the tree and threatened the heavens, that very ball, with my signature three black dots, staring me in the face.

It's anyone's guess how it got there. In all likelihood, someone was behind the tree where I hit my tee shot on the 10th. Then, in searching for their ball found mine, and without looking to identify the small, white orb, played it as their own. Upon identifying the ball on the next green, they thought better of keeping it, or maybe they just didn't care for the make and model, and so left the little surprise in the cup. I don't know who was playing in front of us that day, and never got the chance to speak to them.

However it played out, and for whatever reasons there may be behind this episode, it will always be remembered as the day I hit the 670-yard ace.

~Jay Rylant

98

What's at Stake in a Casual Encounter

A kind word is like a Spring day.
~Russian Proverb

I t had been a routine day at the Marshfield Country Club. I had mowed greens first, raked traps next, then cut fairways, and finally was shaping rough. I was supposedly hard at work atop my tractor, but this task was not work at all. The splendor of the afternoon had transformed this chore into a most pleasing one.

The sun was the only tenant of the sky as it gently massaged vitality into my slender frame. A faint west wind made the tall pines tremble and the air smell clean and healthful. I found nothing quite as peaceful as mowing rough, and in an hour the week's work would be finished.

The boss chased me down in his pickup to hand me my check. Then he pointed down the par-5 4th hole to where golfers were hitting their second shots. The droll manner in which he described the threesome made me smile.

"That's Big Bill Russell way over there on the right and nearly out-of-bounds. He swings like he shoots long jump shots—lefty and lousy. The head sticking from the sand trap belongs to George Plimpton. Good thing he doesn't write like he putts or he'd never get anything published. Bob Brannum, the old-time Celtic enforcer, is the one long and down the middle. I've seen him play before so I know he's got to be wondering what he did right."

My boss explained they were playing a round before returning to Red Auerbach's annual August basketball session for high schoolers at Camp Millbrook in Marshfield, Massachusetts. Brannum was assisting Auerbach, but Russell was there for another reason. Auerbach was attempting to dissuade him from the retirement he had announced at the end of the previous campaign. Plimpton was writing an article for *Sports Illustrated* on Russell's final year and on the 1969 World Championship that went with it. My boss then climbed into his truck and headed toward the clubhouse.

I waited until he had disappeared from my sight, and then I drove the tractor to where I could watch Bill Russell finish the 4th hole. I couldn't deny that I was excited.

To me, Russell was the epitome of what an NBA ballplayer and a Celtic should have been. He was a "winner" in the word's finest connotations. Without Russell, the Boston Celtics would have never won a World Championship. In 1957, Russell's rookie year, the team earned its first; in the next twelve seasons, the Celtics and Bill Russell earned ten more.

During this time period other great Celtics had come and gone—Bob Cousy, Bill Sharman, Frank Ramsay, Tom Heinsohn, and K.C. Jones—but Russell remained and the juggernaut persisted. That spring of 1969 the Celts were mainly veterans in their twilight years and had finished a distant fourth in the division. The experts had discounted any Boston success in the playoffs.

The experts weren't the ones doing the playing; the veterans in their twilight years were. I still don't know how the Celtics did it, but they defeated the 76'ers, the Knicks, and the Lakers to win their eleventh World Championship. I had never lost faith in the Celts, of course, but this faith was more from hope and loyalty than from justification or expectation. The Celts should not have won, but they somehow brought home one more flag to roost in the rafters of Boston Garden.

I loved them.

Russ had been phenomenal. He was not the best basketball player in the league; others had better all-around ability. He was simply the most valuable. In the money games, Russell was a clutch performer. He got the big rebound, blocked the critical shot, made the key pass, or stuffed the decisive basket.

And there was Russ walking down the fairway. His ball lay about 30 yards ahead of me. He would have to walk directly by the tractor. I had to say something to him or burst. I just had to tell Bill Russell how much he and the Celtics meant to me.

As he approached, I took in his familiar 6' 10" frame. He looked a lot different wearing a crocodile instead of a shamrock. I could not mistake, however, the loose, rippling muscles; the enormous, powerful hands; and the long, casual gait. Also, there was his goatee. It was neatly clipped but grew in the same defiant angle it always had. It made him look aggressive and austere. When he would jut out his chin before a jump ball, a rebound, or a shot, the goatee was a warning to beware.

He was only ten feet away from me. I waited until he was within touching distance.

"The Championship made it a great final year, Mr. Russell," I said.

"Yeah, thanks, kid." He barely looked at me as he kept walking.

I guess I was shocked first, then hurt, and finally disappointed. I did not know how he should have reacted, but I did not expect that dismissal. I had heard that he disliked signing autographs, doing benefits, and accommodating the press, but I was not asking him to do anything but accept both my appreciation for a magnificent effort and my homage to a magnificent team.

While I sat bewildered on my tractor, George Plimpton, who had been within hearing distance, walked toward me. I had greatly enjoyed his three books to date, *Out of My League, Paper Lion*, and *Bogey Man*. Each humorously described his misadventures as an amateur in the professional realms of baseball, football, and golf, but each also presented perceptive glimpses into the mettle of the professional athlete.

Plimpton noticed the Amherst College T-shirt I had tied to the back of my tractor seat, and he said wryly, "How's my Uncle Cal been treating you these days?" Then he smiled, needlessly introduced himself. Calvin Plimpton, the president of Amherst, was his uncle. He shook hands with me, and we locked firmly. I was quickly at ease with this man.

He said, "Amherst is one of the best colleges in the world."

I responded, "That's no small compliment coming from a Harvard man."

Plimpton smiled again. He then glanced at Russell's back as Russ walked away from us and toward the green. Plimpton stepped closer to me and said conspiratorially, "Don't be put off by Bill. He really didn't mean anything by his brusqueness. He didn't treat you any differently from the way he treats everybody else outside the ropes."

Plimpton started toward the green to join Russell and Brannum, but after a few steps he turned around to face me. He smiled that knowing smile once more and said, "Bill Russell is not like we are, you know."

I returned his smile as I understood what he meant and what he was doing for me. I no longer felt shocked, hurt, or disappointed. I looked at the big figure with the putter in his hand, and then I started the tractor and resumed cutting the rough. The day remained sunny and warm, and I was left with the peacefulness of my many thoughts.

~Leigh B. MacKay

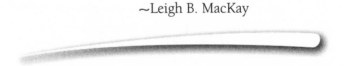

99

Chicken Soup for the Soul

The Stolen Driver

If there is any larceny in a man, golf will bring it out.
~Paul Gallico

I have a good friend named Charlie who took up the game about eight years ago. Equipment companies love guys like Charlie. Every time he's hitting the driver badly, which is pretty often, he buys a new one. At about the time it first came out Charlie bought the Callaway Big Bertha, though he couldn't hit it well either.

Shortly after he bought the Big Bertha it so happened another friend of mine, Lenny, was going on a golf trip to the Poconos. Lenny said to Charlie, "Hey Charlie, let me borrow your new driver for the trip. If I like it I will buy it from you." Charlie agreed, begrudgingly.

When Lenny returned from the Poconos, as he was unloading the luggage from the car, he had a heart attack and died instantly.

Two days later, as Charlie, our wives and I were walking into the funeral home, a few of our other golf friends were walking out. When they saw us they began to laugh. I said to them, "What the hell is so funny?" It certainly seemed inappropriate for them to be behaving in such a way at such a time. They simply replied, "You'll see."

As we walked up to view the body, I saw what was so funny. There, placed in the casket alongside suited Lenny, was Charlie's driver. Charlie said under his breath, "That's my driver." I wasn't sure if he was talking to me or just himself.

As we waited to pay our condolences to the family, I said to

Charlie, "Don't worry. They'll take it out tomorrow prior to closing the casket." When we walked outside to where our other golf buddies were gathered, they were not so reassuring and took the opportunity to razz Charlie.

The next day Charlie and I walked into the funeral home for the final viewing prior to the funeral. Many of the flowers were already removed, but there in the casket was the driver. As we took our seats, Charlie was mumbling, "Lenny's going to steal my driver." I assured him that they would remove it, but he kept saying over and over, "Lenny's going to steal my $300 driver."

After the funeral, we had one of our friends ask one of Lenny's sons about the driver. The son stated in the most reverent tone, "We buried it with my father so that he can now play in heaven."

When the son walked safely out of earshot, we all broke up laughing. All of course, except for Charlie.

To this day, when Charlie starts driving it badly, he still blames the driver and sets about scouring the marketplace for a new one. But every once in a while he'll say on the tee-box after a mis-hit, "It's Lenny's fault for stealing my Callaway driver."

~Robert A. Hedesh

100

The Mix-up at Dunbar

first visited Scotland in the early 1980s and immediately fell in love with the golf, the people and the whiskey—especially the whiskey. I have made annual trips over there ever since. While it was much more of a pure golf experience twenty years ago, before tourism made serious inroads, it is still a journey every true golfer must make.

Half the fun of playing over there is the caddies. In addition to being a bag toter, these unique individuals become your friend, psychologist, humorist and travel guide all at once.

When we first started going over we would arrange well in advance morning tee times at all the well-known courses. Then for the afternoon rounds, we'd count on caddies to tell us about other courses to play, ones that most Americans never heard of. Very often these caddies would join us for the afternoon round at some of these lesser known venues—either as caddies or as fellow players. Many of these turned out to be some of the finest tests of golf I have ever played.

One such special place is Dunbar, on the east coast, below North Berwick.

We were told it was a "wee bit" quirky. Having played Prestwick, I'd gotten used to quirky.

When we arrived at Dunbar the parking lot was empty and the

little golf shop, whose dimensions were only about twenty by thirty feet, was pretty quiet. We were warmly greeted and invited to play the golf course without delay.

I looked out the pro shop window to see a massive stone wall extending as far as my eye could see. In front of it, I counted four greens with four flagsticks. This truly had to be the ultimate in quirky. I elbowed my friend next to me to point out the limitation. I asked the young lad behind the counter about how one plays a four-hole course. He smirked. Probably not the first time some American had asked the question.

The lad explained that after you play the first three holes, you go through a hole in the wall and come upon fourteen magnificent holes right on the sea.

To this day, Dunbar still ranks as one of my favorite courses anywhere.

About five years after this initial visit to Dunbar, I arranged a tee time there with three friends who were visiting Scotland for the first time. I raved about the course, its singular beauty and the fact that it was never crowded — important as every member of the foursome loved nothing better than playing in three hours.

As we approached the club, the street leading to it was much more crowded than I remembered. When we tried to enter the club's car park, only to find it full, I grew a 'wee bit' anxious.

We became more concerned when we tried to enter the small golf shop. It was so filled with people we could barely get through the door. Yet it all seemed the more strange as there was nobody on the first tee and we saw only one group playing on the near side of the wall.

As I approached the counter, a nice young man inquired if he could help us. He looked at me quizzically as I told him I had a tee time at 3:30. When he asked my name, I told him it was Falco, Neil Falco. A sickened look came over his face, which then spread to many others in the crowd. I looked down at the tee sheet. Etched in dark pencil next to the 3:30 P.M. slot was "N. FALDO."

You have never seen more disappointed people in your entire

life. Needless to say, there were to be no glimpses of Nick Faldo playing their local course this day. I overheard some groans as everyone in the shop filed out to the car park or the bar. Within minutes the place was virtually empty, just as I'd promised it would be.

~Neil Falco

Pace of Play

*Golf gives you an insight into human nature,
your own as well as your opponent's.*
~Grantland Rice

One of the more interesting traditions in golf is the handshake at the end of the round. It's an agreeable gesture, and one that suggests the just-finished match was somehow comparable to gentlemanly combat.

But there's another good reason to shake hands. Call it sudden and fleeting friendship. I've seen it happen countless times: at both heavily starched clubs and weather-beaten munis. Some bond occurs during a round. Four strangers meet on the 1st tee, eye one another carefully and set off. A few hours later, they will be striding off the 18th, wreathed in convivial grins and sticking out their paws like old lodge brothers.

Acrimony is possible, of course, even if it's unspoken. Like all social interactions, there is always the danger of some livid fractiousness. Curiously enough, it will likely have nothing to do with politics. The golf course might be the last place left on the planet where snorting political opposites can meet in charmed equanimity. In golf, there is, however, a real social chasm that divides people. Religious differences have nothing on this. Economic disparity, you say? No, it's much more grave than that. It's all about pace.

Take those four strangers on the 1st tee. As they work their way down the fairway, they are glancing nervously at one another's golf game and get-up, dealing with the gnawing fear that one of them might be the jerk who ends up trashing the afternoon round. The gaper who views a round of golf as an excuse for laughing it up with pals and a cooler of beer on the back of a cart, this guy will be a little trepidatious about sharing a round with some lean and hungry police dog of a player. You know the guy—pressed and immaculate, hits a 2-iron farther than you hit your driver, finds time to count everybody else's strokes and penalties. As my mother used to say, a real pill.

But if, like me, you hate carts and love a good, zesty walk and a snappy tempo, the sight of a guy weaving up to the first tee in a golf cart, steering with his elbows as he juggles a mug of beer and a slice of pepperoni pizza... this is enough to make you grind your teeth into powder.

The handicap system might make it possible for players of various skills to play together, but there is no equivalent system for balancing out the fast players and those who play at what might politely be called a leisurely pace.

The brisk players don't call it that, of course. Especially when they're trimming their jets on the tee-box of a par 3, their faces turning steamed lobster red while the cheery schmoozers on the green ahead pause to finish off some magnificent shaggy-dog story. If the jolly putters only dared look back at the tee-box, they would see the walking definition of Lock & Load.

I would count myself among the game's hot-footers, even while I know there are some scratch players among my acquaintance who consider me slower than Bolivian mail. It's all relative. I hate to be one of those seething schmucks, forever jingling the change in his pocket as he waits in the fairway, but that's the way I'm wired.

It was one of those chance meetings on the golf course, however, that changed my whole attitude. After work one day I had stopped off at a short executive course for a fast nine. I had, alas, not quite left the office tensions behind. Ripping along at an over-caffeinated pace, I was just butchering the ball. After hockey-sticking the ball around the 3rd green, I stormed up to the next tee-box and came upon an old man, sitting alone. A sad smile came over him and he waved me through. "Go on, feller," he said.

Stooped, frail and quavery, he was in shocking shape. Studying him more closely, I was gripped by the fear that he was minutes away from death. I throttled back instantly and said, ever so casually, that I'd be glad to join him if he so obliged. He was so tiny, so sparrowlike, I figured that if something happened I could carry him back to the clubhouse on my back.

After bunting a short little drive up the fairway, he confessed that he'd just left the hospital, where his insides had been keelhauled. He had spent four months on his back, dreaming of the watercolors he'd paint someday and thinking of this very course. We poked along in the gloaming, talking of all these matters.

When we were done, I walked him back to his car. He pulled out a little portable canvas seat so he could change his shoes. He told me to look in the trunk, and there I saw some of his new watercolors. The lines were done by a shaky hand, but they were bold. I helped him put his clubs away and we shook hands one last time. As he drove off, it occurred to me that after joining up with him, I had played out the last six holes in level par.

After that, whenever I've felt my nerves ratcheting up like a paint-making machine and my game about to go spiraling out of control, I try to think of the calm deliberation I felt that evening with the old man. Next to him, I felt like Hercules. So why not feel that way all the time?

A year later I saw that man again. He was on the next fairway over and waved heartily as he strode briskly down the fairway. He had a real spring in his step and, while I can't say for sure, he appeared to be a tad impatient to get going.

~Chris Hodenfield

Chicken Soup
for the Soul®
The Golf Book

Meet Our Contributors
Meet Our Authors
Acknowledgments
About Chicken Soup for the Soul
Share With Us

Meet
Our Contributors

Emily H. Allyn received her BS from Eastern Michigan University in 1995. Raised in Michigan, she has lived in Alaska and Alabama. Currently she lives in Michigan and provides care and companionship for seniors. Emily enjoys writing for a wide range of audiences. Please e-mail her at: emyhope@yahoo.com.

Dave Anderson, a *New York Times* sports columnist since 1971, was awarded a Pulitzer Prize for distinguished commentary in 1981. He is the author of twenty-two books and more than 350 magazine articles.

Thomas Ashcraft is a retired Ford Motor Company employee from Detroit, Michigan currently residing in Nashville, Tennessee. Tom is a certified golf addict, who has maintained a single digit handicap for over twenty years.

John Atkinson, a golfer for over twenty years, hopes to get wife, Lori, out on the course someday soon. He is an active father to three children, Machaela, Andrea and Christopher. John's biggest challenge has been battling his advanced stage lung cancer over the last twenty months. His "never, never, never give up" attitude has inspired many.

Brett Avery is the former editor of *Golf Journal*, published by the United States Golf Association. He covered David Sutherland's victory in the 1989 Western Amateur while writing about amateur and college golf for *Golf World* magazine.

Bob Baker played the PGA Tour in the late 70's. He resides in Orlando with his wife of twenty-four years, Lise, whom he met during the Azalea City Open in Mobile, AL. Bob, Lise, Alli (22), Danny(21), and Sarah(17) enjoy jet skiing and enjoying the Florida sun. Please e-mail him at bbgolfb@yahoo.com.

Al Barkow was editor-in-chief of *Golf* and *Golf Illustrated* magazines. His numerous books on golf include *Golf's Golden Grind*, *The History of the Tour*, and USGA Book of the Year (1986) *Getting to the Dance Floor, An Oral History of American Golf*, and *SAM; The One and Only Sam Snead*, a biography.

Nelson Bayne is one of "those guys," who gets up in the morning, goes to work and wishes he were on a golf course! Nelson has worked for a long time. He enjoys playing golf, watching golf, talking about golf and sometimes—miniature golf (he has nephews). Contact him via e-mail at nbayne@nbayne.com.

Philip Beard's second novel, *Lost in the Garden* (Viking 2006), was nominated for the USGA's International Book Award and follows over-privileged, under-motivated, golf-and-sex-obsessed Michael Benedict through a mid-life crisis that Austin Murphy of *Sports Illustrated* calls "rollicking, ribald, poignant and sweet." www.philipbeard.net.

Mrs. Bell, a charter member of the LPGA, has received numerous awards for her tireless contributions to golf, including the USGA's Bob Jones Award. With seven Halls of Fame, she is a master professional, and active in numerous civic, charitable and sports organizations. She and her family live in Southern Pines, NC where they own and operate Pine Needles Lodge & Golf Club.

Trish Bonsall and her Golf Addicted Husband Al are the proud parents of four sons. She enjoys writing short stories, poems and has been busy working on her first book. She loves cruising and spending time with friends. She is a Sales Manager for a building company in Charlotte, NC. Please e-mail her at bonz223@hotmail.com.

Tom Borda earned a BA from Washington & Lee University and a Master of Sports Management from Bond University in Australia. A sporting enthusiast with a love for writing, Tom is honored that his story is included in this publication. Originally from Michigan, Tom now resides in Chicago.

Robert Bruce is a full-time writer and part-time golfer who also loves to cook and cheer for Georgia football. Originally from Cartersville, GA, Robert now lives in Nashville with his lovely wife, Katie. You can contact him at rbrucewriting@yahoo.com, or visit his blog Game Under Repair (www.gameunderrepair.com).

John Buccigross has been a *SportsCenter* Anchor/Reporter since 1996 at ESPN and writes a weekly column on ESPN.com. In 2007 he published his first book with former NHL player Keith Jones. Buccigross has recorded two holes-in-one, including one on the par 4 11th at Newport Country Club.

Kevin Robert Butler born 11-13-86 to Reverend Randy and Joan Butler, moved to Heaven on 01-10-03. He loved his family, Disneyland, July 4th, and golf. But mostly, Kevin loved God and wasn't ashamed of his faith.

Tamara Bowers is a wife, mom, W/C Manager, freelance writer, and now a golfer.

Bob Carney is longtime *Golf Digest* writer and editor, as well as an Evans Scholar alumnus. He caddied at Dearborn (MI) Country Club, graduated from the University of Michigan and now plays golf at Brooklawn C.C. in Fairfield, CT, where he likes to walk and take a caddy.

Reid Champagne plays his zen-like game in Delaware, where he hopes to one day be struck by lightning. His earlier story, "When You

Wish Upon a Par" appeared in *Chicken Soup for the Golfer's Soul: The Second Round*.

Tom Chiarella is Writer-at-Large for *Esquire Magazine*. His collection of golf essays is *Thursday's Game: Notes From a Golfer with Far to Go*.

Sam Christensen received his DDS and Pediatric Dentistry degrees from Iowa University in 1955, and the Distinguished Alumni Award in 1994. He has attended courses at the university's Writers Workshop also. He and his wife of fifty-four years are interested in family, volunteering, travel, sports, reading, and writing. E-mail him at jwcsoc1@aol.com.

Brian Clark learned to play golf with his mother, Frankie, at age seven. Consistent with his story above, he has been runner-up in his club championship four times, without a victory. He has made two holes-in-one and a double-eagle (from the ladies tees!).

Tom Cunneff is a senior editor at *LINKS* magazine. Previously, he was an associate bureau chief for *People* magazine in Los Angeles. He received a BS in Journalism from the University of Florida.

Harry L. Dauberger, grandson of John Dauberger, was given these poems by him. Originally written in German, then translated to English. Harry's grandfather loved golf and made many sets of clubs. Harry used a persimmons putter his grandfather made for years! He hopes the poems bring a twinkle to your eye!

Jaime Diaz is a Senior Writer for *Golf Digest* and *Golf World* magazine. A native of California, he lives in North Carolina with his wife, Stephanie.

Paul Ehmann, a home course 6-handicap, understands the value of a regular foursome. He is passionate about golf, writing and friendship. His essays have been heard on Public Radio. Ehmann lives in

Loudonville, NY with his wife Diane. Please e-mail him at etrain@nycap.rr.com.

Steve Eubanks is a recovering golf pro and retired caddy. He is the author of more than thirty books and has written about sports ranging from amateur golf to professional bull riding for numerous publications. Steve and his obscenely large family live in Peachtree City, GA.

Neil Falco is an executive in the paper industry. He has an undergraduate degree from St. John's University and an MBA from Fordham University. He is a five-handicap who has traveled extensively, allowing him the opportunity to play many of the world's finest courses.

Ron James Fitzsimmons acquired a BA from State University of New York, Geneseo (1965) and a Master's Degree in City and Regional Planning from California State University, Fresno (1973). He plays a lot of golf, babysits grandchildren, and contributes articles to his church newsletters. Please e-mail him at: jsheryl@carolina.rr.com.

Jackie Fleming, a native Californian, was raised in the Bay Area, and then raised three boys on an Island in the California Delta. Her hobby is traveling the world by freighter, yoga, reading and writing. For six years, she wrote columns for two weekly newspapers. She now lives in Paradise, California.

Steve Floyd received his BS degree from the University of Maryland in 1983 and is a diehard Terps fan. Commercial construction management has been his profession for the past twenty-five years, and will continue until he finds a way to get paid to play golf. Hiring? Steve@FloydCM.com.

Mark Fowlkes is from Fort Worth, Texas. His love of golf began in the mid 60's as a caddie at Shady Oaks, home course to Ben Hogan.

Mark never misses a Colonial Invitational, and has never given up on his dream to cure his hook. E-mail him at mark@fnalandscape.com.

Brain Amos Fox is a life long Texan with a passion for golf. Blessed to live where golf is a year-round pursuit, he only takes time away from the course during deer season or when the big bass are hitting. He can be reached at ftworthfox@yahoo.com.

Dwight Freeney has reached the pinnacle of professional football in less than a decade. His fierce pass rush, lightning speed, and signature spin move have led to three consecutive Pro Bowls and the 2007 Super Bowl Championship. He holds the franchise record for career sacks and is the only Colts player with four consecutive double-digits sack seasons.

Fred Funk is one of the most recognizable names and personalities in golf. He has both impressed and charmed galleries in a professional career spanning twenty years. Aside from being devoted to golf, Fred is a family man before anything else. He and his wife, Sharon, are devoted parents and have their children, Eric, Taylor and Perri travel with them.

Kenny G is the world's most renowned saxophonist, with global album sales totaling more than 75 million. His other huge passion is golf. In December 2006, Kenny claimed the #1 ranking in *Golf Digest* magazine's "Top 100 in Music" list, with a +0.6 handicap.

John F. Gaski has been on the faculty at the University of Notre Dame since 1980. He is a Notre Dame graduate and has a Ph.D. from the University of Wisconsin. He is the author of approximately 100 publications, but none of the others have had anything to do with golf. If Professor Gaski had any sense, he wouldn't either.

Matt Ginella is the Senior Travel Editor for *Golf Digest*, and was previously the golf photo editor at *Sports Illustrated*. He is currently featured on the Golf Channel's Travel Time segment. He has a Communications degree from St. Mary's College of California and a Masters in Journalism from Columbia University. He resides in New York City.

David Gould has specialized in golf, travel and lifestyle topics with *Travel + Leisure Golf, LINKS Magazine, Golf Illustrated* and *Golf Shop Operations*. He has published four books, including *The Golfer's Code* and *Q School Confidential: Inside Golf's Cruelest Tournament*. Gould was a Francis Ouimet Scholar at Wesleyan University. He is married to the novelist Rachel Basch.

Harris Green taught English for thirty years before retiring to play golf and do volunteer work. He writes mainly short stories but has completed a novel, *Chinaberry Summer*, in which chronicles the adventures of three boys in a small Alabama city during the summer of 1947.

Vicki Griffin's husband Thomas W. Griffin is the author of two novels and over 200 scientific publications. A former U.S. Army Green Beret, professional musician, university professor, cancer center director, and magazine editor, he lives with his wife in Seattle and Sun Valley.

Chris Hagen was born and raised in New York City. He received his BA from Princeton University and his MBA from Columbia University. He spent his career in real estate in New York and fled to Vermont after burnout.

Neil Haldeman moved to Ann Arbor, MI, after four years in the Air Force right out of high school. At the University of Michigan he studied English Literature and supported himself as a computer programmer. After retirement he took up writing as a hobby, second in importance only to golf.

John Hawkins is a senior writer for *Golf World* and has covered the PGA Tour for the magazine since 1996. He co-hosts the "Grey Goose 19th Hole," a weekly topical-interest program that airs Wednesdays on the Golf Channel.

Robert A. Hedesh is an attorney who moved from New Jersey to North Myrtle Beach, SC. He lives in Barefoot Resort, which is home to four of the greatest golf courses anywhere. In addition to golf, Robert amuses himself cooking. He has written various newsletters and political material in the past.

Nick Henry received his BA from Vanderbilt University in 1997 and his JD from Washington & Lee University in 2001. He is a practicing attorney in Nashville, Tennessee. Nick is married with one child and plays golf whenever possible.

Chris Hodenfield's magazine stories have appeared in magazines ranging from *Rolling Stone* to *Golf Digest* and *Sports Illustrated*.

E. Michael Johnson is Senior Editor, Equipment for *Golf World* magazine. Prior to joining *Golf World*, Mike was equipment editor for *Golf World Business* magazine and also spent ten years with *The Country Club* magazine where he authored over 100 articles on travel destinations and private country clubs.

Ted Johnson, the father of two daughters, has been writing about all facets of golf for twenty-five years. A graduate of UC Berkeley, Ted maintains a freelance business that, aside from providing corporate communications, requires him to travel the world to sample the best places to play.

Josh Kelley started his first band at age eleven, wrote "Amazing" and landed a deal with Hollywood Records while still in college, released six albums, launched DNK Records, appeared on dozens of television shows, including *Ellen, Good Morning America* and *The Tonight Show* *with Jay Leno*, and has been featured in *People Magazine, Us Weekly, Billboard* and *Entertainment Weekly* among others.

Todd Kersting, PGA Professional is a devoted golf instructor from New Mexico dating back to 1985. Todd is working on his PGA Master Professional status for teaching. His passion in life is to develop golf programs to help make the game of golf become a part of people's lives.

Jason Kileen received a BA in Creative Writing from Arizona State in 1999. He currently lives in New York City working as a Film Editor and continues to outdrive his friends on the golf course. Jason enjoys films, writing and photography and plans to continue working in all mediums. Please e-mail him at jjsonic@gmail.com.

Bob Landfield was born in Chicago and has resided in Duluth (The Air Conditioned City) since 1971. The only thing he loves as much as golf is music, thus he works in a record store; still suffering from his art!

Tim Larkin is a graduate of the University of Massachusetts and is an avid, though unremarkable, golfer. He lives in Milton, MA, with his wife, Amy, and their children, Max and Maggie.

Lyn Larsen lives in rural Alberta in Canada. She has studied Education, with an English major, as well as social work. She is now retired from her two careers and enjoys writing both prose and poetry and is working on a novel for early teens.

Y. John Lee retired in 2008 and is writing a collection of essays about golf, business and life. He is interested in all things involving his wife, children and grandchildren. His e-mail is yjohnlee@mac.com.

Mark Long graduated from the University of Maryland in 1986 with degrees in finance and economics. In 1989 he followed his college golf coach Fred Funk onto the PGA TOUR and has caddied ever since. He also makes many of the specialized yardage books used by the players and caddies on TOUR.

Leigh MacKay received his bachelor's from Amherst College and master's from Dartmouth College. A rabid Red Sox and Celtics fan, he taught English and coached golf at independent schools for thirty-three years. Now retired, he has become a freelance golf feature and travel writer while maintaining a single digit handicap.

Mark H. Massé is author of *Inspired to Serve: Today's Faith Activists* and *Delamore's Dream*, a novel. A published writer for thirty years, Massé teaches journalism at Ball State University. He received his BA from Miami University and an MS with honors from University of Oregon. He can be reached via e-mail at mhmasse@bsu.edu.

Ashley Mayo received her BA from the University of Virginia in 2007. She was part of the university's inaugural women's golf team. She's currently a freelance editor for *Golf Digest*, lives in Manhattan, and is happiest when on a golf course. Please e-mail her at ashleykmayo@gmail.com.

Jim McCabe was born in Boston and has lived in the area all his life. For twenty-three years he worked at the *Boston Globe*, the last ten as the newspaper's lead golf writer, though he recently moved on to write for *GolfWeek Magazine*.

Bruce McCall is a Canadian-born writer and illustrator in New York and a longtime contributor to *The New Yorker, Vanity Fair* and other magazines. He has published four books of humor and has in his time seen Emperor Hailie Selassie, a flying saucer and Ted Williams hitting a home run, as well as getting a letter from Norman Rockwell.

George McDonald graduated from Pacific University College of Optometry in 1966. He and his wife Carol live in Luverne, MN, where he practiced optometry for forty years. He is an avid golfer and enjoys freelance writing as a hobby.

Craig McLean has been the Head Golf Professional at the Dorset Field Club in Dorset, VT for twenty-one years. Prior to that Craig was the Assistant Pro at the Mohawk Club for eight years in Schenectady, NY where he grew up. Craig has been active in the PGA throughout his career and is currently the President of the PGA's New England Section.

Gregg Mills received his degree in Physics from Franklin and Marshall College. He resides in Haddonfield, New Jersey, with his wife Courtney and is expecting his first child. He dedicates this essay to his father and to his wife for her love and support.

Tony Mohr's essays and short stories have appeared in the *Christian Science Monitor, The Sacramento Bee*, two anthologies, and several literary magazines including *The LBJ: Avian Life, Literary Arts, Literary House Review*, and *Word Riot*. He lives in Los Angeles.

Tom Munson has co-written a screenplay and a book titled *First Adventure*. He has written blogs on various websites on topics ranging from sports, entertainment, and politics. He is also an avid golfer and loves to play the game despite the fact that he has an average handicap.

Tim Murphy has been the managing editor for *Golf World* since 2000. Prior to that he was the editor of *Golf Shop Operations*, which he joined after twelve years as a sportswriter for the *Worcester (Mass.) Telegram & Gazette*. Please e-mail him at tim.murphy@golfworld.com.

Robert Scott Nussbaum has been a golfer for half of a century and an attorney for thirty years. He has been married for thirty-one years with two children. No family members have followed in his footsteps for a lifetime of joy and frustration on the links.

Arnold Palmer was the first person to make one million dollars playing golf. Palmer attracted legions of fans—known as "Arnie's Army"—who hung on his every shot, celebrating his successes and suffering his failures along with him.

George Palmer is a retired attorney, living in Pawleys Island, SC. He teaches tenth grade English at nearby Georgetown High School and plays golf at his member clubs, True Blue Plantation and Caledonia Golf and Fish Club. He previously wrote for *The Weekly Fisherman* newspaper in Islamorada, Fl.

Mark Parisi's "off the mark" comic, syndicated since 1987, is distributed by United Media. Mark's humor also graces greeting cards, T-shirts, calendars, magazines, newsletters and books. Check out www.offthemark.com. Lynn is his wife/business partner. Their daughter, Jen, contributes with inspiration, (as do three cats and one dog).

Jeff Patterson graduated from Middlebury College in 2008 with a degree in English. He played on the men's golf team, shooting everything from 73 to 95, and wrote for *The Campus* newspaper. A native of Old Saybrook, CT, he once played 126 holes—walking—in a single day.

Don Patton is a recently retired engineer living in Tucson. Among his many interests is writing fiction and nonfiction stories. Don plays golf as often as possible and aside from aspiring to break par he has always hoped to have his stories published.

Gary Player, who has been dubbed the "International Ambassador of Golf," has 24 PGA Tour victories, 19 Champions Tour victories, and 110 International victories to his credit. The native South African operates The Player Foundation, whose primary objective is to promote education for underprivileged children.

Kay Conor Pliszka is a frequent contributor to the *Chicken Soup* *for the Soul* series. She and her husband, former teachers, live in a Florida retirement village that boasts having over thirty golf courses. Kay says it's hard deciding which is more fun—writing or golfing! Please e-mail her at knpliszka@comcast.net.

Ron Read is the USGA's Western Region director. He graduated from Drake University. His interests include jogging, bridge, reading, the outdoors, dogs, travel, and of course golf. He is affiliated with the Royal & Ancient Golf Club of St Andrews. Upon retirement, he will write about his golf experiences over fifty years.

Peter Richmond's work has appeared in *The New Yorker, The New York Times Magazine, Vanity Fair, Rolling Stone, Parade, GQ, Details, Architecture, Parade, Golf Digest, Travel + Leisure Golf* and *TV Guide*, among others. His journalism has been included in many anthologies, including *The Best American Sportswriting of the Century*.

Bruce Robinson is an award-winning, internationally published cartoonist whose work has appeared in numerous periodicals, including *National Enquirer, The Saturday Evening Post, Woman's World, The Sun, First*, and *Highlights for Children*. He is also author of the cartoon book, *Good Medicine*. Contact him at cartoonsbybrucerobinson@hotmail.com.

Neil Rosen is CEO of an Internet software company in Connecticut. He has master's degrees in education and psychology. He enjoys tennis, bridge, and spending time with his wife and three children. Neil is the author of *Open Your Heart With Writing*, published by Dreamtime Publishing. E-mail neil@ewaydirect.com.

Steve Rushin is the author of a forthcoming novel, *The Pint Man*, as well as two previous books, *Road Swing* and *The Caddie Was A Reindeer*. His website is www.steverushin.com.

Mark Rylak wrote this poem as a freshman at Bucknell University to commemorate his one and only round of 69 while a student at North

Hunterdon Regional High School. He is now a practicing dentist in Whippany, NJ and still enjoys golf.

Jay Rylant graduated from Mountain View College in Dallas, TX, after which he went on to spend fourteen years as a freelance musician in and around the Dallas area. Moving on to a new career in retail, he now pursues a career as a writer and novelist. He is currently the editor of *Different Strokes*—a weekly newsletter for golfhelp.com.

Cliff Schrock has combined his love of golf and journalism since his high school days in Illinois. The Illinois State University English major has written many bits and pieces as a longtime editor at *Golf Digest*, plus four golf books. He collects original *Hardy Boys* books, but believing we should always be learning, he aspires to learn the piano.

Nick Seitz is editor at large for *Golf Digest* where he's been based for most of his adult working life. His handicap has gone unlisted.

Craig Shankland, sixty-three, teaches at LPGA International in Daytona Beach, FL, and is one of *Golf Magazine's* Top 100 Teachers.

David Shedloski is an award-winning writer from suburban Columbus, OH. He has covered golf for more than twenty years and is the author of three books on the game and contributed to three others, including this one.

Whit Sheppard lives with his wife and infant daughter in Richmond, VA, where he's at work on a biography of the late Arthur Ashe. He lived and worked in France from 2001-2006. An avid golfer and squash player, he can be e-mailed at whit.sheppard@comcast.net.

Ed Sherman covered golf at the *Chicago Tribune* for twelve years. His timing couldn't have been better, as the first tournament he covered was Tiger Woods' landmark victory in the 1997 Masters. Sherman currently is a contributor to several golf publications and is the author of *The Great Book of Chicago Sports Lists*.

Jared Slater is a master carpenter who splits residences between Chicago and Jackson, Wyoming, where he spends much of the winter snowboarding.

Mark Soltau received his BA degree in Communications from Cal-State University Chico in 1977. He works for *Golf Digest* as a Contributing Editor and is also the editor of Tigerwoods.com. He lives in Northern California with his wife and daughter. He can be reached by e-mail at msoltau72@aol.com.

Mark Spangler received his Associate of Arts, with honors, from Minnesota State University, Mankato. He is a former radio broadcaster and currently teaches students at Mankato West High School as a paraprofessional. His fiction, commentary and poetry have been published in *Esquire, Mankato Free Press, Lyrical Iowa* and other publications.

Mike Stachura is a senior editor at *Golf Digest*. He has been on the staff of the magazine since 1992 and also has written for *Golf World* and *The New York Times*. He is the author or co-author of three books, including *Classic American Courses*. Please e-mail him at mike.stachura@golfdigest.com.

Eric Stark lives in Northeast Scotland where he took early retirement from a pharmaceutical company so he could work in the mornings and golf in the afternoons. He normally keeps his golfing stories for evenings in the golf club, but decided to put this one on paper.

Kaameran Stenberg is a high school junior.

Caroline Stetler graduated from Wake Forest University in 2003 and has worked for magazines such as *Golf Digest* and *Golf For Women*. She is pursuing a master's in Journalism and Public Affairs at

American University in Washington DC, and is a graduate assistant at the Investigative Reporting Workshop. E-mail caroline.stetler@hotmail.com.

John Strege has written five books, including *When War Played Through*, which in 2005 won the United Stated Golf Association International Book Award, and *Tiger: A Biography of Tiger Woods*. He has written extensively for *Golf World* and *Golf Digest* magazine. He lives with his wife and daughter in San Diego, CA.

James Swigert works in the steel industry. He graduated from Newcomerstown High School in 1975. He enjoys spending time with his children and grandchildren, traveling, working on the family home and collecting sports memorabilia. And of course, any minutes he can steal away for golf. He can be contacted at jcswigert@yahoo.com.

John H. Tidyman is a Cleveland, OH, native, an award-winning journalist, and author of a half dozen books, most recently on the Cleveland Police Department and another on golf travel. He plays with persimmon woods, Haig Ultra forged blades and a putter that changes every week. He has yet to break 80 and, let's face it, time is running out.

Terri Tiffany counseled adults for seventeen years before owning a Christian bookstore. She resides in Florida with her husband where she writes full time. Her stories have appeared in Sunday school take-home papers, women's magazines and numerous anthologies. Please visit her at http://terri-treasures.blogspot.com.

Ross Troike graduated from the Naval Academy in 1991. He served thirteen years active duty and is currently a Commander in the Navy Air Reserve Forces. Ross was selected as a finalist for the 2008 Golf Digest U.S. Open Challenge for his essay on handling pressure.

Rick Weber received his BA in journalism from Penn State University.

He has won the Casey Medal For Meritorious Journalism and been honored twice by the Associated Press Sports Editors. His book, *Pink Lips and Fingertips*, will be published in late 2009.

Guy Yocom is a Senior Writer for *Golf Digest* in Wilton, CT. A winner of several national awards for golf writing, he has written seven books, including four with U.S. Open champions Tiger Woods, Johnny Miller, Corey Pavin and David Graham.

Bob Zahn is exclusively represented by CartoonFile.net which offers thousands of his cartoons for visitors to enjoy. After his untimely passing in January 2008, it is hoped his work will live on through this unique web catalog. Anyone with questions about Bob's work can make contact by e-mailing: syndicator@gmail.com.

Meet Our Authors

Jack Canfield is the co-creator of the *Chicken Soup for the Soul* series, which Time magazine has called "the publishing phenomenon of the decade." Jack is also the co-author of eight other bestselling books including *The Success Principles(tm): How to Get from Where You Are to Where You Want to Be, Dare to Win, The Aladdin Factor, You've Got to Read This Book*, and *The Power of Focus: How to Hit Your Business and Personal and Financial Targets with Absolute Certainty*.

Jack is the CEO of the Canfield Training Group in Santa Barbara, California, and founder of the Foundation for Self-Esteem in Culver City, California. He has conducted intensive personal and professional development seminars on the principles of success for over a million people in twenty-three countries. Jack is a dynamic keynote speaker and he has spoken to hundreds of thousands of others at more than 1,000 corporations, universities, professional conferences and conventions, and has been seen by millions more on national television shows such as *The Today Show, Fox and Friends, Inside Edition, Hard Copy, CNN's Talk Back Live, 20/20, Eye to Eye*, and the *NBC Nightly News* and the *CBS Evening News*.

Jack has received many awards and honors, including three honorary doctorates and a Guinness World Records Certificate for having seven books from the *Chicken Soup for the Soul* series appearing on the New York Times bestseller list on May 24, 1998.

You can reach Jack at:
Jack Canfield
P.O. Box 30880 (Santa Barbara, CA 93130
phone: 805-563-2935 (fax: 805-563-2945
www.jackcanfield.com

Mark Victor Hansen is the co-founder of Chicken Soup for the Soul, along with Jack Canfield. He is a sought-after keynote speaker, best-selling author, and marketing maven. Mark's powerful messages of possibility, opportunity, and action have created powerful change in thousands of organizations and millions of individuals worldwide.

Mark is a prolific writer with many bestselling books, such as *The One Minute Millionaire, Cracking the Millionaire Code, How to Make the Rest of Your Life the Best of Your Life, The Power of Focus, The Aladdin Factor*, and *Dare to Win*, in addition to the *Chicken Soup for the Soul* series. Mark has had a profound influence in the field of human potential through his library of audios, videos, and articles in the areas of big thinking, sales achievement, wealth building, publishing success, and personal and professional development. He is also the founder of the MEGA Seminar Series.

He has appeared on *Oprah*, CNN, and *The Today Show*. He has been quoted in *Time, U. S. News & World Report, USA Today*, the *New York Times*, and *Entrepreneur* and has given countless radio interviews, assuring our planet's people that "You can easily create the life you deserve."

Mark has received numerous awards that honor his entrepreneurial spirit, philanthropic heart, and business acumen. He is a lifetime member of the Horatio Alger Association of Distinguished Americans.

You can reach Mark at:
Mark Victor Hansen & Associates, Inc.
P.O. Box 7665 (Newport Beach, CA 92658
phone: 949-764-2640 (fax: 949-722-6912
www.markvictorhansen.com

Max Adler is an Associate Editor at *Golf Digest* and a member judge of the Hot List, the magazine's annual comprehensive evaluation of new golf equipment in the marketplace. Max's articles and stories appear regularly in *Golf Digest, Golf Digest Index*, and *Golf World*. His original short fiction has been published in several outlets.

Max played NCAA golf at Washington & Lee University, where after graduating he was awarded the Ernest L. Ransome Scholarship to study abroad at St. Andrews University in Scotland. In two years there, he obtained a Masters of Letters degree (with distinction) in English Studies and competed on the men's university golf team. Now living the working life, he still plays a full schedule of summer amateur events and was the 2007 GWAA (Golf Writer's Association of America) medal play champion.

You can reach Max at:
Golf Digest
20 Westport Rd
Wilton, CT 06897
max.adler@golfdigest.com

Acknowledgments

Thanks to Amy Newmark, a great publisher and editor.

Thanks to D'ette Corona, Barbara LoMonaco, and Kristiana Glavin for their administrative support and editorial skills.

Thanks to Brian Taylor at Pneuma Books, our book designer.

Thanks to Jessica.

Thanks to Meaghan Delahunt and Douglas Dunn, two terrific professors.

Thanks to Drew, a good golfer but a better teacher.

And thanks to my parents.

Thanks to all those who submitted stories we weren't able to accept. We read every one, and even those that were not used made an impact on us and helped to shape the book.

Finally, none of this would be possible without the business and creative leadership of Chicken Soup for the Soul's CEO, Bill Rouhana, and president, Bob Jacobs.

Chicken Soup for the Soul

Improving Your Life Every Day

Real people sharing real stories—for fifteen years. Now, Chicken Soup for the Soul has gone beyond the bookstore to become a world leader in life improvement. Through books, movies, DVDs, online resources and other partnerships, we bring hope, courage, inspiration and love to hundreds of millions of people around the world. Chicken Soup for the Soul's writers and readers belong to a one-of-a-kind global community, sharing advice, support, guidance, comfort, and knowledge.

Chicken Soup for the Soul stories have been translated into more than forty languages and can be found in more than one hundred countries. Every day, millions of people experience a Chicken Soup for the Soul story in a book, magazine, newspaper or online. As we share our life experiences through these stories, we offer hope, comfort and inspiration to one another. The stories travel from person to person, and from country to country, helping to improve lives everywhere.

Chicken Soup
for the Soul®

Share with Us

W
e all have had Chicken Soup for the Soul moments in our lives. If you would like to share your story or poem with millions of people around the world, go to chickensoup.com and click on "Submit Your Story." You may be able to help another reader, and become a published author at the same time. Some of our past contributors have launched writing and speaking careers from the publication of their stories in our books!

Your stories have the best chance of being used if you submit them through our website at

www.chickensoup.com

If you do not have access to the Internet, you may submit your stories by mail or by facsimile. Starting in 2010, submissions will only be accepted via the website.

Please do not send us any book manuscripts, unless through a literary agent, as these will be automatically discarded.

Chicken Soup for the Soul
P.O. Box 700
Cos Cob, CT 06807-0700
Fax: 203-861-7194

Golfers are a special breed. They endure bad weather, early wake up calls, great expense, and "interesting" clothing to engage in their favorite sport. This book contains Chicken Soup's 101 best stories about golfers, golfing, and other sports. Chicken Soup's approach to sports books has always been unique — professional and amateur athletes contribute stories from the heart, yielding a book about the human side of golf and other sports, not a how-to book.

978-1-935096-11-5

Check out our
great books on

Chicken Soup has a slam dunk with its first sports book in years, and its first on basketball, with the Orlando Magic's very own Pat Williams, well-known author and motivational speaker. Pat has drawn on his basketball industry connections to compile great stories from on and off the court. Fans will be inspired, surprised, and amused by inside stories from well-known coaches and players, fascinating looks behind the scenes, and anecdotes from the fans.

978-1-935096-29-0

SPORTS

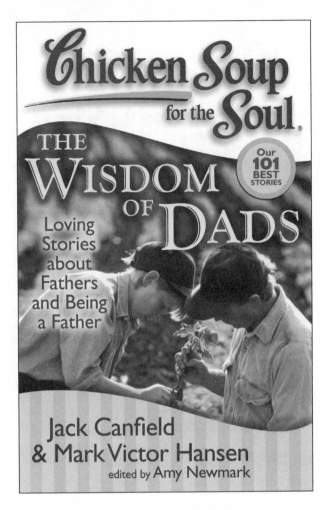

Children view their fathers with awe from the day they are born. Fathers are big and strong and seem to know everything, except for a few teenage years when fathers are perceived to know nothing! This book represents a new theme for Chicken Soup — 101 stories selected from 35 past books, all stories focusing on the wisdom of dads. Stories are written by sons and daughters about their fathers, and by fathers relating stories about their children.

978-1-935096-18-4

*C*heck out our
great books for

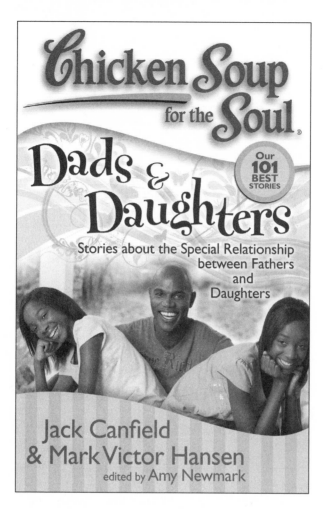

Chicken Soup for the Soul

for the Soul.

Dads & Daughters

Our **101** BEST STORIES

Stories about the Special Relationship
between Fathers
and
Daughters

Jack Canfield
& Mark Victor Hansen
edited by Amy Newmark

Whether she is ten years old or fifty — she will always be his little girl. And daughters take care of their dads too, whether it is a tea party for two at age five or loving care fifty years later. This wide-ranging exploration of the relationship between fathers and daughters contains selections from forty past Chicken Soup books. Stories were written by fathers about their daughters and by daughters about their fathers, celebrating the special bond between fathers and daughters.

978-1-935096-19-1

DADS

Chicken Soup for the Soul

www.chickensoup.com